FRANCE'S YELLOW VESTS: WESTERN REPRESSION OF THE WEST'S BEST VALUES

RAMIN MAZAHERI

Badak Merah Semesta

2022

FRANCE'S YELLOW VESTS:
WESTERN REPRESSION OF
THE WEST'S BEST VALUES

Cover Photo: Adnan Farzat
Cover Design by: Rossie Indira
Layout by: Rossie Indira

First edition, 2022

Published by PT. Badak Merah Semesta
Jl. Madrasah Azziyadah 16, Jakarta
http://badak-merah.weebly.com
email: badak.merah.press@gmail.com

ISBN: 9780578396415

Dedication

To God for all things, and for shepherding my co-workers and me through so many demonstrations without any major injury.
To my cameraman colleagues: We made it!
To the French and to France.
To the Yellow Vests.

Special Thanks

Special thanks to PressTV: They understand revolutionary spirit, and thus they understood the importance of thoroughly covering the Yellow Vests.

www.presstv.ir

Special thanks to two websites: The Saker and The Greanville Post. These articles first appeared in a serialised form on those two admirable websites, and without their help and support this book would not have been made. I extend my sincere thanks to all of their staff.

www.thesaker.is

www.lesakerfrancophone.fr

www.greanvillepost.com

By the Same Author

I'll Ruin Everything You Are: Ending Western Propaganda on Red China

Socialism's Ignored Success: Iranian Islamic Socialism

How This Book is Arranged

This is a book which is rather split into two halves.

Chapter 1 through Chapter 8 deals with French history from 1789 until World War II. Chapter 9 through Chapter 18 deals with the Yellow Vests.

For those looking only for a history describing why the Yellow Vests were produced, the history of their movement, an analysis of them and an explanation of their victories - perhaps turn directly to the second half.

For those who want a comprehensive, undoubtedly Yellow Vest-inspired re-telling of modern political French history since 1789 - I think you'll be rewarded by starting at the beginning.

Interspersed throughout the book are nearly 100 quotes taken from actual, marching Yellow Vests. I got them as an on-the-street reporter first in French, then translated them into English for use in scores of hard-news reports (the police brutality endured to produce these regular Saturday reports does give a new meaning to "hard-news") for Iran's 24-hour English-language PressTV, and then translated them back into French for the French version of this book.

Aware or unaware, you are our king,
And, good or bad, can swear to anything.
Kings rule the world, and aren't afraid to say
Whatever they might wish, in any way.
If what you've said turns out to be untrue,
Who here would dare to point that out to you?

— *Fakhruddin Assad Gorgani*

11th century Persian poet
Vis and Ramin

CONTENTS

Preface

As the journalist - in English or French - who has covered more Yellow Vest demonstrations than any other, I thought it was my responsibility to give them something I can't find anywhere: an objective, accurate and complete history.

Soon after starting this project I quickly realised: France doesn't need an accurate rendering of the massive repression of progressive politics which began on November 17, 2018 - they need an accurate rendering of the massive repression of progressive politics which began in 1789. If they lied and misrepresented the Yellow Vests in 2018, wouldn't they have also done the same in 1936, 1871, 1848, 1789 and in between?

It is that realisation which led to this book.

My previous books have dispelled the lies about modern China and modern Iran - after more than a dozen years living here, I think I can do the same for the good people of France.

This is going to be the most comprehensive book on the Yellow Vests you can find, and from the journalist who talked with them more regularly and over a longer period than any other; who got gassed and harassed right alongside them; who wore out shoes on their weekly, 15km+ races across Paris chased by riot police. Most importantly, this will also be the book with the most space devoted to the actual words of the Yellow Vests, as I'll soon explain.

This book was written during the run-up to France's 2022 vote. I thought this book would talk much about that vote but then I realised: How much more vital and interesting is a Yellow Vest-fuelled rethinking of two centuries of French and global politics than one election featuring not one but four essentially far-right candidates?

Right in 1789, right in 2019 - why don't Western historians admit France keeps being right

When it comes to reading Western commentary on French political history from 1789 into the 21st century what always baffles me is: they are so terribly critical of France and its revolutionaries even though by the 1970s much of what they fought for would be absolutely insisted upon by the average European. I think the Yellow Vests will continue this trend of being ahead of the curve.

The book is divided into two broad sections: the first is French history from 1789-2018, and the second is an analysis of who, how, why and what the Yellow Vests are for.

What's certain is that it's a necessary book: The English-language books on the Yellow Vests (less than a handful) are analyses from overseas and not worth mentioning. The leading French-language books on the Yellow Vests were seemingly all published by spring 2019: they give the whys but not the actual history of the Yellow Vest movement, which this book will; they were published too soon to grasp the depth of their victories, as this book does; they include a fraction of actual Yellow Vest words, most crucially.

This book is not detached analysis: I have interviewed hundreds of Yellow Vests in my work for Iran's 24-hours English-language news channel PressTV and their quotations will be interspersed throughout every chapter. I think this unique condensation of three years of covering Yellow Vest demonstrations shows how long-running the fight for progressive politics truly is, how similar progressive political demands have been since 1789 and how the Yellow Vests undoubtedly deserve a place in the pantheon of French revolutionaries.

I can promise you that the first part of this book is not some boring leftist genuflecting at the 1794 glories of Robespierre, Danton and Marat - they are not analysed at all.

As an immigrant journalist to France I have been forced to try and make sense of French history from 1789 until today. In the same way that historians like to sum up centuries of history from the Achaemenid or Safavid eras in Iran - it can be done, after all - I'm looking for patterns and threads, and I think the Yellow Vest phenomenon has both capped and sparked an absolutely major part of French history.

I have covered France for 13 years, but it's a special 13 years: This is the era when the recently born "neoliberal empire" - the European Union - made its Age of Austerity power plays to become entrenched and obeyed. These are not spur of the moment creations - the European Union and the eurozone are institutions which are centuries in the making. They might last centuries, but only upon the broken bones of the truly once-in-a-century, undemocratic repression of the Yellow Vests.

The Yellow Vests provide us with a new mountain ledge in history - thanks to them the patterns and threads from 1936, 1871, 1848 and 1789 become much clearer. Thanks to the Yellow Vests we can better grasp what today's establishment institutions truly want; we have been reminded of the episodes of bloody repression from times incorrectly thought to be bygone. Thus, by incorporating the Yellow Vest experience we can give a more scientific historical analysis of French history and - because of France's unusually prominent role in modern political thought - even global political history.

The second-most important thread which emerges from 1789 to the Yellow Vests is this: The failure of Western Liberal Democracy as a system which can produce broad security for the average person and not just the elite. They Yellow Vests remind that, still, Western Liberal

Democracy can only be imposed by force and without democracy - it is not chosen by popular mandate in a democratic "marketplace of ideas".

In the 21st century I think it may take someone who is personally familiar with the evils of monarchy and shah-dom to realise that the French had it right long ago: Monarchy, and its ideological partners and inbred ideas, are not from some bygone era but are still in force today. Macron means autocracy: that is a fair and common judgment of his five-year tenure. Autocracy is still a problem, the Yellow Vests gorily remind us.

The Iranian Revolution, which in 2022 is still the great revolution of the contemporary era and which was waged against the "king of kings", also reminds us that the shortest summation of the progressive goal of human political efforts is this: To move away from autocracy.

Autocracy - opposition to popular democracy of any sort - is the spring from which all political evil flows, and we saw it in the Yellow Vests, and in the method of governance from Brussels and Paris which provoked the Yellow Vests.

For the Englishmen who insist wizened Queen Elizabeth II could never hurt a fly, unfairly collude with a bank/landlord or covertly join in suppressing opposition to her royal brethren in Morocco, Saudi Arabia and elsewhere - they must also necessarily fail to see that the oligarchy produced by Western Liberal Democracy represents only the barest broadening of the spoils of autocracy. The Yellow Vest grasp this: the "rubber bullet Liberalism" of Macron needs no prefix - Liberalism has always been violence in support of government policies by and for a tiny elite instead of by and for the people.

This book combines understanding of politics today with an understanding of the autocrats who insist on the politics of yesterday

You know about the Yellow Vests, and thus you know what repression Western Liberal Democracy will wage to preserve itself, and you likely also know what a "neoliberal empire" is. But, and forgive me if I am presumptuous, do you know how Western Liberal Democracy truly got here?

It's not easy, because they don't give an accurate accounting of their own history any more than they do for the Yellow Vests.

I am always amazed at how much the history of the 19th century in the US, France and UK is so very ignored by those countries even though this era saw the very formation of the Western Liberal Democracies which their leaders champion so violently today? The reason for this is because this era is full of elitist nonsense, unpatriotic treasons, violence and ever-repeated repressions of the average person. Continuing ignorance about this has only produced domestic political misunderstanding, and thus domestic political chaos. Abroad, this era literally created the disparities which we now refer to as the "Third World", but domestically they were just as awful to their very own people. This is, "... because class warfare" but also, and Karl Marx himself doesn't stress this enough, "... because monarchy", which is autocracy by and for elites; which is perfectly acceptable to Western Liberal "Democracy".

Some contemporary political analysts talk about a "neo-feudal" model because, I believe, of the widespread misunderstanding of the actual history of Western Liberal Democracy, which began in 1789 and the fight against monarchy. But the failure to see Western Liberal Democracy also as international 1%er collusion against the masses implies the failure to see Western Liberal Democracy as also autocratic. Make that mistake and you misunderstand the political foundations of the modern world since 1789, and thus the class struggle, modern imperialism and today's "Bankocracy" - which is to say the entire factual foundation for the sensible and successful choice of Socialist Democracy.

Make that mistake and you'll ask: Why are the French told to have a conflicted and even negative view of Napoleon Bonaparte, even though he was the most influential figure of the 19th century? How can the French 3rd Republic's president, Adolphe Thiers, treasonously and openly collude with Prussia's Otto von Bismarck and still be a Western Liberal Democratic hero? Why do 21st century Westerners call people "neo-nazis" even when such people have zero socialism in their platforms and seemingly no familiarity with the Marxist view of 19th century history? Why are they the "Revolutions of 1848" when they only succeeded in one place - France? If the French Revolution is done and dusted then why is modern Western conservatism still based around the ideas of Irish-Anglo Edmund Burke and his knee-jerk *Reflections on the Revolution in France* from 1790? The first part of this book about the Yellow Vests answers these vitally important questions.

Burke, Karl Marx - the leading historian of the 19th century - and Leon Trotsky - the leading historian of first decades of the 20th century: this book relies on them heavily to help us understand the 2020s. Why am I employing philosophical leaders from the far-right to the far-left? Because, mostly, all three were aware that Western Liberal Democracy was a sham democracy and doomed to failure for everyone but a most unmeritorious elite. They thought these things for different reasons but, just like the Yellow Vests, they are all the most trenchant critics of Western Liberal Democracy.

If the repression of the Yellow Vests doesn't merit a new and serious criticism of Western Liberal Democratic history... then I guess one is avoiding such objective and honest talk until the aftermath of World War III?

So while I may be painted as a naive leftist, an Islamo-leftist, a communist, an apologist, a spy, a reactionary, a fake-journalist - I have heard all these things, amusingly - we still need a cogent critique of modern French history which accurately describes and includes the Yellow Vest era.

This book rests upon the voices of the Yellow Vests: I am simply the facilitator - the one who was on the daily hard-news job when it became clear what "neoliberalism" and "neo-imperialism" means for 21st century France, Europe and beyond.

<—>

Introduction:

A Yellow Vests' history must rewrite contemporary & recent French history

Yellow Vest: "Yes, I am proud of the Yellow Vest movement. We are trying to fix France's many fundamental problems, and we never stopped despite all the repression. What's shameful is that we didn't start sooner, and that our leaders totally ignore us."

The reasons for the Yellow Vests are historical in scope and complexity, but we can never agree on what the movement actually means without having a basic agreement and understanding of French and European history.

The second part of this book analyses the Yellow Vests in detail, but it necessarily rests upon the first part of this book, which is an analysis of the historical, economic and political context which existed up until the arrival of the Yellow Vests. Therefore, this introduction chapter is needed to give the broad strokes of what has happened - with the eyes of a Yellow Vest - over the past several centuries.

Consider the following as a "brief glossary of revolution years", to clarify where this particular writer is coming from, given that historical outlooks are both not universal and easy to incorrectly presume.

1492: Economic revolution: Victory over the Western hemisphere makes war, imperialism and trade newly hyper-profitable for Europe.

1688: England's Glorious Revolution: The trading Whigs use these new types of profits to force in a foreign king, pass the English Bill of Rights and to soon establish the prominence of parliament for the first time in English history - absolute monarchy is thus slightly widened into the creation of an aristocratic oligarchy. For modern Western conservatives this is the start and end of both political and human and rights.

1776: Victory of the new aboriginals (those born in the Western hemisphere) over all classes of Europe. Not a major revolution because no overturning of the social order was attempted. European imperialist/trade designs begin to turn back towards the Eastern hemisphere.

1789: Victory of the burghers, city workers and rural peasants over the clergy and noble classes. Noble class restored by 1815. The modern basis of political rights elaborated in the Declaration of Rights of Man and of the Citizen - first revolutionary attempt at overturning the social order.

1917: Victory of the city workers and rural peasants over the burghers, nobles and clergy. The basis of human rights, including the right to equality, established.

1949: Victory of the rural peasants (confirmed during Cultural Revolution) over the city workers, burghers, nobles and clergy.

1979: Victory of workers and peasants in all areas and the clergy over the nobles and burghers.

1999: Economic debut (eurozone) of 1993 political revolution (European Union debut): Victory of burghers, nobles and new atheist/secular clergy over all workers.

In these eight dates are the most significant political-economic revolutions of the modern era.

The USSR, China and Iran must be included because they built upon the European ideas of 1789 - France was no longer able to do so. Via a class analysis we can see which class triumphed and what changed - which class fell, rose again or was completely altered. We also see that the European Union is as revolutionary a change - in a reactionary sense - as 1789 was, and why.

These eight dates are the simplest definition of what political-economic modernity is and what it became. A leftist-inspired view explains why, and I think this chronology extends deeper in time the Marxist view. Now a bit more detail, which I hope will be refreshing and informative:

In 1491 landed money dominated, as land was the primary source of wealth. Gold and silver was earned by trade and business. But the opening up of the New World was a staggering and revolutionary expansion of both commerce and war (imperialism). Europe is the part of Earth which profited the most, and we can fairly point to 1492 as the rise of the "bourgeoisie" in Europe because it represented an economic revolution as staggering as the industrial revolution: Just as Marx's histories of 19th century France showed how landed, monarchical wealth "became bourgeois" (i.e. similar to and joined with the new forms of industrial-financial wealth), so we can show how imperialist-capitalist wealth "became bourgeois" much earlier. After all, this post-1492 trading class had just as much revolutionary power as 19th century industrial wealth: this is reflected by the 1688 Glorious Revolution, which forced in a foreign (Dutch) king to respect the very first (but still elitist) Bill of Rights of 1688.

The American Revolution initiated the first reversal of Europe's staggering good fortune. In order to sustain their profits and New World investment/ponzi schemes, Europe's trading/imperialist class was forced to attempt unprecedented colonisations of the Old World. The French occupation of Algeria in 1830 was the harbinger of EU neo-imperialism - Europe colonising Europe. (This will be explained further, but it's rarely discussed today how France and Algeria were brothers in a culture much older than "Europe" - that of "Mediterranean Culture".) The American Revolution attempted no overturning of the social pyramid - it only heralded the continuation of more imperialism, which goes on until today.

The primary economic revolution of the French Revolution was not caused by the killing of the king but bythe nationalisation of the lands of the Roman Catholic Church. This produced the *assignat,* truly the wrongly-maligned Bitcoin of its day: It was a new type of paper money - paper which represented the value expected from the sale of the confiscated lands of the Roman church. Edmund Burke, a Whig, the *nouveau riche* trader-based group which rose to power to effectuate the 1688 English Revolution, is universally considered to be the father of modern Western conservatism in not only because he railed in favor of rule by an oligarchical bourgeois-aristocratic elite, but also because he railed against this new "paper money", which would necessarily gain power at the expense of "proper, well-mannered" landed wealth and trader wealth, much as Bitcoin threatens the monetary status quo today.

During the Soviet Revolution of 1917 the nobility fell to never return, truly. Also gutted, finally, was the trader/burgher class. This is the first sustained people's revolution, and it reappropriated the expropriating power of the "bourgeois", which by 1917 was the combination of the different classes of monarchist-landed wealth, trader-imperialist wealth and industrial-financial wealth. Explaining how the different "classes" of wealth combined to thwart the masses - and thus, "... because class warfare" - is one of Marx's greatest contributions. I think, however, he made a mistake not to go back to 1492 and include my aforementioned economic revolution in trade/imperialism. Lenin and his cohorts did not make this mistake of underestimating imperialism, however.

The Chinese Revolution would go further than in 1917 in that the rural masses would no longer be the bottom of the pyramid, but be pushed onto the top. No longer were factory workers and urbanites considered to be the primary repository of and motivator for redistributions of economic and political power, but the average person - period - and that meant the average peasant.

The Iranian Revolution of 1979 marks the return of the clergy class to power, but in a completely different context: Unlike in 1789 the clergy was not stocked by and for the nobility, but here was firmly allied with all workers against the burghers and nobility, while also being conscious of Marxism, Leninism-Stalinism and Maoism.

1999 marks the lamentable return of both the nobles and the burghers, as well as an awful new type of clergy. It's a "neoliberal empire", but it's merely a modern version of what the Whigs installed in 1688. The burghers and nobility/aristocracy/neo-aristocracy (whatever you prefer to call them) have restored their rule over all workers, urban or rural. Its only "revolution" is to institute a secularism - latent and superficial Christianity combined with a strong atheism - which is fully allied with the burghers and elite and against all workers. It's like the French Revolution never happened - oligarchy dominates. The Yellow Vests arrive in 2018 when Emmanuel Macron's "neoliberal revolution" hits the birthplace of political modernity, France.

That is a class analysis which sums up the last 500 years of European history quite succinctly. This analysis correctly reduces the traditional socialist emphasis on the Industrial Revolution, which allows us to expand the importance of the imperialism which began in 1492 and continues into today. After all, reduced wages for factory workers gives the elite much riches, but not as much as imperialist domination and war! And it is not with the railroad but the increase in the power and reach of the ship which marked the true start of West European commerce's ability to create an expanded and more politically-powerful trader class - Henry VIII of England (reign 1509-47) is known as the "father of the English navy", and is one of many proofs I can give to buttress the above timeline and analysis which re-emphasises the power of 1492 and of imperialism's longstanding political influence in Europe.

And for those who want only short aphorisms: The economic life of humanity can be summed up most easily as "slavery, wage-slavery, debt-slavery". Western Liberal Democracy is the desire of the elite for debt-slavery to persist, while Socialist Democracy desires to end both slavery and the elite.

These ideas are obviously both broad and condensed - fleshing them out with more detail is why the first part of a book on the Yellow Vests requires a historical overview which goes back further than just 2018.

> *Yellow Vest: "We have to understand the social misery which is the reason this movement was created. This also is the reason why there is so much social violence. But were the marches to stop now, that would be the movement has failed, and so they must keep marching."*

But there is the world to consider, and then there is just *la belle France.*

The need for a new leftist history of France which incorporates the EU and the Yellow Vests

It's often said that the French are the intellectuals Europe - they are, but not in practice. What's accurate to say is: The French are the *ignored* intellectuals of Europe.

The European Union is undoubtedly the combination of English parliamentarianism with Teutonic fiscal elitism. European history since 1789 is most easily defined as Anglo-Germanic monarchism fighting implacably against the political advances which arose in France.

Those last three words - "arose in France" - are so widely assumed to be true, ethnocentrically, that it requires many, many books to overcome this false arrogance of Europe's sole ownership of political modernity. Therefore, I will spend only this one paragraph on it in this book about the Yellow Vests: The ideas of political freedom and equality obviously spread from the New World to the Old World, contrary to European claims. More accurately, all great cultural advances are the result of cultures inter-mixing. This idea of political equality passing from "west to east" across the Atlantic is proposed in the anthropological book *1491: New Revelations of the Americas Before Columbus* (Charles C. Mann, 2005) and the author's coda is dedicated to calling for more examination of this idea. The truth of this couldn't be more obvious when we realise how much it must have changed colonial Europeans, who were so inured to absolute monarchy, by coming into contact with thriving Native American egalitarianism. We cannot debate this point, though Europeans will, foolishly.

Concepts of political equality are thus not native to Europeans, but why did they sprout first in the French part of Europe? Clearly, geography destined Western Europe to make the first Old World contact with the New World, but why didn't "*Liberté, égalité, fraternité*" arise in England, Spain or the Netherlands?

Again, another difficult question to which I will devote just this one paragraph in a book about the Yellow Vests: In my opinion, entirely too much precedence is given to the modern idea of "Europe" when for France the multi-millennia "Mediterranean Culture" has obviously had a longer and more profound influence. France's history is dominated by 2,500 years of contact with North Africa - Scandinavia and Slavs are but recent friends. In the long-thriving "Mediterranean Culture" France was a major power, but not a primary power: Unlike Greece, Rome or Egypt, France was always a runner-up and never a leader. Therefore they know what it is to be permanently denied empowerment, self-determination, sovereignty, etc. France is seemingly a perennial #2 or #3, even in the past two centuries of imperialism. Significantly, also, they were not re-shaped by Protestantism, which - as exemplified by English and American culture - is often synonymous with an arrogant idea of "bequeathed natural merit, outstanding personal exceptionalism and God's chosen grace". Thus the ever-losing French, with their Catholic (the word means "universal") outlook, would perhaps be especially open among the European colonisers to the enlightened ideas of equality of Native Americans, I believe. This is more difficult to prove, but *voila* - I have laid out my theory, and now turn back to far more practical, knowable matters.

Whatever the reason for France's enlightened political intellectualism, and no matter how much it was smothered by the Hapsburgs, Hanovers, Windsors (name change in 1917: formerly called the house of Saxe-Coburg and Gotha), Bismarcks and Metterniches of Europe, the fact of it remains, as does today's fact that they remain Europe's ignored intellectuals.

The European Union is not based on the ideals of 1789 but the ideals of what is most often termed today as "neoliberalism". But for neoliberalism to ignore 1789 across all of Europe we must realise that ideals of 1789 are suppressed in France today as well, just as the Yellow Vests are suppressed.

> *Yellow Vest: "There isn't democracy any more in France. Macron is a king who hasn't given us anything - he is no different than the king of Morocco or Saudi Arabia - and that's why we can't stop until he leaves."*

In the French book *Le fond de l'air est jaune* (There's a Yellow in the Air) the French historian Sophie Wahnich wrote this about domestic teaching regarding the French Revolution: *"It has practically disappeared from universities."* She attributes this, unsurprisingly, to the Mecca of neoliberalism, the University of Chicago. During the cultural coverage of the bicentennial of the French Revolution - essentially the very timeframe when "neoliberalism" was starting to emerge with Ronald Reagan and Margaret Thatcher - French historian Francois Furet emerged as the most prominent (revisionist) historian of the

Revolution's bicentennial debates. Furet was a commonplace success: the former leftist who renounced leftism for reaction and was thus feted by a capitalist-imperialist mainstream media. Furet replaced the idea of popular action with great man-ism; deemed the French Revolution inherently totalitarian and anti-democratic; and rejected the indispensable Marxist interpretation. Essentially, the French elite silenced the average Frenchman's pride in the French Revolution and forced them to adopt the view of the winners. Which is, as George Orwell wrote, "*To the average Englishman, the French Revolution means no more than a pyramid of severed heads.*" To many young French students now as well, sadly, but not to the Yellow Vests, certainly.

France is more than just the French Revolution, but it is certainly the inescapable foundation of all modern politics. It is only historical nihilism which would insist that there is no differentiating between eras of human history - between caveman and pharaonic, feudal and modern, etc.

Therefore, just as I divided European political-economic history into just two handfuls of key events, we can reject the neoliberal, reactionary view of people like Furet and instead rely on a popular, Marxist-inspired view to help us succinctly update the history of France since 1788:

1788: Absolute autocracy exists across the European Continent, with very mild exceptions of absolute oligarchy, such as in the UK or Hungary.

1789: The move away from autocracy begins - the beginnings for both Western Liberal Democracy and Socialist Democracy. In 1792 the 23-year "European War Against the French Revolution" begins. This era is usually divided into the "French Revolutionary Wars" and the "Napoleonic Wars" in order to distort history.

1794: The apex of Robespierre, wealth redistribution, democratisation and rights for the 99% with the Constitution of 1793 - it is never implemented.

1799: The overwhelming election of Napoleon Bonaparte, the "centrist revolutionary" as First Consul. He takes a middle path between Jacobinism and constitutional monarchy.

1815: Restoration of Bourbon absolute monarchy - political failure of the French Revolution following 23 years of monarchical-led wars to topple it.

1830: Replacement of the land-based House of Bourbon monarchy with the House of Orleans monarchy, which had an industrial-financial base. Conquest of Algeria - a former part of the "Mediterranean Culture" which France has been a key part of since 600 BC - begins.

1848: European-wide revolution as the result of the ideals of 1789 finally being embraced in Germanic lands. Ends in total failure everywhere but France: Western Liberal Democracy begins here, implemented as the 2nd French Republic.

1851: Failure of Western Liberal Democracy provokes the self-coup of President Louis-Napoleon Bonaparte, which would be sanctioned by what was then the largest popular vote in history. He, too, is a "centrist revolutionary" - against both the despised and ineffectual first attempt at Western Liberal Democracy and the absolute monarchs which reign across Europe, still.

1871: Louis-Napoleon Bonaparte is deposed during the Franco-Prussian War of 1871. Paris Commune occurs in response to the popular rejection of monarchy, Bonapartism and Western Liberal Democracy: Socialist Democracy established for first time. Collusion of French Western Liberal Democrats with Germanic & French royalists in the four-month siege of Paris results in the forced restoration of Western Liberal Democracy, implemented as the Third French Republic: "Neoliberalism" begins here. To quote Marx on the Paris Commune: *"The republic has not subverted the throne, only taken its place; become vacant."*

1914: "World War to Forestall Socialism" begins, aka World War I.

1936: Last legislative election of the Third Republic sees French leftists win nearly 60% majority following Western Liberal Democracy's bloodletting, popularly called World War I, and subsequent economic mismanagement, popularly known as the Great Depression.

1940: "Second World War to Forestall Socialism" begins, aka World War II. Majority of France occupied by Germanic National Socialists and Vichy collaborators, who reject both Socialist Democracy and Western Liberal Democracy.

1945-75: Era of Social Democracy begins, greatly influenced by Socialist Democracy's victory across Eastern Europe, China, Cuba and elsewhere. Following the second great bloodletting and economic collapse, both of which were caused by the perpetual failure of Western Liberal Democracy, some economic and political concessions are wrested from the 1%. Known in France as the "30 Glorious Years" due to the economic stability the average French person enjoyed.

1976-99: In the Anglophone world Liberalism gets fully restored - Social Democracy's gains were always fewest there. Liberalism re-wins over the French elite but the French masses fight to maintain the gains of Social Democracy. French popular rejection of "neoliberalism" and the European Union evidenced in successful mass protests, referendums, etc.

2009: Socialism's "20 Years In the Wilderness" ends - a similar era is called the "Special Period in the Time of Peace" in Cuba. Socialism With Chinese Characteristics explodes past Western Liberal Democracy, which has been crippled by the "Great Recession", the anti-democratic methods and aims of European Union & Eurozone, and the wasteful warmongering of the United States.

2010: For the first time in the postwar era France's elite refuses to heed massive French protests after Brussels orders retirement age to be raised. Era of Social Democracy ends, replaced with "Neoliberal Empire" of European Union.

2018: One year after "neoliberal revolutionary" Emmanuel Macron takes office, completing the historic third imposition of Liberalism, the

Yellow Vests appear. Massive repression guts the credibility of Western Liberal Democracy. Final victory of Liberalism in France if Yellow Vests fully repressed?

Yellow Vest: "We are in a dictatorship, and Macron is the dictator. This tyranny existed in France before, but Macron has been arrogant enough to make it obvious to the whole world. Our president is now the enemy of the French people."

Thus we see the reason why the second part of this book is needed: If the Yellow Vests fail then "neoliberalism" will prevail in France across on the continent as fully as in England or the United States.

The Yellow Vests: Are the torchbearers of 1789 the West's last hope against liberalism's complete restoration?

There are those (like me) who constantly decry "fake leftism", which is centrism/rightism posing as leftism. It would be a huge, unforgivable error not to shout eureka when real leftism shows itself - and it does with the Yellow Vests.

What the above quick-histories should indicate is that France's model for the past 70 years - a type of Social Democracy which is as strong as any on the Continent, including the often-cited "Scandinavian model" - has been wilfully dismantled despite spectacular popular disapproval, and thanks to foreign elite domination aided by domestic collusion from French elites. The goal of this unwanted breakdown of Social Democracy is to implement a return to the first post-feudal order (the original feudal order died in 1789) - that of Western Liberal Democracy (born in 1848) - which has already been ideologically defeated by Socialist Democracy (which began in 1871).

To re-paraphrase Marx for 2022: A throne of autocracy still exists, even in Western constitutional republics like France - the people do not sit on it, but an oligarchy. The United Kingdom - the only country to fight against the French Revolution in all seven Coalition Wars against it, from 1792-1815 - is thrilled about that. The Yellow Vests may or may not be revolutionaries for Socialist Democracy, but they are - undoubtedly - fighting to maintain the hard-won postwar concessions which Western Liberal Democrats were forced to temporarily give.

> *Yellow Vest: "We must instill in the French people a thirst for democracy that must never be quenched. This is the only way to free ourselves from the oligarchy that governs us. The mask of France's dummy democracy has fallen, now we must do what it takes to install direct democracy. "*

Call this restoration of Western Liberal Democracy "neoliberalism" if you insist, but a soiled rose always smells unsweet: Western Liberal Democracy joins together landed monarchical money, commercial money, imperialist money, and bourgeois financial-industrial money to put the state at the service of this economic elite and not at the service of the people. To maintain their supremacy this economic elite engages in constant, global class war, with the goal of making no concessions at all to the political and economic redistributions championed by Socialist Democracy.

The above analysis is needed because it precisely explains why the oppression of the Yellow Vests is on a scope which has not been seen in France in nearly a century:

The imperialist wars in Afghanistan, Iraq, Mali, Syria and elsewhere - all of which were raging in 2018 - were not nearly as important to the Western ruling class as the crushing of the Yellow Vest rebellion, which threatened "neoliberalism's" victory over both Social Democratic and Socialist Democratic ideas. Such a victory would entail a redistribution of wealth and power which far exceeds the loss of cheap African uranium, weapons sales to the Middle East or client regimes in paltry

Third World economies. Ask yourself if Marx would disagree - that the oppression of the Yellow Vests, which threaten the entire "bourgeois order" of the 5th Republic, wouldn't be more important to French and Western elite than Tuareg rebellions to wrest control of the sandy northern part of Mali, Assad's ageing Baathists or the Taliban's control of one the world's poorest countries?

> *Yellow Vest: "There has been enormous repression never seen before in France. Even in 1968 it was not as bad as this. But this has been the policy chosen by the president in order to break the movement. We will keep improvising new solutions to win our demands."*

There's a reason their success was so stunning and threatening: The Yellow Vests achieved a 75% approval rating despite a massive police, media and state propaganda war against them and, crucially, despite the reigning context of total rejection of all political actors (unions, media, political parties, political personalities, religious leaders, etc.). They miraculously united a French populace which was seemingly impossible to unite - their only opponent was a 20% "bourgeois bloc", headed by Emmanuel Macron, which - it's vital to recognise - is the direct legacy of absolute monarchy, industrial-financial-imperialist wealth and aristocratic/oligarchical elitism.

From November 2018 until June 2019 France was undoubtedly in a revolutionary situation, in which the mass of the pyramid completely rejected the governance style and governors of the elite. It was only via a Great National Brawl every Saturday, then legalised by a raft of repressive anti-Yellow Vest laws, which frightened an already-apathetic populace back into apathy. No Western imperialist country has ever seen such a long episode of police brutality, lockdowns, assaults, pre-emptive arrests, laws designed to revoke the most dearly held rights of Western Liberalists, propaganda campaigns and everything else heaped on top of the Yellow Vests in order to to scare French citizens from expressing publicly their dissatisfaction with public policy.

The "spectre" of Yellow Vest rebellion thus became synonymous with the "spectre" of the French Revolution and the "spectre" of Socialism - i.e. a long-running, class-based, often Anglophone and Teutonic bias against any change in Europe from what is the barest improvement from absolute monarchy: Western Liberal Democratic parliamentary oligarchy/presidentialism.

This book places the Yellow Vests in this historical context: Yes we can understand these political, economic and social trends. Yes we can understand our own - the people's own - history. Yes we will remember yesterday. Yes we do know the Yellow Vests will be out there next Saturday.

At the heart of the gradual reformism which underpins Western Liberal Democracy is the insistence that we must wait for equality. Why? Why must we wait for the enjoyment of political rights, and for social and economic policies which promote equality? Why should we listen to orders which are issued by those who have the most of the pie to lose, and their sycophants?

The Yellow Vests are not the first to ask these questions, but you must agree that they have asked it the most insistently and courageously seemingly anywhere in the West - and certainly in France - in nearly a century. That alone makes this book necessary reading.

In 2022 two things are certain:

1. Europe's theocratic absolute monarchs - who were truly the first "globalist 1%" - and their ideology of autocracy and elitism have been subsumed by, not opposed by, Western Liberal Democracy.
2. Despite all the repression, maiming, prison sentences, court cases, slander, return of apathy and general climate of fear, at countless traffic roundabouts and demonstrations every

> Saturday the Yellow Vests are essentially doing what Lenin has said the dictatorship of the working classes should do: "Teach every cook to govern the state." They are talking about politics, and they are getting more and more ready to govern.

The Yellow Vests victories are real and must be understood, as they are a potentially international answer to the historic problem of how to progress towards Socialist Democracy, equality and peace. Certainly, they have already re-smashed Western Liberal Democratic totems both old and recent.

We now have a necessary historic overview to begin discussing modern France. Let's begin to break with the Western Liberal Democracy's arch-conservative stranglehold with the next chapter.

<—>

1

The UK's endless reaction: 1789 & feudalism's end creates modern conservatism

It would be boring to defend the French Revolution by showing the moral and intellectual worth of its left spectrum - of Danton and Robespierre, Marat and Babeuf. What's far more interesting is to examine the right's assessment and criticisms of 1789. If we do so we will be exceptionally rewarded - after all, we unearth the very foundation of Western conservatism, and thus the most recalcitrant and blinkered supporters of Western Liberal Democracy.

Edmund Burke's *Reflections on the Revolution in France* is the Bible of modern conservatism, with Burke regarded as that ideology's indisputable philosophical founder. It is no exaggeration to call him the "Marx of conservatism".

It's not only Burke's political philosophy which has become dominant in the West, but his economic philosophy prevails today as well. Read Adam Smith's evaluation of Burke: *"...the only man I ever knew who thinks on economic subjects exactly as I do, without any previous communications having passed between us."*

Additionally, just as conservatives today despise the "fake money" of Bitcoin - which is creating a new class (both a class of monied persons and a class of investment type) - so Burke railed against the French Revolution's creation of paper "fake money". The *assignats* were paper bonds created by the projected bonanza which would be reaped from the sales of the newly confiscated estates of the Roman Catholic Church in France. Burke's condemnation of this - and his promotion of wealth only based in land, gold and commerce - has become adored by stingy conservatives who distrust going off the gold standard in 1971, Quantitative Easting, Modern Monetary Policy and cryptocurrency. Burke was a member of the Whig Party, which established the Bank of England - the first central bank - giving him even more economic relevance to our era of banker domination.

As Burke fears a newly monied class will reduce the power of the established upper class, *Reflections* is full of apparently tolerant concerns (Burke was a Protestant) for the future of the Roman Catholic Church in France. Burke's concerns are nothing but false piety masking his class interests, but *Reflections* is considered by today's conservatives to be a righteous and modern call to defend your true church. Burke defends Christian monarchy as being free from despotism, it being Christian, after all. Such is typical of his logic when it comes to honest self-examination of his motivations. As for the aristocracy beneath the holy autocrat, Burke simultaneously insists that aristocrats in Christendom have always practiced the true faith… but they have been converted to atheism en masse in France over the last century. This mix of multicultural tolerance (as long as that culture is Christian) and loyalty to an unchanging establishment religion (no matter how infested with nobility and disregard for the poor) is quite similar to the faux-religious stance of modern Western conservatives.

Burke also rails against calls for subverting the aristocratic world - a world full of hard-won merit, he insists - by a new media-political-intellectual class which has become divorced from the longtime forces of traditional wealth and the church. In the 21st century technocrats and meritocracy's (allegedly-deserving) victors denounce a new intelligentsia: that of the masses, which is found on Facebook, social media, blogs, etc., which dare to contradict the mainstream media of sacred Western Liberal Democracy, which is - in fact - actually being run ever so well by the establishment's elite.

Burke writes little about 1789's abolition of seigneurial rights, mainly because it's such an indefensible position - in typical English fashion it was certainly bad "manners" to talk of such things openly. Or rather, it had just become bad manners. Burke insisted that a truly noble nobility justifiably rules and oppresses because of the English triumph of socially-concerned "manners" over ancient, individualistic and barbarous Greek "virtue". This idea would help create the alliance between culture and aristocracy which so dramatically moulded the art of the subsequent Victorian Era. Again, Burke's importance resonates with Marxian reach here as well. The Western condemnation of "deplorable" Yellow Vests, Trumpers and Brexiteers for their lack of respect and awe is above all a continuation of Victorian repugnance for the "ill-mannered" and certainly ill-bred masses.

But wait, there's more!

It's said that much of Burke's modern appeal is that he allegedly discovered the roots of modern totalitarianism: He was first intellectual to be spooked by the "spectre of 1789", which is synonymous with the spectre of Socialism, which modern conservatives falsely conflate with totalitarianism. What's obvious to all is that the accusations against Socialism as "totalitarian" from a class of hyper-privileged persons who fear losing their privileges - even if these privileges are abused and then revoked by popular, democratic revolution - are intellectually invalid barring extraordinary proofs of intellectual objectivity. Burke fails that test all over. Therefore the true base of Burke's appeal to modern conservatism in this instance is so hard to categorise that we can only call it psychological. It is easy to define, however: A desire to privilege illogic and inefficiency - the role of an "invisible hand" - in both economic and social affairs, something rejected by Socialism's central planning and demands for equality. Logic, science and mathematical reasoning must always appear terribly totalitarian to those who, like Burke, invariably resort to using an "invisible hand" in their equations which explain and order societal affairs. Burke does not use an "invisible hand" that is truly Godly, because it is not all-embracing and all-levelling, but instead the unplanned order found in hereditary right, unregulated markets, slavishly following an unchangeable tradition/past, and the unplanned order of the unpredictable eccentricities produced by a totally unchecked individualism/autocracy. Modern conservatives agree: an "invisible hand" ultimately rules, somehow, and all humans can do is work around it. Planning against the "invisible hand" is personally anathema to modern conservatives, especially rich ones.

Therefore, in economics, religion, intellectualism, culture and psychology you should see why I am starting off this book with Burke - he combines to become the absolute cornerstone of Western conservatism. *Reflections on the Revolution in France* distills what reasoning is used, and which is used still, to oppose every modern, progressive revolution.

Burke is the man who stood up to the Yellow Vests of 1789 and shouted them down as people who were trashing and upending the economy, who were godless demons that respected nothing, who were too stupid to be listened to much less be allowed to help govern, who were unmannered berserkers, who failed to comprehend that incomprehensibility in human affairs must be endured, and who must stop their critiques of monarchism on pain of being sent to the Bastille, which must be immediately retaken.

Marx had Burke's number: In a single word - "sycophant".

Yellow Vest: "Our recent governments serve only the rich class, instead of serving the people – that's the problem. France has enough money and produces many goods, but these are not distributed fairly. At the same time, our government is taking away the social rights we fought decades to win."

Burke hated 1789, but few realise he wrote just as poorly of nascent Western Liberal Democracy

However, it would be unfair and incorrect to say that conservatism in Western Liberal Democracy can be reduced to encouragements to become a slavish sycophant to the status quo because "conservatism" has universal values like family cohesion, respect for religion, thrift, hard work and modest pride in a modest amount of property. Such traditional concepts are easily also found in Confucianism, Hinduism, the Islamic World and even nomadic life. Therefore, to pin all the West's faults on "conservatism" is illogical, foolish and doomed to failure.

Of course, many Western fake-leftists do exactly that - in the US, for example, the constant claim is that the Republican Party is the sole party responsible for all the evils at home and abroad. This totally ignores the failures of the Democratic Party and of Western Liberal Democracy itself. It's easier to blame conservatism than to refine and enlighten one's own leftism.

But read Burke's masterwork and it's truly impossible not to be struck by what a tremendous toady this Irishman was to English royalty! If the noble class were one-tenth as noble, blameless and competent as he repeatedly claims then nobody would have ever had the slightest notion to overthrow them. If the revolutionary class in France - which is to say, millions of people - were as vile, clueless and without merit as he claimed then they could not even have had the intelligence to tie their shoes much less envision an unprecedentedly democratic and egalitarian type of society.

Examples of his toadying are legion - his fairy-tale account of meeting Marie Antoinette produced eye-rolling even in Burke's own day - so

I will not waste time listing examples. Simply open *Reflections* to any page, stick your finger on a sentence and it will likely be describing the noble class as nothing but people who make Marcus Aurelius look unwise, every small-town cleric as improvers upon the philosophy of Jesus son of Mary, and the king as being an entity of - per the writing of one similar Hindu toady (whose name I forget) - such cosmic goodness that lighting bolts of pure enlightenment shoot out of his big toenail.

Burke's book has become a manifesto because Western conservatives want to be affirmed in the idea that slow reformism of the status quo is the only sociopolitical solution, universally. "Keep calm and carry on", universally, as opposed to discussing and implementing changes which aim to improve equality immediately. He's wrong: oligarchy disguised as ineffectual parliamentarianism (with a monarch or a prime minister or a president) is a less democratic and egalitarian system than that proposed by Socialist Democracy, and this was precisely the cry and proposed solution from the French Revolution up to the Yellow Vests.

But few read Burke for this: His book is also the ultimate takedown of modern Western Liberal Democracy *at its very conception.*

Therefore, we can read him and - undiscussed by modern conservatives - find some very just and salient criticisms of Western Liberal Democracy precisely when the child has first been placed in the cradle. This is the opposites of what modern conservatives usually mine *Reflections* - to find criticisms of Socialist Democracy.

What's vital to realise is that Burke's critique of Socialist (and Liberal) Democracy was not written after "the Terror" or after the rise of Napoleon or - shockingly - even after capital punishment was pronounced for Louis XVI. It was written at the very start of the revolution, in 1790: Burke is writing merely after the fall of the Bastille and the declaration of the end of feudalism! The king lives, but the god has been defiled by the hands of commoners, and Burke pauses in his sucking-up to write a very long letter, in an extremely protracted but impressive style, to a fellow aristocrat in France.

This change in the nature of medieval society is enough to shock Burke the Whig, who is a proto-Western Liberal Democrat because of his acceptance of monarchical oligarchy. He's an aristocrat shocked at losing his privileges over the life and property of his workers. He can't imagine that society doesn't openly declare that his DNA is a cut above the "*swinish multitude*". Burke's shock helps explain why, as I will discuss in the next chapter, the 1688 Glorious Revolution - the birth of English parliamentarianism - is not the birth of modern democracy.

This shock at the very start of the French Revolution form the completely counter-revolutionary basis of his passionate reflections, which are sent in letter form to a fellow aristocrat in France. The letter becomes history's best example of intellectual opposition to the French Revolution from the point of view of both monarchy and modern Anglophone conservatism, and thus early Western Liberal Democracy. By examining the text which first criticised the actions of the obvious forebears of the Yellow Vests, we can see how the criticism of the Yellow Vests' demands is not recent, but goes back over 230 years.

> *Yellow Vest: "For us it was not the 'Great Debate' but the 'Great Smokescreen'. This is why many Yellow Vests quickly refused to participate. We know that nothing concrete will come from those one-way debates. It will ultimately make people even more disappointed in the government, and turn to the Yellow Vests with even more support."*

The notion of ending aristocratic rule: As shocking to the elite of yesterday as it is for today's Western elite

The opposition to monarchy/autocracy and a demand for an equitable redistribution of wealth and political power - this is the battle of modern politics. Whether or not the autocrat is Emmanuel Macron, ruling by executive order and smashing the Yellow Vest demonstrations, or Louis XVI makes no difference in 2022: both their means and their ends are the same - political autocracy. From the time of *Reflections* publication to the Yellow Vests the demands of the average citizen have always been the same: More grassroots rights to political power and wealth for the masses than Western Liberal Democracy is willing to offer.

The great, galvanising crime for Burke was threefold, and I think only the last would be seriously debatable today, and even then only by a few: making the king finally answerable to a single parliament (no House of Lords) composed mainly of non-nobility, the abolition of feudal titles and rights, and France's nationalising of the Roman Catholic church.

Beginning with the last: It should be reminded that what we can call the "nationalisation" of the Roman Catholic church and the dissolution of the Roman Catholic monasteries occurred in England under Henry VIII - via the creation of the Church of England - more than 250 years earlier than in France. The Whig Burke decried this for France even though the Whig Party's early members came to economic prominence in a large part from royal land grants of former Roman Catholic Church lands in England! This book will not debate the merits of Europe's Protestant Revolution - I will simply take that revolution as a grassroots, honest desire for greater emancipation from the Vatican in many ways, economics included. Therefore, England had already profited from their spiritual independence for centuries, yet France should be faulted for doing the same so very much later?

What 1789 demanded was not a complete separation between republic and church, but a pledge of allegiance of the Roman Catholic Church to the new republic in order to create a better, more progressive and more locally-devoted clergy. Fifty-five percent of French clergy would accept to take this new Constitutional Oath, which (again, I am not entering into religious discussions here) can be fairly viewed as a modern and progressive demand to serve your local laypeople well and firstly. Contrarily, the Church of England in 1789 was precisely the same as their aristocratic parliament: a hierarchy headed by sycophants, largely limited to fellow nobles, who were engaged in maintaining the deeply embedded socioeconomic class disparities created by English feudalism. Napoleon's Concordat of 1801 will make peace with the Vatican regarding these changes, and also cement a new and more progressive clergy for France. A complete separation between church and state would not occur until the passage of the "1905 French Law on the Separation of the Churches and State". This pledge from a clergy towards a national democratic revolution was frightening to Burke because it exposed the alleged progressivism of England - which in 1788 had a claim to be perhaps the most progressive country in Europe - for what the nation remains today: an unmodern oligarchy with a rich, landowning church that refuses to engage in a serious questions of redistribution of wealth or political power.

Nationalising the church, attacking the social and economic privilege of the nobility via ending feudalism and constraining the king's power with a parliament which doesn't aim to collude in preserving an aristocratic oligarchy - *these three crimes alone* joined together to galvanise Burke into warning how the French Revolution heralded the slow death of the autocratic order of the oligarchy.

So the French Revolution has just begun and barely a drop of royal blood has been shed but Burke simply can't believe his eyes - he thought that the era of aristocratic autocracy, supported by a clergy which looked the other way and an intelligentsia restricted to sanctioning the first two estates (as Burke did), would go on for ever.

> *Yellow Vest: "France has turned into a system of oligarchy which is run by high finance, and we cannot take it anymore. This is why the Yellow Vests are demanding citizen referendums, especially*

regarding France's banks and our economic policy. That's the only way we can create jobs, schools, hospitals and peace in our country."

The Western Liberal Democrats who oppose the Yellow Vests are precisely the same: they are modern day aristocrats who support the autocracy of the French executive, the elite-only justice of the judicial branch, care not that the legislative branch is stuffed with oligarchs, are unhindered by any appeals from a politically-active clergy, and who either decide to join or bow down to the dictates of the 21st media mainstream media intelligentsia.

This is why reading *Reflections* is so important - to find the initial but enduring justifications for autocracy, faux-meritocracy, technocracy of the inept, spiritual guidance from the unrighteous righteous and minds bent on subservience, i.e. the modern Western conservative whose conservatism exceeds just limits because it is rooted in pre-1789 ideas.

Natural law: We can do nothing about that which justifies every inequality

Burke's ultimate rejoinder to attack the ideals of 1789 is that - and here we see the same justifications of Western Liberal Democratic leaders from the slave-trading time, to the start of imperialism in the Western hemisphere, to the eugenics movement, to today's false "the rich deserve to stay rich because of 'meritocracy'": because caste is "natural".

Indeed, it's that simple to Burke.

Don't kill the messenger - I can't be faulted for relating the faults of modern conservatism: logic, nor a study of history which aims to be as scientific as the subject will allow, nor humanity's finest emotions and desires are a basis for society, but only an invisible hand of "natural" laws which dictate that a high and a low must be created and perpetually preserved.

This "natural" law is the basis of "conservatism" from England, to the caste of India, to the rigid hierarchical view of Confucius, to the frightened and walled-off worldview of tribes and nomads, etc. It's a "bad" conservatism, as it refuses to be compatible with equality and modern - not medieval - justice.

Over and over in *Reflections* Burke justifies the privileges of the aristocracy based on some sort of "natural" superiority and the "natural" need for a subservient class in society in order to prevent proto-Socialist "anarchy", which a modern reader sees Burke confusing with the barest "equality".

Absolutely crucially, he backs their theocratic right to rule - divinity is God-given via birth and bloodline. Burke believes that the "highness" is real and natural of "His and Her Royal Highness". It's so astoundingly forgotten that until the bloodletting of World War I nearly all of Europe was not just feudal police states but also theocracies: kings were kings by "divine right" and were often the heads of churches. England still is this way!

This is something which appears staggeringly obvious to Muslim readers of modern European history, but this incredibly awful theocratic rule in Europe seems to be totally unrecognised in Western descriptions of their political history and situation? It is totally unrecognised how this legacy affects Europeans of today? Europeans act as if they are as many millennia removed from caveman-ism as they are from being ardent supporters of the most irreligious type of theocracy?

Burke is not from the final era of total scoffers at the French Revolution's Rights of Man and of the Citizen, but the very first. Again, it is glossed over in the West how even Liberal Democratic rights are so very new in Europe, as well - the upcoming chapters will remind how the entire 19th century was a victory of the mostly Anglo-Germanic monarchical repression of 1789. The wilful historical blindness of the

Western mainstream - in order to promote ideas of Western exceptionalism and superiority - has lead to total ignorance regarding how monarchy is the cardinal sin of domestic politics and culture.

Beyond this "natural law", it's clear that to Burke and conservatives that money matters, and it matters so much because the presence of money, to conservatives, bestows merit; papers over hypocrisies; make criticism easy to luxuriously ignore. Beyond the ending of harvest taxes, church tithes and other redistributions of wealth from the bottom upwards, the confiscations of the church estates in France began the rise of a revolutionary new "paper" *assignat* money, and as Burke scholar J.G.A. Peacock wrote: *"This is the key to all his analyses of the Revolution, and is bound to remind us of earlier Tories who, in the reign of Queen Anne* (reign: 1665-1714) *had attacked the Whig 'monied interest' and declared that 'the Church was in danger'."* I see his point, but beyond just the arrival of a paper money which went beyond the crux of the English economy at this time - an unparalleled extension of credit (also the crux of the United States in our time) -, the key to Burke's analyses of the Revolution is more accurately: that of a typical modern conservative to any Socialist redistribution of wealth or political influence.

> *Yellow Vest: "We will be marching every Saturday to demand our human rights and our human dignity. We are here because there is no economic justice in France. France is an oligarchy composed of political elite, union leaders and high finance. They suck the life and riches out of the real producers of our nation's wealth - the workers."*

Critically, the Whigs were modern conservatives in their view that all money - whether landed, trade gained from imperialism or industrial wealth - were in harmony, unity and striving towards progress. Burke opposed the paper *assignat* - his class would soon relent and profit from this type of financial instrument. As Marx would put it decades later - all wealth, to the rich, eventually "becomes bourgeois". Modern conservatism will, eventually, accept Bitcoin wealth because they eventually sanction any and all wealth. This is why Burke is a proto-Western Liberal Democrat despite his opposition to the end of absolute monarchy. Both Burke and the modern conservative believe the class war is wrong - the only just war is to fight your way up in class.

Conclusion: A Whiggish clerisy to sanction monied nobility until Judgment Day, which doesn't exist

Many Whigs of the 21st century are attached to their own religion, but there, too, has been a reconciliation. It's an accommodation just as significant as between monarch and president/prime minister in Western Liberal Democracy - that of secularism, the new Western state religion. In France it is called *laïcité*, and it has been employed as a major cultural distraction since the start of the Great Recession. The spate of terror attacks - in which France's foreign policy in Syria, Mali, Afghanistan and elsewhere was seemingly always cited - gave *laïcité* even more media space.

In modern conservatism secularism is the iron law. Secularism necessarily promotes the production of a spiritually-indifferent, neutered, class-unconscious clerisy; secularism doesn't make every citizen this way, but it necessarily produces a class dedicated to preserving secularism. This new clerisy can be attached to an established religion, or public agnosticism, or outright atheism, or even a bizarre new polytheism - as long as said new cleric does not promote mixing religion and politics/economics.

Yellow Vest: "The fire at Notre Dame touched everybody, but there is a big controversy over how we could raise a billion euros for a church so quickly, and why we can't raise such an amount for poor people. There is a lot of anger, and a fire at Notre Dame is not going to change this mental reality."

Western society considers itself to be the apex of progress because it has deposed the clergy but not nobility. The basis of this society is shaky: while it declares humans radically equal irrespective of religion it also declares humans radically unequal as regards to class.

Modern conservatism is Whiggish in that it conflates not just love of the nobility, or the neo-nobility, with patriotism, but religion with mere property: property is sacred, even though it is merely property, and to attack property is heresy in Western Liberal Democracy.

(Except, of course, when that property is of those who choose a path different from Western Liberal Democracy, like Iranians, Cubans, Russians, etc. To such persons and nations religious feeling is not extended.)

Burkean conservatism is not modern but ancient. As applicable to modern society as Marx is Burke is as inapplicable, despite Burke's present-day proponents. He is not modern because he writes not to defend the average person's home, goods and religion but only those of a hereditary aristocracy, which any modern person must disavow. I am speaking of the vital difference between the right to personal conservatism and a political, social and economic conservatism which combats society's efforts to introduce modern, humane equality.

Therefore it is vital that modern leftist wrest unjustified conservatism from the elitists like Burke in favor of a conservatism which also supports revolutionary political ideals.

Conservative types of values are what help anchor society, and that includes revolutionary societies - the difference is in the political-economic bedrock on which your society is founded.

<—>

2

The Glorious Revolution of 1688: England declares 'death to all other revolutions'

Modern conservatism was hugely inspired by Edmund Burke's constant assertion that one is not permitted to remake society into something new because to wipe out the historical context which shaped that society would be immoral. It's the crux of his anti-revolution thesis.

This is the precise logic of modern reformism - i.e., slow reform and improvement of English-style parliamentarianism, which is the political backbone of Western Liberal Democracy.

But it's a cardinal error of the ardent and overdramatic conservative - to give entirely too sweeping a brush to any revolution. Nobody could totally wipe away a nation's historical and cultural context - what's done is done and won't be forgotten, but it can be looked at differently. The past often should be left behind in order to implement a new, more humane legal foundation.

Modern conservatives and Burke, the acknowledged philosophical founder of Western conservatism, ultimately want to continue to be the elite arbiters of what legal, economic and cultural changes get made, whereas Socialist Democracies insist that the mass of the people

- the Third Estate, the proletariat & peasantry, the 99%, etc. - should be the arbiters.

Burke had the opportunities and status he did because he was an aristocrat (the House of Burke was a centuries-old noble dynasty), an imperialist (of Ireland - Burke was born there) and, ironically, because of revolution. Burke's *Reflections on the Revolution in France* is equally a defense of England's Glorious Revolution of 1688 - both of its methods and its results - as it is an assault on the new ideas of 1789 France. It's truly a book which covers two revolutions, and it distinctly marks the political-cultural schism between both Anglophone and Francophone cultures and between revolutionary and conservative cultures.

The methods: A royal coup in England which installed a foreign royal (William of Orange, from the Netherlands). What the English like to focus on is not this anti-patriotic, "monarchy-as-the-original-globalist-1%ers" class aspect, but the fact that it was done without bloodshed, and that it ended a four-decade era of civil war and political changes.

The results: The coup was effectuated by the Whigs, the new social class which had been created off the new profits from Western Hemisphere imperialism and its explosion in commercial trading. I mentioned this in the Introduction: 1492 created a slow but certain economic revolution by making war, imperialism and trade newly hyper-profitable for Europe. By 1688 the Whigs were able to use these profits to force in a foreign king, pass the English Bill of Rights and establish the prominence of parliament for the first time in English history.

Burke was a Whig and, sycophantic Whig that he was, wrote that all revolutions to the post-Glorious Revolution status quo should be denounced as awful - this explains how *Reflections* marks the birth of Western anti-revolutionism. Burke is writing about France but also saying, expressly, that the 1688 intra-elite coup which encoded rights to the noble class is the only revolution which should ever be glorified, and long live the reign of the Whigs.

Thus it's total self-interest; it's total class war long before Marx; it's an alliance of the allegedly-noble rich - whether landed, royal and theocratic rich or *nouveau* imperialist-trader rich; and it's totally reactionary (which is defined as: opposing progressive political or social reforms). It is this eventual unification of all types of wealth - land-based, commercial/imperial, then 19th century financial/industrial - and then their united struggle against the 99% which is what made the Marxist analysis of 19th century European history so provokingly revolutionary. Marx drained the nobility of their Burkean pretensions to a deserved grandeur by pointing out: all you care about is money.

The Glorious Revolution has gone global, partially, like every successful revolution inevitably does - it has become inseparable from Western Liberal Democracy. Ultimately, the Yellow Vests are rebelling against merely the latest failure of Western Liberal Democracy. 1688 is the feudal-era basis of this ideology, which hasn't been "modern" since 1789.

> *Yellow Vest: "It's clear that the government is selling us a democracy which is actually a total illusion. When we see how much violence there has been to the peaceful Yellow Vests, it's clear that French democracy is a dream and not reality."*

Why England's and America's revolutions are not the start of modern politics

Crucially, because the 1688 revolution is based not on the empowerment of the average person and democracy but is instead based on protecting elite privilege, it cannot be considered as the revolution which births modern politics.

It's far more accurate to say that 1688 was the last organised resistance by European elite aimed at containing modern politics.

1688 erected the most vigorous bulwark against modern politics, sadly. The religious emphasis of the English Civil Wars also make the 1688 Revolution far less suitable than 1789 to mark the start of the modern political era, which is defined by class politics - religious wars belong to the earlier era. Nor should the culmination of the colonisation of Ireland during this era permit 1688 to serve as the start of the neo-imperial project of the European Union (that date is 1871, as I explain later) - for one thing, England is not even in the European Union anymore. The proof is also right there in the pudding: from 1688 until today the British Isles are the seat or co-seat of seemingly every effort *worldwide* to fight against the ideals of 1789 and socialist democracy.

But history is a slow process, and we should acknowledge the merits in the Glorious Revolution lest we lose the key thread of political history - the move of away from autocracy. Is that not what the average person has been fighting for since 1789? A major effort of this book is to show how monarchical concepts - such as autocracy and rule by a small elite - must not stop with 1979 Iran and still drastically shape Western Liberal Democracy today.

1688 was important, and not just for its shortcomings:

Firstly, it produced the Bill of Rights of 1688, which should be considered far more important than the Magna Carta of 1215, though the latter is better remembered. The Magna Carta is only a big deal within England - it wasn't even the biggest expansion away from absolute monarchy in its very own era. In 13th century Hungary their aristocracy was far more inclusive and egalitarian: 5% of the country was nobility and the "Golden Bull" decree of 1222 made them all equal, even giving them the right to vote in the most weighty matters of state. (Indeed, the parallels and legacies between this longstanding Hungarian elite class and the elitism of the modern "Austrian School" of political economics are too numerous to list here.)

Secondly, 1688 effectively ended the world's worst - and most historically prevalent - type of theocracy: the divine right of kings. The Puritan Revolution and Oliver Cromwell had done its work and could not be reversed: "Christ, not man, is King" is the epitaph on his tomb. I think a better epithet would be "God, not man, is King", but I'm Muslim. I certainly appreciate Cromwell's point. The awful lovers of monarchy, such as Burke, who opposed Cromwell and his Protectorate republic (1653-59) exhumed his corpse in 1660, the year monarchy was restored - they stuck Cromwell's skull on a pike and placed it on the roof of Westminster Hall for 30 years.

Thirdly and lastly, the Bill of Rights can be best described as a "Rights of Man and of the Citizen… but only Aristocrats are Men or Citizens". It took 100 years for the idea to take root that all humans - and not just nobles - have rights. The aristocrat Burke opposed 1789's attempts to spread this idea just as much as kings, prior to 1688, opposed the idea that nobles have rights.

But the Glorious Revolution was indeed a true advance, and it's with some justification that England thought itself the most progressive nation in Europe. However, 1789 changed this self-perception, and the allegedly post-feudal United Kingdom was now behind the times. It remains there, sadly.

England's Bill of Rights has 13 key articles, and it is nearly identical to the 10 articles of the United States Bill of Rights. Indeed, it is a part of United States domestic propaganda to portray the US Bill of Rights as some sort of spectacular advance when it was clearly modelled on something a century old. The American Bill of Rights was written in 1789, the same year as the French Revolution's Declaration of the Rights of Man and of the Citizen. Absolutely crucially, the 27 articles of France's declaration goes so very, very much further than the American declaration.

It's entirely accurate to say that the Americans did not join with the French conception of political rights but with England's: The Glorious and American Revolutions did not remake their social orders but merely established a limited view of political rights. This explains why modern Western Liberal Democracy easily embraces both the constitutional monarchies of Europe (Spain, Sweden, etc.) as well as the constitutional republic of the US (and France, Italy, etc.).

The US merely codified an oligarchy - American oligarchs were now in charge on the Eastern seaboard, not English oligarchs - and this allows us to explain why modern politics doesn't begin with the American Revolution of 1776 either.

For the common man the Glorious English and American Revolutions are truly "internal coups" more than "revolutions". In neither was there an attempt to fundamentally reshape society - an autocracy expanded slightly to oligarchy is hardly a revolution. 1688 and 1776 are important, no doubt, but it is a complete misunderstanding of modern politics to believe that they are as important as 1789.

It's incredibly telling that Burke barely commented on the revolutionary experience of the United States - it's not that he didn't know what to make of it, which is one reading of his reticence, it's that he both found it entirely good sense but also threatening to the English empire to which he was such a toady.

> *Yellow Vest: "Macron is a puppet. He has a program which aims to ruin the French people in order to benefit a few billionaires. Look at how he refuses to allow a referendum on the proposed privatisations of the airports of Paris. He wants everyone to shut their face and accept whatever he wants, but that's not the way France should be."*

But, history is a slow process, and we should acknowledge the merits in the American Revolution lest we lose the thread.

The American Revolution was an undeniable advance as well because it represented the start of the end of 284 years of European domination of the Western Hemisphere - now the locals (some locals) had some rights and sovereignty. Of course, the aboriginals were not included in the new system of rights in the United States - more proof of how elitist, and not progressive, the American Revolution was.

Yes, the French Revolution was overturned, and The Declarations of the Rights of Man and of the Citizen wouldn't be firmly embedded in a French constitution until 1945, but that's only due to the anti-1789 machinations of its enemies. The French Revolution, while overturned in 1815 via a restored monarchy, was a true advance in Europe's very low level of political consciousness and away from monarchical and oligarchical despotism.

The Russian Revolution would be an even greater advance because it finally extended modern political and human rights to all - even the poorest landless peasant - inaugurating an entirely new era of political history. All revolutions after 1917 (China, Cuba, Iran, etc.) are socialist-inspired and their main obstacle is the same as France's was from 1792-1815: all these other nations, led by the United Kingdom, which seek to pull them back to the old era of political history, one of rights limited to monarchs, sheiks and the affluent. This is the clear, simple pattern of Western politics and global history.

This analysis can only be considered invalid if one believes that Western Liberal Democracy is truly the apex of political thought. The longstanding demand of many French leftists, and not just the Yellow Vests, to found a new republic undermines that claim, as does the incredible repression of the Yellow Vests.

Burke himself was emphatic: 1688 was actually NOT a revolution

It's not just me who argued that 1688 wasn't a major revolution - it's a key thesis of Burke's book!

The glory of England's Glorious Revolution is that change had come without civil war, without any absence of government and without any rule by revolutionaries - thus we see how today's conservatism has absolutely carried this Whiggish banner which demands that change only come through peaceful reformism.

However, the great unsaid of English parliamentarianism and then Western Liberal Democracy is that this peaceful reformism must be entirely guided by the ruling oligarchical elite. Class analysis, and an objective accounting of modern history, tells us that this oligarchy will always fear losing their power and privileges to the people - thus, Western Liberal Democracy is aristocratic to its marrow. Thus there's a constant criticism of Western Liberal Democracy that it is unable to be genuinely reformed into a system which focuses on the 99%, and not the 1%

Part of the conservative retort to revolution has always included that even a temporary absence of government is a fearful Rousseauian "state of nature", which can only result in either the falsely-alleged anarchy of Socialism or a civil war that features pure hysteria and zero ideology. Order must be kept... because the oligarchy must not lose power, of course. "Keep calm and carry on" - the English phrase which swept the Anglophone world during the economic collapse of 2008 - perfectly incarnates this view of a slave which loves the order provided by his master.

The analysis that England's 1688 Revolution is the true foundation of modern democracy is something which Anglophones will persist in, mainly because they have not actually read Burke.

Specifically what shocked Burke in *Reflections* was the presumption: "*that we have acquired a right:*

1. *to choose our own governors*
2. *to cashier them for misconduct*
3. *to frame a government for ourselves*"

Burke does not only reject these basic democratic rights for the French in 1789 but he asserts that the Glorious Revolution did not employ these rights either!

Therefore don't believe my opinion that 1789 is the true start of modern politics - Burke himself says that 1789 cannot claim to be following any democratic precedent allegedly set by 1688. Burke himself says that the Anglophone system rejects anything but an unaccountable autocracy.

1789 was thus rejected by English conservatism, just as they obviously also reject 1917, 1949, 1959, 1979, etc. We all expect English and modern conservatives to reject everything from 1917 on, but what's rarely admitted is how modern conservatives fully reject 1789. This rejection persists in the 21st century even though by the 1970s the ideals of 1789 had become commonplace across the West.

Burke continues after his 3-part list:

> *"This new and hitherto unheard-of bill of rights, though made in the name of the whole people, belongs to those gentlemen and their faction only. The body of the people of England have no share in it. They utter disclaim it. They will resist the practical assertion of it with their lives and fortunes. They are bound to do so by the laws of their country made at the time* (1688) *of that very Revolution which is appealed to in favor of the fictitious rights claimed by the Society which abuses its name."*

Both "*their faction*" and "*Society*" refers to the Revolution Society of England, a group which supported the French Revolution. Burke correctly notes that none of these three principles are found in the Bill of Rights, which is the practical and legal embodiment of the principles of the Glorious Revolution of 1688.

French revolutionaries, Napoleon Bonaparte included, had initially been inspired by England as a model. This is expressed by Burke in the above phrase, "*of that very Revolution which is appealed to in favor*". They soon realised that they were seriously mistaken. Burke repeats this French disenchantment with English oligarchy in greater, necessary detail:

> *"Your leaders in France began by affecting to admire, almost to adore, the British constitution; but as they advanced they came to look upon it with a sovereign contempt. The friends of your National Assembly amongst us have full as mean an opinion of what was formerly thought the glory of their country. The Revolution Society has discovered that the English nation is not free. They are convinced that the inequality in our representation is a 'defect in our constitution so gross and palpable as to make it excellent chiefly in form and theory'."*

Yes, France's revolutionaries took a closer look and realised that they were totally mistaken about England's relationship with democracy. Perhaps someone misinformed them that Cromwellism had prevailed?

The conservatives who knowingly or unknowingly cling to 1688 or 1776 are either rewriting or misunderstanding history, but Burke was well aware that the admiration of the British model quickly changed to contempt in France - all it took was a proper understanding of the limited rights England offers the common man. France's riposte was the Declaration of the Rights of Man and of the Citizen, a spectacular leap ahead of Britain and the US.

Indisputable: 1789 launches modern politics - the fight against monarchs and Macronian autocrats is the fight of today's politics

Burke's account of the Glorious Revolution in *Reflections* would eventually dominate English thought on two subjects. He became the explainer of two revolutions - one "preserving" and one "destroying". His flaw is being totally wrong on which one should receive which treatment.

> *Yellow Vest: "There is no way the Yellow Vests will stop until the government responds to our needs and our democratic demands. As long as the government doesn't change, neither will our insistence on real changes."*

The modern Western conservatism which thwarts all progressive revolutions is not interesting, but the enormous flaws, egotisms and the lust to implant illogic in human affairs which abound in Burke's philosophy must be exposed for its fallacies.

And yet, the coming chapters will see me further quoting Burke for his accurate predictions for and criticisms of what will become known as Western Liberal Democracy, which becomes rooted in the disastrous 2nd Republic of 1848-52 France.

Above all, Burke is vital to remind us of what exactly modern conservatism has to "conserve": an anti-patriotic, 1%er, class warfare view of human society. The only name for this used to be "monarchy", the first system which put class loyalty above national loyalty:

> *"But a more decisive proof cannot be given of the full conviction of the British nation that the principles of the* (Glorious) *Revolution did not authorise them to elect kings at their pleasure, and without any attention to the ancient fundamental principles of our governed, than their continuing to adopt a plan of hereditary Protestant succession in the old line, with all the dangers and all the inconveniences of its being a foreign line full before their eyes and operating with the utmost force upon their minds."*

Burke admits that the principle of hereditary possession, of religious segregation and of democratic repression override any patriotic concern.

Burke also admits that the invasion of a foreign Dutch army was just solely because it ended the threat of Cromwellian republicanism possibly flowering into the ideals of 1789, thus threatening the Whig oligarchy.

> *"The Revolution of 1688 was obtained by a just war, in the only case in which any war, and much more a civil war, can be just.* Justa bella quibus necessaria. (Livy: Wars are just when they are necessary.) ***The question of dethroning*** *or, if these gentlemen like the phrase better, 'cashiering kings', will always be, as it* ***has always been****, an extraordinary question of state, and* ***wholly out of the law - a question*** *(like all other questions of state) of dispositions and of means and* ***of probable consequences rather than of positive rights****."*

The emphasis of mine is added to make clear:

Modern conservatism means that no one has the right to depose a king or president - no matter how repressive, or poorly they govern - because it's not about rights but of consequences, the consequences being the end of the oligarchy's dominance. Political leadership is a "*question of state*" - i.e. a question for the elite to handle among themselves because they are the state.

Modern conservatives collude, for the absurd reasons enumerated by Burke's book and summarised in the previous chapter, to uphold this undeserved dominance. Modern conservatism has not changed from Burke - they continue to use his same faulty, elitist rationales.

The status quo cannot be dethroned?! The French Revolution disagreed, and Napoleon Bonaparte - the focus of our next chapter - would not be enthroned but voted into the throne, something Burke surely would have fainted at.

<—>

3

Modern political history makes no sense if Napoleon is not a leftist revolutionary

"The peasant was a Bonapartist because the Great Revolution, with all its benefits to him, was, in his eyes, personified in Napoleon."

— Karl Marx

To be against Napoleon Bonaparte in the 19th century was to totally reject grassroots, democratic French opinion, and thus to be against the French Revolution itself. It was to cede the view of Napoleon Bonaparte to his enemies: the English snob, an in-bred Austrian king, a colluding and traitorous Italian noble, a Hungarian aristocrat, etc.

Modern Western political history simply makes no sense - it loses the thread of expanding power away from the absolute ruler - if we do not take the view that Napoleon Bonaparte was a leftist, as his citizen contemporaries did. Making Napoleon a demon of bloodlust and ambition, just another fascistic military man, a secret reactionary, etc. - all is designed to obscure the importance of 1789 and to reverse it.

The willing desire to lose the thread of progressive history was especially evident in the awful reporting surrounding the 200th anniversary of his death, in 2021. The coverage in France was surprising sparse and can be summed up with three words: "tyrant" and "controversial legacy". A fake-leftist, and thus totally deluded, view was routinely proffered, typified by state media France24's article: *"Napoleon: Military genius or sexist, slaving autocrat?"*

The official anti-Napoleon smokescreen was personified by President Emmanuel Macron's speech on the bicentenary, which ended with: *"I have no intention to say if Napoleon realised or instead betrayed revolutionary values. I will of course steer clear of such territory."* Of course he will steer clear - Western Liberal Democrats always do, because they are the ones who work to ensure that the revolutionary values of 1789 are never realised.

Here is your simplest retort to those who accuse "tyrant": Napoleon was voted First Consul for life and then emperor by millions of people, and the "voted" part is what made it these appointments spectacular political advances for its era. The other monarchs of his era were merely more unelected dictators. Secondly, his constitutions were also ratified by many millions - another spectacularly leftist advance. These things simply cannot be dismissed because it would be more than a century before they would be emulated in most of Europe. The number of referendums on monarchy in global history only total a few dozen, and nearly all were after 1950.

Simply ask if the king of Saudi Arabia, Morocco or the behind-the-scenes monarchs of Europe would ever put themselves to a public vote? When it comes to the schism between the Muslim and Western worlds perhaps the single largest problem is that the latter totally forgets the violent threat, the crude insult, the perpetual theft which is hereditary monarchy. Because the West forgets this they also fatally misunderstand their own European history since 1789, and thus they fail to see Napoleon Bonaparte as a leftist hero.

Making Napoleon Bonaparte worse than his absolute monarch peers is a preposterous revision of history and totally excludes the political view of the European peasant and working class. Ask a subject who never voted for his monarch: There is no "controversial legacy".

> *Yellow Vest: "We are here to protest against the abusive government and this kingship-presidency of Emmanuel Macron. The Yellow Vests are here to promote a true vision of democracy and to redistribute our nation's wealth. Every election there is more and more abstention because people don't believe in mainstream politics anymore."*

What an objective view reveals is this: Revolutionary France saw not just one but seven "Coalition Wars" to restore monarchy, privilege, feudalism, torture, inequality, racism and the oppression of an aristocratic elite. From 1792-1815 Europe's elite refused to make peace with the socio-political advances of the French Revolution, which the French people democratically chose again and again and again. England was the only nation which participated in every war, and it repeatedly paid off other nations to join them.

The simplest retort to those who call the French Revolution "imperialist" is this: The French Revolutionary Empire at its greatest height - in 1808 - *was the result of defensive wars which it won.* All the Empire's territory was gained as punishment for aggressive wars against France or lost by rebelling populaces choosing to side with France, with the sole exception of Portugal. All seven Coalition Wars were attacks on France, all to prevent democracy from spreading across autocratic Europe.

The "Napoleonic Wars" have absolutely no reason to be set off from the more accurate "European Wars Against the French Revolution" unless that reason is obfuscation. This 23-year period must be looked at as a whole, because it wouldn't have mattered if it was Napoleon in charge or not as long as the ideals of the French Revolution were being employed - the Revolution would have always been aggressed. Like Iran, Cuba and the USSR know, 23 years of military intervention by royalists or Western Liberal Democrats to stifle progressive, anti-elite political systems is simply *de rigeur*.

This chapter is not a whitewashing of Napoleon Bonaparte, but a refusal to say that his entire revolutionary career from 1789 to 1815 should be judged on the basis of the last few years. Napoleon's primary leftist and anti-revolutionary failure was his development of dynastic intentions. However, we are not taking about this turn to personal gain until 1810, when he married Marie-Louise, a princess of the Austrian Hapsburgs, the corrupt and wasteful absolute monarch ruler of most of the continent. In *Napoleon, or, the Myth of the Savior*, Jean Tulard, perhaps the pre-eminent French historian of this era (and not a pro-Napoleon one in my estimation) wrote, *"On St. Helena, Napoleon, 'brutally awakened from his dream of monarchic legitimacy' confided that he should have married a French woman and, above all, not a princess. He saw clearly, but too late."* Napoleon's error was in forgetting that he already enjoyed more leftist legitimacy than any monarch ever - he was the first to be voted in. The counter-revolutionary monarchs of everywhere else would never accept that because the French Revolution was - above all - against unsanctioned autocracy. Similarly, putting his brothers in charge of countries which willingly joined France was another leftist error in line with dynastic intentions, but this wasn't really unpopular until the imposition of Joseph Bonaparte as King of Spain, who replaced the feudal Bourbons, in 1808. Napoleon himself said that one of his greatest mistakes was reintroducing the ranks of the nobility, also in 1808. The three criticisms here are all related - the restoration of elite privilege and hereditary oligarchy - but we would be inaccurate and unfair to not emphasise that this trend only occurred two decades into Napoleon's spectacularly successful revolutionary career and amid constant refusal to make peace with Revolutionary France!

Was Napoleon's vision of the French Revolution that of the left of the Revolution, epitomised by Robespierre and Marat? No, but calling a lifelong revolutionary soldier like Napoleon Bonaparte a "non-revolutionary" because he was not completely on the left side of the revolutionary spectrum is to absurdly say that there is no "revolutionary political spectrum". It is to say that the "revolutionary political spectrum" is the same as the non-revolutionary, typical "political spectrum", in a total falsehood. It is to undemocratically excise the revolutionary viewpoints of his millions of comrades, and also of the democratic majority of his time. What is certain is that it is to reveal essentially no first-hand experience with any real revolution at all, as such a view of revolution is a fool's fairy tale of pure idealism.

By distorting Napoleon - by saying that Elvis was always "fat Elvis" and never the king of rock and roll who shook the world - today's 1% can keep 1789 totally dead.

Napoleon is the key to keeping 1789 alive and continuing to implement its most progressive, leftist ideals.

It is simply astounding that the left doesn't find so much to embrace in Napoleon Bonaparte. What I list here are only the absolutely critical facts of his political career, and they undoubtedly demonstrate his leftism.

The 1790s: Napoleon's leftism was vetted over and over by the revolution

Prior to the Revolution Napoleon was born a minor noble in Corsica, putting him in the top 2% of France. However, being a minor noble in poor Corsica was to have title and little property - it's not Burgundy. When half of France's nobles exiled themselves over the Declaration of the Rights of Man and of the Citizen Napoleon was already in the 1%. Napoleon Bonaparte - like Mao, Castro and others - was another leftist hero who defied the dominant view of his elite class.

Napoleon grew up in the aftermath of the repression of Corsica's independence movement. The incredibly progressive Corsican Republic

(1755-69) included a Liberalist constitution, the first implementation of female suffrage and was the first-ever practical application of the modern political ideas of people like Voltaire and Rousseau. France took control of the island, and they were a big improvement from the previous landlord, Genoa. When the French Revolution began Napoleon saw it as capable of bringing even more progress to Corsica. Thus Napoleon was one of the very first of many "foreigners" (he was born shortly after France took control of the island, and thus was truly French) to seek domination not by France but by the ideals of the French Revolution.

As the 1790s went by Napoleon obviously had to be vetted over and over by the leaders of the Revolution. In 1793, Napoleon was friendly with none other than Augustin Robespierre, Maximilien "The Irreproachable" Robespierre's brother, who surely would have sniffed out someone not committed to the ideals of 1789. When the brothers were executed in 1794, marking the end of the leftist Jacobin era and the start of the Directorate era (1794-99), the Directorate tried to get him to quit by downgrading him to the infantry.

Lucky for them Napoleon refused to leave: in Paris on October 5, 1795, he would save the Revolution from a major royalist revolt using what was the undoubted foundation of his military genius - his mastery of new artillery technology.

He became a national hero, and thus the Directorate spied on him to check for dangerous traits. Their spying general wrote back to the Directorate: *"It is a mistake to think he is a party man. He belongs neither to the royalists, who slander him, nor to the anarchists, whom he dislikes. He has only one guide - the Constitution."* Facts: Robespierre was anything but an anarchist, and being a constitutionalist in Europe in 1796 made one a revolutionary. Failure to accept this will create misperceptions which will extend to misunderstandings of our present day.

Confidence renewed, the Directorate gave Napoleon command of the Army of the Alps, and his subsequent campaign in Italy cement his status. He started by immediately court-martialling two of his soldiers for shouting "long live the king".

Of course the Italians and others embraced the revolution being offered by France's peasant army! In liberated lands we find the same actions of the French Revolutionaries over and over: feudal dues and tithes abolished, Jews not forced to wear the star of David and Muslims no longer second-class citizens, the first uncensored newspapers allowed to open, slavery abolished, the first constitutions legalised. Keep all that in mind the next time you read of how Napoleon "enslaved Europe" - such total reversals of reality are only used for the truly great leftist leaders. It was so popular ex-Papal states petitioned to join the new Cisalpine Republic. *"In annexed countries teaching was allowed to keep its own identity; French did not become an obligatory second language, there was no attempt to destroy the soul of conquered provinces,"* writes Tulard. The French Revolution, itself intensely patriotic, fostered patriotism elsewhere - this would be called "nationalism" and is part of the reason the French were eventually forced out in annexed countries, ironically.

The great man-ism inherent in Western Liberal Democracy wants to talk about Napoleon's military genius in things such as issuing bold flanking orders. It's foolish: We can credit Napoleon's military genius for doing something without precedent - storming a bridge under heavy fire - or we can credit the revolutionary inspiration of the actual troops that did the storming. Napoleon's ability to inspire (well-known, and real) is still not at all the same as the zeal inspired by revolutionary principles. To not realise is this is, again, to have no experience with revolution.

Napoleon biographer Vincent Cronin writes in *Napoleon Bonaparte: An Intimate Biography*: *"In analysing why Napoleon won battles in Italy, one is also analysing why he always - or nearly always - emerged successful from a battlefield. The first quality was discipline. Napoleon, with his legal forbears, was a great person for law and order. He insisted that officers issue a receipt for everything requisitioned, be it a box of candles or a sack of flour. … In letter after angry letter he condemned sharp practice by army suppliers.… Napoleon was merciless towards these men and when one of them made him a gift of fine saddle horses, hoping that would close his eyes to embezzlement, Napoleon snapped: 'Have him arrested. Imprison him for six months. He owes us 500,000 ecus in taxes.'"* Here we see the moral legitimacy which won him followers in the army, and that is better than issuing bold flanking orders.

The Egyptian campaign: After examining and giving up the idea of invading England, an invasion of Egypt was the best way of striking always counter-revolutionary England. It was not mere adventurism - Revolutionary France was fighting for its life, so there was no time nor funds for tourism to see the Pyramids. Napoleon read the Koran on the way to Egypt and declared it "*sublime*". He was inspired enough to say in his first declaration, "*Cadis, sheiks, imams - tell the people that we too are true Muslims.*" The French Revolution was universal in scope, like Islam, and Napoleon did not believe in the Trinitarianism of Roman Catholicism, and nor does Islam. The muftis found Napoleon sincere as a person but not actually willing to become a Muslim - they proclaimed Napoleon's God messenger and a friend of the Prophet. With humanitarian ideals and actions, and replete with its famed scientific corps, it is thus totally different from France's imperialist invasion of Algeria in 1830.

In August 1799 he got his first news from Europe (due to the British blockade) that the 2nd European War Against the French Revolution had begun and that France was collapsing: Russian-Anglo forces in the Netherlands (which had joined the Revolution willingly), while Austro-Russian forces were in Switzerland (joined willingly as well) and Italy (joined willingly as well), with Turco-Russian forces in Corfu, Greece. Napoleon waded into that for personal glory, some say - to keep fighting to save the Revolution, say the less cynical.

As First Consul: Good leaders get elected and then re-elected - this truly all started with Napoleon Bonaparte

Napoleon made a political alliance with none other than Abbot Emmanuel Sieyès, the same "abbé Sieyès" whose 1789 manifesto *What is the Third Estate* became the manifesto of the French Revolution and the literal groundwork for the entry of the lower class into politics. (The pamphlet begins, famously: "*What is the Third Estate? Everything. What has it been hitherto in the political order? Nothing. What does it desire to be? Something.*") Still not leftist enough for some, though…?

The undoubtedly revolutionary principle of constitutionalism upon which Napoleon rested is reflected in the poster put up after his participation in the coup of 1799 (Coup of 18 Brumaire) and the start of the Consulate era (1799-1804): "*THEY HAVE ACTED IN SUCH A WAY that there is no longer a Constitution.*"

Was constitutionalism the only demand of the French Revolution from 1789-1799? No, it was simultaneously revolutionary and "middle-of-the-road". Napoleon never did side with the royalists - that would have been an undeniable betrayal of the Revolution - nor with the Jacobins, nor with their executors the less-leftist Thermidorians who ran the 5-man Directorate (one of whom was currently asking for 12 million francs to restore the Bourbons). Instead, Napoleon placed himself above party politics and alongside the concept of constitutionalism, which, along with his repeated military defences of France and the Revolution, won him popular acclaim. Of course Napoleon embraced many other primary political ideals of the Revolution: an end to feudalism, an end to absolute monarchy, the division of common land, civil equality, the suppression of tithes and seigniorial rights, and nationalisation of the property of the Roman Catholic Church. What's vital to recognise is that the social aspects of the revolution - free education, health care, food - weren't even much discussed until 1796, via leftist hero Gracchus Babeuf, the continuer of the now-executed Robespierreian left. Faulting Napoleon for not holding out for free education for the masses is to critically forget that these social questions were in the infancy of political expression, and certainly were limited to the progressive vanguard of an already unprecedentedly progressive revolution.

In 1800 his coup and his constitution were both overwhelmingly approved by millions in a vote - a vote totally unprecedented in scope, reach and political progress. People who wish to ignore these votes are simply baffling, and biased. The coup was bloodless, as well. Napoleon - the alleged new dictator - is credited with giving the new constitution the idea of universal male suffrage and not just voting rights for property owners.

France went on to win Second European War Against the French Revolution - a bit of peace, finally. Napoleon the general became Napoleon the elected public servant. His administrative energy was as amazing as his martial energy: "*The ox has been harnessed - now it must plow,*" he said.

Napoleon took great interest in consolidating the best of Roman, custom/precedent and Revolutionary laws into the new *Code Civil*: equality before the law, end to feudal rights and duties, right to choose one's work, inviolability of property, right to divorce and freedom of conscience. All were unprecedented leftist advances. The *Code Civil* is not at all the "Napoleonic Code" but more accurately the "French Revolutionary Code". It was "*an instrument of war against feudalism,*" to quote Tulard, and its influence is inestimable and global.

Napoleon curbed widespread brigandage, and pacified rebellions which had lasted years. He brought peace to France after a decade of civil war, and yet he did not give the army a privileged position. He even forbade them from getting involved in civil matters, something he considered "*madness*".

He declared an amnesty for those living abroad, which anyone personally familiar with revolution knows has an inestimable positive effect, but also some negative ones.

Napoleon ended yet another war in 1801, when French churches finally reopened after the signing of the Concordat. The agreement okayed French nationalisation of Church lands (the sales of which did the most to effectuate an economic revolution downwards), maintained religious freedom, did not declare Roman Catholicism the official religion of the state, allowed the French state to pay clerical salaries (giving them a decent standard of living), had the clergy swear an oath of allegiance to the state, and banned nearly all the monasteries (viewed as parasitical and useless in France, whereas the useful teaching nun orders would soon be doubled). Of course, this recently-installed Pope would ultimately side with the monarchists against the Revolution, but there's no doubt that Napoleon secured the Revolution's aim in neutering the Church's power in France, a major goal.

On only two occasions did he involve himself in local governance of the *prefects*: one of them was to stop a prefect from forcing vaccinations - draw your own inference regarding the coronavirus epidemic of 2020-22.

The currency never had to be devalued, the cost of living became stable, he spent more on education than anything else, built three great roads, canals and ports each, attained full employment, stable prices, a positive trade balance, increasing population, and presided over a 180-degree shift in public spirit after a decade of civil and foreign violence.

So of course he was popular - he was making the principles of the French Revolution law, which broke with the absolute monarchy that reigned essentially everywhere else in Europe.

Elected emperor: Democracy combines old forms with new ideas - conservatives are overdramatic

By 1802 Napoleon had committed the crime of making the Revolution workable, peaceful and - worst of all - attractive. A Third Coalition was declared; at home royalists kept trying to assassinate him.

> *"Thus the need to establish monarchical power in France for the sake of permanent peace was put forward. The word 'form' was essential. The spirit of the Revolution would be respected but the outwards appearances of executive power would need changing; it required a a title which would fit in with those of other European countries,"* writes Tulard.

In 1802 he was was voted Consul-for-life by 3.5 million people (against 0.008 million opposed), a staggeringly progressive occurrence for the time - ignoring this is to lose the entire thread and principles of what progressive politics are! However, what should be well-known to all readers is that progressive revolutions are not allowed to evolve in peace, and that foreign powers constantly place pressure on them to make unplanned compromises.

> *"It was in fact precipitated by the renewal of conflict with England. … Rather, there was a tendency to increase his power in order to ensure the defence of the land. A dictatorship of public safety was needed. How could it be entrusted to anyone other than Bonaparte? At this moment the Royalists inopportunely chose to renew their plotting.… The revolutionaries saw in the consolidation of the First Consul's power… the only bulwark against attempts to restore the monarchy."*

It is with this lifetime appointment in 1802 that many republicans were dismayed and many leftists say the Revolution ended. If one wants to call it "despotism", it's false. It's a bit contradictory, it's totally different and revolutionary, it's provoked by foreign aggression, it's better than anyone else's around and it's still incredibly progressive for its era! *"It seemed, above all, to be the surest means of maintaining a stable government, putting an end to intrigue and plotting. This in no way represented the acceptance of a Bourbon-style dynasty. The Empire was first and foremost a dictatorship of public safety, designed to preserve the achievements of the Revolution."* Again, that's from an author, Tulard, who is not strongly pro-Napoleon - he is, however, a Frenchman who understands his country's history.

Napoleon has still not betrayed the revolution at this point in any serious way! In a move which was preceded by much discussion, he took the crown of Emperor from the Pope's hands in a public (another first) coronation not because of the bosh about how it was his own arrogant and usurping personal power which won the crown, but because it was the people which had crowned him. This is all a huge difference from the divine, theocratic right of kings, which Prussia, Russia, Austria and countless other local kings would insist on in total autocratic form until 1914.

If the French Revolutionary Emperorship was a typical emperorship - and thus no ideological threat - why did it not cause the European Wars Against the French Revolution to stop? The answer is obvious to those who are objective.

In 1806 the Fourth Coalition saw Prussia and Russia attack - France wins again and Prussia is compelled to finally renounce serfdom.

In 1808, popular revolt against the Spanish king in the "Tumult of Aranjuez", which is still celebrated today, ended the Bourbon dynasty. The overthrow of the Bourbons, and the sheltering of the new ideals of the French Revolution, allowed Latin America to win their independence.

The French Revolution has spread to the New World. It had already spread to the oldest of the Old World: Mohammad Ali founded modern Egypt in 1805 after France had defeated the Mamluks.

The French Revolution starts to topple - revolutionary zeal starts to wane following decades of foreign attacks

This is where things start to turn badly: 1808 Spain is not yet at the point of 1789 France. Proof? After 1815 Spain is the only place where feudalism would actually be restored. The guerrilla war saps France, which is supported by Spain's progressives, abolished the Inquisition and ended feudal rights - hardly a terrible legacy.

The war in Spain coincides with when Napoleon starts to let the emperorship go to his head and thinks more of preserving his dynasty than of the Revolution - he is always thinking of France, however. His Continental Blockade against England would have bankrupted them… if France didn't also have to fight in Spain and Russia, too. The French Revolution is always attacked from all autocratic sides - this must be remembered because it so greatly shapes their possible choices. After a few years the Continental Blockade turns into pro-French economic imperialism, in a non-leftist mistake. Spain, the Blockade, dynasty - these are the three key mistakes Napoleon made. However, he does not deserve a permanent "Ogre" caricature for these three because two of them are fights against autocracy.

The Fifth Coalition of 1809 saw the awful Hapsburgs' last stand, the arrival of huge modern wars of attrition, conscripted armies, and the growth of nationalist movements which Revolutionary France had expressly fostered.

Tsar Alexander refuses to allow Napoleon to marry into the royal family, so he marries into the Hapsburgs instead. The marriage did not cement an alliance for peace - which was entirely the aim - because

Austrian royalty, like the simply awful Metternich, were not only Teutonic racists but completely aware that France represented revolutionary change which was incompatible with autocracy. It was Metternich (who takes the mantle from France's Talleyrand as the most dreadful and shameless politician of his generation) who is credited with the propaganda theme of "Napoleon as mere personal ambition".

France invades Russia because Moscow refused to end their threats to the revolution - first Russia, then England, then peace, finally, was the plan.

Why didn't the French Revolution free the serfs? Certainly leftists today would have acclaimed Napoleon more. Napoleon reflected: "*They wanted me to free the serfs. I refused. They would have massacred everyone; it would have been frightful. I warred against Tsar Alexander according to the rules*; *who would have thought they'd ever burn Moscow?*" Such objections miss the entire point of the French invasion of Russia - to force the Tsar to accept peace towards the French Revolution, and there would have been no peace if the serfs had been freed. France was already trying to administer the Netherlands, Belgium, Switzerland and other places - how could they administer huge Russia as well?

Indeed, who could have guessed that the Tsar would defeat his own peoples in order to defeat Napoleon, i.e. the scorched earth tactic, which Clausewitz proved "*were only applied accidentally by headquarters*," per Tulard. Say slaver monarchs defeated Napoleon - it makes fools of Russian serfs to say that their sacrifices were correct instead of manipulated; they would get their revenge against such misguided, brutal managers a century later.

Napoleon was keeping 250,000 seasoned troops in Spain at this time, let's recall. He said his two main mistakes were not wintering in Vitebsk, Belarus, and instead going to Poland. He ignored the original option - staying in Moscow - which had plenty of noble-abandoned supplies to live off of. The second mistake was in trying to get peace from the Russian absolute monarchists, who never wanted peace, like all monarchists. "*I thought that I should be able to make peace, and that the Russians were anxious for it. I was deceived and I deceived myself.*"

After the disastrous retreat from Moscow the monarchs of Europe jumped on Revolutionary France in 1813 with the immediate Sixth Coalition, the first knockdown blow to the French Revolution after more than 20 years of trying. Not far from Paris Napoleon resolved to die in battle - to pass the throne on to his son - and though he went where fire was thickest and his uniform was tattered by shot he was not killed.

The fall of Paris was shocking: Paris, which hadn't seen a foreign invader since Joan of Arc 400 years earlier, spectacularly fell without even a full day of fighting - the re-propertied nobles had spread defeatism, paid for subversion and colluded to reverse the French Revolution, which of course they still hated. The elitist concept of royalism would still play a major role in French politics for another 65 years, keep in mind.

After decades of fighting not only were his marshals old and worn out, but so was the original revolutionary generation. What Napoleon needed was a Cultural Revolution to refresh the ideals of the French Revolution, but of course such a solution had not been conceived of yet. Such a leftist idea would have probably led to more civil war in France, which was only able to end its original civil war with the moderate Napoleon adopting many of the forms of monarchism, after all. The Seven Coalition Wars Against the French Revolution should show just how very different French leftists were back then.

Banished to Elba, he famously returned. When France saw that the Bourbons wanted to push the clock back to 1788 this did have the immediate effect of a Cultural Revolution, restoring the vitality of the ideals of the French Revolution. Napoleon landed and dared people to fire on him all alone, ever the patriot who opposes civil war. He was literally pushed all the way to Paris by the peasants and urban proletariat - the army would only rally to him later. He entered Paris like a hero and totally avoided bloodshed - all it took was the sight of him in his overcoat and bicorne hat. It's really rather stunning, and something only a leftist - a man of the people - could have ever done.

The Bourbons fled, of course. The "Additional Act" was added on to the Constitution, which added checks to the power of Napoleon, granted total freedom of expression, an enlarged electoral college, the right to elect mayors in towns less than 5,000 inhabitants, trial by jury and was approved by 1.6 million voters. It wouldn't be until 1867 that Britain's electorate would reach that size.

The vote enraged royalist autocrats continent-wide, of course, and they resolved to immediately overturn the progressive democratic will of France, again. Metternich spread the fiction of Napoleon as ambition personified and rejecting peace. It's incredible how durable this false image has been, but absolute monarchists won and winners write the history books (though not this one).

Above all, what France needed was a period of peace to consolidate these changes - Napoleon's aura was not the same, Liberalist ideas away from a super-powerful executive were taking further root and France had been awakened to the fact that their revolution was powerful but not invincible. They almost had it: Wellington declared Waterloo "*the nearest-run thing you ever saw in your life*", but instead of wiping out Wellington the next day Napoleon spent the morning visiting the wounded - Napoleon the quick had become a sentimental old soldier. The Coalition refused to make peace - of course. Instead of dissolving the National Assembly, as a dictator would, he trusted it and asked for full powers: instead, they told Napoleon to abdicate or be deposed.

Now the French Revolution was truly over. It would be 33 years until there would be another vote for the chief executive.

The defeat of Napoleon - tyrant, slaver, sexist - heralds not a left-wing renaissance, but a right-wing one, really?

Just as Napoleon and the French had warned for decades, the clock was wound back across Europe: Poland was re-wiped off the map by Russia and Prussia, Hapsburgs in north Italy, Bourbons in Naples and Spain, Pope Pius VII restored the Inquisition and the Jewish ghettoes, England responded to calls for parliamentary reform with the massacre at Peterloo - vicious counter-revolution everywhere. The censorship imposed by Metternich is total, with spies everywhere - Europe is a true police state for the benefits of monarchs and aristocrats... again. The French Revolution was truly over, and because a monarchical oligarchy conspired to stop it.

In 1821, living in cruel imprisonment imposed by Britain on the island of St. Helena, Napoleon died of stomach cancer, like his father, at the age of 51. His last words: "*France - army - head of the army - Josephine*".

They act as if Napoleon waged wars on the peoples of Europe, instead of on the autocrats of Europe?

They act as if he won his royalty by birth, marriage or violence, instead of by vote?

They act as if his administration was marked by corruption instead of revolutionary ideas, progress and domestic unity?

Bah... the haters of Napoleon - what can be done? To smear Napoleon Bonaparte is to smear the French Revolution. The two are not synonymous, as Napoleon once claimed - but now, I think, you know what he meant.

In 1823 his memoirs, *The Memorial of Saint Helena*, would become the 19th century's best-selling book, moulding the worldview of several generations.

It is truly amazing how relatively few things there are in France named after Napoleon. However, his stunning tomb at Invalides is - thankfully - not a military shrine but a monument to his 10 greatest achievements as a domestic revolutionary politician. It's truly amazing: comparing the negative view which so many have Napoleon with the 10 progressive political advances etched in marble at Invalides.

The common leftist criticism that Napoleon Bonaparte used foreign war to liquidate the revolution, domestic conflict and class conflict completely ignores the fact that the Seven European Wars Against the French Revolution were defensive and not initiated by France.

The criticism which equates Bonaparte with Bourbon - calling them two absolutist systems, with the former merely being more allied with the *nouveau riche* bourgeois class - completely ignores the historic votes, constitutions, and the quality of governance. It also totally ignores the peasant gains stemming from the French Revolution's ending of feudalism.

The claim that the French Revolution was "imperialist" totally ignores the fact that the French Revolution wasn't even "French": Italy, the Netherlands, Switzerland, Belgium - these are just the countries where the people were able to join the Revolution, and certainly many more wanted to.

All great revolutions are always externalised - ideas do not know national boundaries. The 1979 Iranian Revolution, for example, both spread and was a part of an idea that spread: in 1978 the Saur Revolution in Afghanistan established the socialist People's Democratic Party of Afghanistan; in 1979 the Grand Mosque of Mecca was under siege for two months to oppose the House of Saud monarchy; in 1982 Saddam Hussein committed the massacre of the Islamic Dawa Party, the crime for which he would be ultimately sentenced to death. Where does Iran 1979 fit in this, who can say with total precision? France, Haiti, the Cisalpine Republic, the Batavian Republic (Netherlands 1795-1806) even the USA and League of Iroquois - where does 1789 France fit, precisely? What makes France and Iran different is that their revolutions succeeded and lasted, and thus they must be celebrated and learned from.

In a quote of Trotsky's which sounded the death knell of capitalism entirely too early, Napoleon Bonaparte represented "*the bourgeoisie's impetuous youth*". We must, therefore, look at the "*impetuous youth*" of Bonaparte's bourgeois victory as a victory for the people precisely because it was the only victory which could be permanently extracted in that awful autocratic era - the Liberalist rights which 1789 fought for *were advancements;* bourgeois rights *were advancements;* peasants, not nobles, getting land should not be derided as a "bourgeois revolution" but *were advancements.* It is the West's total blind spot regarding the social evil of monarchy - which is the only accurate standard of comparison Napoleon and the French Revolution can be compared to: their peers - which blinds them to the obvious historical truth.

We can expect the right to paint Napoleon poorly, but what the left seems to ignore is that what every historian eventually admits is that the peasants and the working class - the mass of the people - wanted, trusted, elected and re-elected Napoleon Bonaparte as the French Revolution's chief. This makes Napoleon Bonaparte like Lenin, Stalin, Mao, Castro, Khomeini, etc.

Now we grasp the Western Liberal Democratic campaign against Napoleon's legacy: he was a true, beloved leftist.

Napoleon truly must be reclassed with those figures along the left. We cannot allow reactionaries to say that Napoleon, the dominant personage of that 26-year era - somehow did not embody it, but rather embodied its negation. What an absurdity!

Perhaps the whole point of this chapter - to fellow leftists - is to prove: We can admire Robespierre, Danton, Marat and Babeuf while also admiring Napoleon. Napoleon certainly must be reclaimed from today's aristocratic bourgeoisie - this chapter should make it clear why they would don't even claim him: Napoleon was a leftist.

Gaining the trust of the democratic mass explains - *more than any other factor* - how Napoleon was able to lead France to stability in 1799 and beyond. Western Liberal Democrats have never been able to do either - gain the trust of the masses or provide stability for them - and from its very conception. As de Tocqueville observed:

> *"On coming to power Bonaparte imposed an additional 25 centimes of tax and nothing is said. The people do not turn against him; on the whole what he did was popular. The Provisional Government was to take the same measures in 1848 and was to be cursed immediately. The former was making a much-desired revolution, the second was making an unwanted one."*

What was unwanted across Europe in 1848 was the success of the counter-revolutions, which successfully refused to finally implement the ideals of 1789. In France, however, what was quickly unwanted was the first implementation of Western Liberal Democracy.

<—>

4

The 'Counter-Revolutions of 1848' stillborn child: Western Liberal Democracy

The primary cause of the Revolutions of 1848 was the fact that it took 50 years for the sociopolitical ideas of the French Revolution to spread in a Europe dominated by autocratic monarchs. That's how radical 1789 was, and how slow political history moves.

The secondary cause was the economic changes caused by the refusal to end feudal mindsets anywhere in Europe but in France, and amid the start of industrialisation. 1789 had changed all Europeans, but all monarchs - including the two dynasties in post-Napoleonic France - refused to govern according to the entirely new needs and demands of their citizens. It's expressed in the primary slogan of 1848, "Bread and work, or lead!"

The primary result of the 1848 Revolutions was total failure everywhere but France. 1848 provided new upheavals to replace Europe's memories of the Seven European Wars Against the French Revolution (1792-1815), and what replaced them was even worse absolute monarchies. Political gatherings and demonstrations were outlawed, censorship was not just rampant but total - in short, all European political life was back to where it was in 1847: underground, publicly nonexistent and ruthlessly repressed. There were no revolutions - plural - and any accurate reading of European history would call this period the "Counter-Revolutions of 1848".

So why isn't it called that? For the same reason behind this long historical preface before an analysis of the achievements of the Yellow Vests: Western mainstream history and education is a catastrophe of elite bias and propaganda.

The secondary result of the Revolutions of 1848 was the very first establishment, and immediate popular rejection, of what we can finally start calling Western Liberal Democracy. It would last just three years before a coup against it was popularly approved 11 to 1 in what was then the largest democratic vote ever in history. It took just three years for Western Liberal Democracy to prove to voters its total, eternal inability to care for the masses and not for an elitist oligarchy.

This chapter will make that conclusion perfectly clear not only because we have 175 years of hindsight, but because we have the world-shattering journalism and analysis of one Karl H. Marx. His on-the-ground analysis of the actions of 1848 would shape politics for over a century, and inspire both true socialists and Socialists-turned-Fascists into breaking with Western Liberal Democracy.

Napoleon always draws the crowds - but his nephew? Many don't even know he had one who was important. In between Napoleon Bonaparte's demise and World War One there is an abyss of historical understanding in the West. In fact, they are instructed to think of this era as insignificant - this chapter and the next hopes to explain why, and why that's false.

Marx on France: The only country that mattered in 1848... and 1849

Simply look at the results:

Italy carried the torch of 1789 the most. After initially giving false hope, the Pope openly said that the Papacy could not be the leader of a unified Italian state. His refusal to mix religion and politics, even in a country which was so overwhelmingly of the same religion, was a major error. After 1848 the Papacy became totally anti-liberal, anti-national and supportive of absolutist regimes.

Hungary gave up after their ethnic-based revolt failed to take root - unsurprisingly - with the rest of the extremely multiethnic Hapsburg empire. Indeed, many seem to think that Germanic racial elitism was founded by Adolf Hitler?

Revolutionary France had ended the Holy Roman Empire in 1806, but the autocratic Hapsburgs held on after 1848 - the counter-revolutionary victory was primarily theirs… it's a common theme.

Tsarist Russia was not affected by 1848. They would, in large part to keep Prussia weak, prop up their Austrian autocratic brethren.

Just like in the aftermath of Russia's 1917 success, and the 1930s, and the Great Recession, Germany totally disappointed Europe. The Germanic areas were especially brutal in repressing their revolutions, and it would require World War One to finally end Germanic despotism, at least in the monarchical form.

> *Yellow Vest: "We were so numerous in the beginning, but when people began to see how violent and ferocious the government repressed the Yellow Vests, then many got too scared to protest. The government did everything they could to make us disappear, just so they can govern us according to their selfish whims."*

The broad outline of what happened across Europe in the year of

1848 is simply this: The *nouveau riche*, professional, and managerial classes were always quite content with mere Liberalist reforms, which were opposed by the monarchists. Those three groups initially allied with the artisans, students and the masses to push back against Anglo-Germanic-Russian enforced absolutism and repression. When this "bourgeois" triumvirate got the mild reformism they wanted (i.e. rights for themselves) these Liberalists would no longer support the artisans and students - of course they never wanted to ally for long with the peasants and proletariat. They instead supported repression of the artisans, students and lower class, and thus we have the Counter-Revolutions of 1848. These Liberalist reformers never wanted a revolution, but merely a bill of rights for rich people against autocratic monarchy. As all mere reformists do, they refused to incarcerate, confiscate or execute the counter-revolutionaries, and thus the counter-revolution won, as it always will when facing half-hearted reformism. 1848 stands as proof that the alleged heroes of Liberalist reformism are actually right-wingers opposed to genuine democracy.

The tertiary result of 1848 was the growth of nationalism, but rarely pointed out in the Anglo-Saxon world is that this nationalism was required to expel Anglo-Germanic theocratic autocrats. We certainly can't blame the French revolutionaries who departed decades ago, but only after they planted the seed of anti-feudalism, anti-monarchism and patriotic pride. The rebellions across Europe were against the poor governance of the aristocratic oligarchies who had colluded to wipe out 1789. Some leftists see this rise of nationalism as a bad thing, but they have totally lost the thread.

1848 addressed the "political question", of how governance should be arranged, and everywhere but France failed to install something which anyone could call "progressive". Furthermore, France's revolutionary victory also allowed for the first political discussions of the "social question" - how shall we transfer socially from feudal monarchy: Liberalist capitalism or Socialism? - to be addressed and fought out in their new political structure. At least it was assumed at the start of 1848 that this would be a fair fight.

It took France 33 years (the length of a human generation), from the fall of Napoleon until 1848, for the French to get rid of an unelected executive - once again they were alone in this achievement. Universal (male) suffrage was also spectacularly achieved for the first time, as was the founding of a "right to work". While all other Europeans gave up achieving any move away from pathetic monarchy France founded the 2nd Republic.

French history from the fall of Napoleon, and thus the end of the French Revolution, until 1848 can be quickly summarised: In 1815 Napoleon was imprisoned on St. Helena, and the Bourbons returned after having fled, yet again. The Bourbons only ruled until 1830, when Louis Philippe I of the House of Orleans was installed during that year's "July Revolution". For France 1848 was the result of 18 years of awful neglect from the Orleanists, who cared only about bleeding the country dry at the behest of the burgeoning financial elite, as it was this "bourgeois" who originally helped push the House of Orleans into power. 1848 deposed the House of Orleans, and France looked forward to this new system we term "Western Liberal Democracy" - they would be disappointed.

In a country with universal male suffrage you would think the new parliament would endeavour to represent the interests of the masses, no? If so, you misunderstand who Western Liberal Democracy aims to serve. Marx summarised the Second Republic thusly, and according to his ideas of political progression: *"Under the bourgeois monarchy of Louis Philippe only the bourgeois republic could follow; that is to say, a limited portion of the bourgeoisie, having* (from 1830-48) *ruled under the name of the king, now the whole bourgeoisie was to rule under the name of the people."*

Western Liberal Democracy inevitably turns out that way, but the revolutionaries of 1848 had certainly expected some power and wealth to be devolved to them. In a truly post-feudal France former serfs now had higher opinions of their value to society, their right to earn bread to eat, wanted the necessary stability provided by central planning, social welfare, etc. However, while the souls of the French serfs had grown, the power of the new financial-oriented class had grown at a usurious rate! This is thanks to the start of industrialisation, but also to the usurious abuses of the serfs-turned-sharecroppers. I say "start of industrialisation" because at the time of Napoleon the average workshop had just four workers and the only large businesses were arms manufacturers - not so 30 years later.

As the short-lived 2nd Republic progressed it became clear that this new form of governance was only there to benefit the old landed royalists, the post-1492 corporate trading enterprises and these new "bourgeois" industrialists and rentiers. The 2nd Republic is the start of when powers began to slowly stop being royal and start being monetary powers; when power became corporatised. This is what makes 1848 France so vital to understanding the 21st century.

> *Yellow Vests: "Our system has become totally rotten. They make the laws to suit their own needs, or the needs of corporations, and they have done nothing to resolve the huge problems of the average person. This is why the Yellow Vests will keep marching in the streets."*

It took the French three years to learn this, then to clear a path for 1848's popularly-elected president to bloodlessly abolish the always-oligarchical parliament of Western Liberal Democracy. That president was Louis-Napoleon Bonaparte, the nephew of Napoleon Bonaparte, whose father was Louis "the Good" Bonaparte, who was appointed King of Holland in 1806 in a failed bid to make the Batavian Republic less subject to monarchical attacks.

The above analysis which condemns Western Liberal Democracy is why this chapter is needed: The mainstream historical analysis of 1848-52 France places way too much emphasis on economic changes - i.e. the industrial revolution - and the alleged dictatorship of a guy who was allegedly elected only because stupid French hillbillies thought a very elderly Napoleon had broken free from St. Helena. This faulty analysis exists because it allows for the sidestepping of what actually happened politically: the mismanagement of France's first Western Liberal Democrats, their obvious bias against the bottom 90%, and the eventual rejection of this form of governance which only entrenches inequality and creates regular crises.

On the social level what they were pushing for in 1848, but what the 2nd Republic failed to legislate, is what postwar Europe looks like! The revolutionaries of 1848 were proven right, and that can't be disproven.

1848-1948 was an awful century for the European masses, it must be emphasised. However, it was an awful century for the masses everywhere else - European imperialism created the tragedies, famines and inequalities which literally moulded a new "Third World": prior to 1848 a peasant in Europe was in the same socioeconomic condition as a peasant in India, China, Latin America, etc.

> *Yellow Vest: "The movement will hold firm in the future. It will not disappear because their demands are so very solid and true. There are real reasons for a revolution in France, and we will always continue to play our part."*

Learning how the 1848 Revolution got off-track in the country where it had its greatest success is a major key to understanding Western governments of today, because it is this form of government which has ultimately prevailed despite instant and lasting popular disapproval.

Thus, the 'Counter-Revolutions of 1848', indeed.

Marx's genius: tying together 1848 and 1789, which is the only way to understand 1848

There are three critical contributions Marx made to the understanding of France's 1848-52 period. They are so critical because they illustrate how Western Liberal Democracy starts with fake-leftism and ends in oligarchy over and over and over. It should be considered quite important that the complaints of the 2nd Republic are the exact same as the ones heard today!

Firstly, Marx condensed the economic evolution of France in a time when society and economics were changing rapidly even without the complications of a successful 1848 revolution. He laid out how class economic interests twisted the 2nd Republic into something which nobody who was actually at the barricades would have fought for.

Shortly after the February Revolution of 1848 forced the abdication of the House of Orleans the "June Days" uprising scared the royalists and bourgeois republicans (i.e. anti-monarchists) to unite into the "Party of Order". The Bourbons - who represented the power of landed property, the oldest basis of money - finally ended their royal squabbles with the Orleanists - who were installed to defend the increased power of *nouveau riche* industrial/financial property. This new unity is what Marx meant by writing, "*...landed property has become completely bourgeois through the development of modern society.*" Gone were disputes of old or *nouveau* - it was just *riche* versus poor. Thus, 1848 in France is the birth of modern class warfare - and the rich started it!

Secondly, Marx documented what actually took place in the hectic few years after the 1848 Revolution, which culminated in the popular vote which sanctioned the coup of Louis-Napoleon Bonaparte against the unicameral National Assembly. Marx's charted the lifecycle of this new political structure, and how it discredited itself via the same oligarchical flaws which are eternally apparent in this system.

Thirdly, Marx showed how the new professional politicians,

doctors, small-town lawyers, bank managers and other professional-types, who are the cadres in this new Western Liberal Democracy, joined with the richer categories of wealth (royalist, usurious, landed wealth and financial, means-of-production wealth) to engage in a style of governance which put all their own interests first and demonised the interests of anyone else as "Socialism!". Yes, as epitomised in the awful politics of the United States 175 years later, Marx was flabbergasted to see even calls for the most basic reforms and moves to reduce inequality tarred as "evil Socialism" at the very first implementation of Western Liberal Democracy. Marx goes even further to permanently indict Liberal Democracy as being far inferior to Social Democracy. This is an old debate, and it should have been decided in the latter's favor by 1852 France.

By succinctly condensing - in just the one paragraph below - Marx's summary of the events from 1848 to the voter-backed coup of Louis-Napoleon Bonaparte in 1852, all three historical contributions will be made clear.

An uprising truly led by the people (i.e. a popular revolution) in February 1848 forced out King Louis Philippe of the Orleanists, but the modern leftist demands of the people would be betrayed by June. The people's hopes for a "Democratic and Social Republic" were betrayed by the Social Democrats, mostly the small traders who were content with merely cementing the unprecedented achievement of universal male suffrage. However, the Social Democrats were soon betrayed by the bourgeois republicans - those richer cadres of Western Liberal Democracy - who don't want universal suffrage but merely Liberalist rights for the upper class only. However, the republican bourgeois are betrayed by the "Party of Order" coalition in parliament, half of which *still wants* a royalist restoration and the other half of which wants a republic but cares not much for Liberalist rights but especially universal suffrage. This faction prevails and eventually guts universal suffrage, and also votes the subordination of the constitution to the majority decisions of the parliament - i.e. two true legislative coup against the people. After three years of inefficiency, grandstanding and state-sponsored looting of the country's natural, social and labor resources the "Party of Order" is betrayed by the Bonapartist party - the National Assembly is dissolved, and what is restored is the Bonapartist idea of a popularly-elected emperor who puts the will and good of the nation first.

This is why Marx famously wrote his opening lines in *The 18th Brumaire of Louis Napoleon (*18th Brumaire is the French revolutionary calendar date for the coup of Napoleon Bonaparte in 1799*)* of history repeating itself as farce: instead of the revolution trending upwards in the first several years with leftist successes, as in 1789-94, a similar time period in 1848 sees failure. *"Accordingly, the revolution moves on a downward line. It finds itself in this retreating motion before the last February-barricade is kicked away....* "

Having condensed Marx's timeline of 1848, his comparison with the timeline of 1789 will be especially illuminating of both 1789 and 1848. This book does not dissect the pre-Napoleonic events of 1789-94, in large part because they have been perfectly analysed by Marx in one paragraph. I include in parenthetical my explanations of key 1789 terms/parties which may not be fully known by the average reader (Marx is in bold)

"In the first French revolution, upon the reign of the Constitutionalists (i.e., the start of the French Revolution via forcing the king to accept a constitution and to renounce total autocracy. Napoleon Bonaparte's commitment to constitutionalism is precisely what made him a political revolutionary of his day.) ***is succeeded by the Girondins*** (Truly, the early martyrs of today's Western Liberal Democrats. Most were from the department of Gironde, home of France's slave-trade capital - Bordeaux -, and were committed to free market, decentralisation and imperialist war. It's decapitating them which Westerners call the "Reign of Terror", precisely because neo-Girondins are what still rule in the West in the modern era.) ***and upon the reign of the Girondins follows that of the Jacobins. Each of these parties rests upon its more advanced element. … Just the reverse in 1848."***

It's clear why outside of France the "Revolutions of 1848" are such a failure, but why is the French Revolution of 1848 such a failure for Marx? It's because he was so very anti-Bonapartist. In 2022 it seems like a major mistake which loses the thread of political history: moving away from autocracy. I'll deeply criticise his overly-strong condemnation of Louis-Napoleon Bonaparte in the next chapter, but what's needed first is his analysis of France from 1848-52 - it's critical because it is so reminiscent of Western politics today.

Both revolutionary eras fought against the very same political principle: autocracy, anti-democracy and the rule of an aristocratic elite. The Yellow Vest fight in the exact same way, even if the autocracy is only slightly less barbaric, although you should tell that to one of the many mutilated Yellow Vests.

What happened to France's progressive revolution of 1848, then? Western Liberal Democracy happened!

The short answer is that Marx places the blame for the failure of 1848 on the half-revolutionary actions of France's left wing in 1848, as well as the role played by Louis-Napoleon Bonaparte.

In the above section I related in one paragraph Marx's summary of the events from 1848 to the popular coup of Louis-Napoleon Bonaparte. A bit more information is needed on the major political events in between that start and finish.

The February Revolution of 1848 re-ended monarchy, but April's voting results saw the new constituent (temporary) Assembly filled with royalists, elite and professionals who did not incarnate the Socialistic demands which had propelled the popular revolution: the opposition to free markets and the demand for government works to create jobs. National Workshops had been immediately created in 1848 in order to fulfil the "right to work" and thus introduce governmental central planning into the economy.

So one should imagine the hundreds of thousands of workers now trying to ply a trade in Paris while, concurrently, the new temporary parliament to draw up a new constitution is full of capitalistic Western Liberal Democrats. Naturally, the people saw they were getting left behind. On May 15 a leftist demonstration entered and dissolved this temporary National Assembly. The National Guard - which had always played the decisive role in French revolutionary affairs - sided against the protesters. The ardent republicans and protest leaders were arrested; a banker would be installed as the new Paris Chief of Police; a lawyer would now head the restored Assembly.

In June the conservative National Assembly announced that the National Workshops would be closed, and the newly-unemployed workers could either join the army or go back home to the provinces - this sparked the June Days uprising. We see here how Western Liberal Democracy is never - not from it's very earliest days - going to allow anything but an "invisible hand" to guide the economy, and also that imperialist war (which is not at all revolutionary war) is its primary answer to the economic question. Over 10,000 people were massacred, or 60% as many as were guillotined during the "Reign of Terror" (but without any trial). It also marks the last time French Catholic clergy tried to play a role in elections: The Archbishop of Paris literally entered into the Paris street fray as a mediator - he was shot, almost certainly by the conservative forces. The popular revolution was thus ended: death, prison and exile to Algeria for the leftists.

Yet the trader-class Social Democrats did not condemn the repression - they threw their weight behind November's Constitution of 1848, which granted universal male suffrage. Louis-Napoleon Bonaparte was overwhelmingly elected president in December, and like his uncle he took a middle-of-the-road pro-revolutionary approach: he was neither like the leftist Socialist candidates, nor the anti-Socialist/pro-republican army chief who led the June Days repression, nor a Liberalist lawyer. Marx was unwilling to reconcile with Louis-Napoleon Bonaparte, who was also a leftist writer - his most famous book was the pro-working class *The Extinction of Pauperism*, which undoubtedly helps explain his massive victory. It should be noted that the political ideology of Bonapartism also strongly existed in the interim between the two Bonapartes - it's not as if the legacy of Napoleon Bonaparte and all of his comrades simply vanished from the political scene. Far from it, in fact, and the popularity of Louis-Napoleon Bonaparte as due in large part to the enduring strength and influence of Bonapartists.

After Louis-Napoleon Bonaparte was elected 1850-onwards was an ineffective and nation-destroying combat between the executive and the legislative branch:

The legislative branch - as it will always do for the next 175 years - lost all popular support by rejecting to represent the populace and not just the upper class. The popular, bloodless coup of Louis-Napoleon Bonaparte would be deemed "fascism installed by country rednecks", and Marx's own analysis is very similar to that, sadly.

The executive branch - as it will always do for the next 175 years - would jealously fight to acquire as much autocratic, dictatorial powers as it could, and employ jingoistic, imperialist wars to win popular opinion while mostly advancing the needs of the elite.

It took only three years to realise such a system was unworkable, and yet is this not still the alleged apex of governmental structure and efficiency for Western Liberal Democrats of today?

Yellow Vest: "After three years nothing has changed, except for the fact that things have gotten even worse for the average French person. Life has gotten so much more expensive, but Macron doesn't care. Macron doesn't see the demands of the Yellow Vests, or even the French people, as worthy of his attention."

Weak leftism against a strong executive - France has the same problem today

In May 1849 the first National Assembly of the 2nd Republic was officially seated. This Assembly would eventually go on to approve total non-support for any other popular revolution sweeping Europe; to ban the reborn *Sans-Culottes* and other political parties; similar to Macron today, they would end the longtime practice of the National Assembly of hearing petitions from grassroots groups.

Louis-Napoleon Bonaparte would immediately use foreign war to establish to the "Party of Order", which had 64% of seats, that he, too, was a mighty man of (executive) "Order". Even before the new parliament sat he violated the new constitution's prohibition of military interference in the freedom of other nations by bombarding Rome to prop up an exiled Pope. This was at the expense of the nascent but doomed Roman Republic, which undoubtedly did not have popular support. This does not make either Bonaparte the equivalent of an absolute monarch, one must point out. France had arrived expected to be received as liberators, and also sought to prevent an invasion by Austria.

The opposition Social-Democrat Mountain Party, with 26% of seats, boldly voted to impeach Louis-Napoleon Bonaparte, who had been elected by a whopping 75% landslide. Propping up the Pope was popular among the average person, and now France's "left party" (though actually petit-bourgeois small traders and minor professionals) were taking on an extremely popular president?

What cannot be disputed is how ineffectually the Mountain Party fought their fight. Marx's superb analysis will remind people of the halfhearted, non-revolutionary struggle of fake-leftist parties across Western Liberal Democracy. We should remember that Marx was living in Paris at this time. He surely must have hoped that the Mountain were genuine leftists - after all, "fake-leftism" in a Western Liberal Democratic context had not yet ever been seen!

Following the Mountain's impeachment vote the unarmed protests of June 1849 were held. The National Guard was there - in uniform, but unarmed. This pacifistic decision was fatal: they had no way to defend themselves from the subsequent army attack. The demonstration ended in total failure - it was the last "Revolutionary Day" of the 2nd Republic - and there were no casualties. Marx writes: "*The chief error of the 'Mountain' was* ***its certainty of being victorious.***" (emphasis his) I don't think France has had an official "Revolutionary Day" since, and probably because most French don't know this history either?

Marx saw that the real leftism had been chopped out of the Mountain by the June Days of 1848 and replaced with a smug, ultimately conservative, sense of false certainty. He saw these fake-leftists were doomed precisely because they accepted Western Liberal Democratic terms:

> "*If the Mountain wished to win in parliament, it should not appeal to arms; if it called to arms in parliament, it should conduct itself in a parliamentary way in the street; if the friendly demonstration was meant seriously, it was silly not to foresee that it would meet with a warlike reception; if it was intended for actual war, it was rather original to lay aside the weapons with which war had to be conducted. But the revolutionary threats of the middle class and of their* (Social) *democratic representatives are mere attempts to frighten an adversary....*"

This certainly describes France's union-led demonstrations and the "walks in a park" which are other European Social Democrat-led demonstrations. This same entrapping logic is what the Yellow Vests are told to submit to and what they still so bravely faced down Saturday after Saturday.

> *Yellow Vests: "France is waking up. The government continues to accuse all of us of being Black Bloc or thugs to make the country turn against us. But we are all united to prevent the destruction of France, and this unity will continue to increase."*

The *"superstitious spell"* the National Guard had on the French imagination - i.e. its ability to sway the army to back the people and the elite - was crucially broken here. They would be suppressed under Louis-Napoleon Bonaparte and then banned at the start of the Third Republic in 1871, when Western Liberal Democrats would wrest back control from the Louis-Napoleon and the Bonapartists.

A clear difference between imperialist Liberal Democracy and anti-imperialist Social Democracy: the former clearly uses foreign war to gut the possibility of a marital spirit which would seek to protect the rights of the people domestically. It also uses perpetual imperialist war to insist that such domestic rights are not convenient, and that such discussions certainly cannot involve anything but words.

The subsequent crackdown caused the remaining true leftist politicians, including many in the Mountain Party, and journalists to be arrested or go into exile - Marx went to London. With the real left gone the new Mountain Party was no opposition. The National Assembly embarked on a series of right-wing measures which turned everyone against them.

On June 13, 1848, they voted the subordination of the constitution to the majority decisions of the parliament - it was a coup against the constitutional rights of the people.

"So, indeed, did the republic understand it, to-wit, that the bourgeois ruled here in parliamentary form, without, as in the monarchy, finding a check in the veto of the Executive power, or the liability of parliament to dissolution. It was a 'parliamentary republic', as Thiers styled it."

Thus we see the true emergence of the unstated dream of Western Liberal Democracy: a country ruled by a parliament of the rich; an expansion of absolute monarchy to a tiny coterie of aristocratic elite.

The last straw would come on May 31, 1850, when the assembly would vote to drastically undermine universal suffrage by millions of voters. Marx wrote, *"The law of May 31, 1850, was the 'coup d'etat' of the bourgeoisie."* Against the voters, he means.

Thus the first coup in the 2nd Republic was actually made by the parliamentarians and not by Louis-Napoleon Bonaparte! Bonaparte would restore universal suffrage, to his great credit.

Those two absolutely crucial facts are always left out of any discussion of the 2nd Republic and Louis-Napoleon Bonaparte's "self-coup" (a coup where a legally-elected executive dissolves the legislative branch). In 2022 they should drastically guide our assessment of him, and break from Marx's negative, rather biased view.

From the beginning Western Liberal Democracy showed what it wanted: A country ruled by a parliament of and for the rich

Marx writes in summation of the political discussion permitted in the first Western Liberal Democracy:

"Whether the question was the right of petition or the duty on

wine, the liberty of the press or free trade, clubs or municipal laws, protection of individual freedom or the regulation of national economy, the slogan returns ever again, the theme is monotonously the same, the verdict is ever ready and unchanged: Socialism! ***Even bourgeois liberalism is pronounced socialistic****; socialistic, alike, is pronounced popular education; and likewise, socialistic national financial reform. It was socialistic to build a railroad where already a canal was; and it was socialistic to defend oneself with a stick when attacked with a sword.*

This was not a mere form of speech, a fashion nor yet party tactics. The bourgeois receives correctly that all the weapons which it forged against feudalism thorn their edges against itself; that all the means of education which it brought forth rebel against its own civilisation; that all the gods which it made have fallen away from it. It understands that all its so-called citizens' rights and progressive organs assail and menace its class rule, both in its social foundation and its political superstructure - consequently have become 'socialistic'. ***It justly scents in this menace and assault the secret of Socialism, whose meaning and tendency it estimates more correctly than the spurious so-called Socialism is capable of estimating itself*** *and which, consequently, is unable to understand how it is that the bourgeoisie obdurately shuts up its ears to it, alike whether it sentimentally whines about the sufferings of humanity; or announces in Christian style the millennium and universal brotherhood; or twaddles humanistically about the soul, culture and freedom; or doctrinally matches out a system of harmony and well-being for all classes.* ***What, however, the bourgeoisie does not understand is the consequence that its own parliamentary regime, its own political reign, is also of necessity bound to fall under the general ban of 'socialistic'.****"* (Emphasis mine)

If you still believe in Liberal Democracy, may I suggest you read that again.

Not only does Marx show that Western Liberal Democracy refuses to protect the rights which Western Liberal Democracy claims to have created and to believe in, but that Western Liberal Democracy is a phoney "third way": there is either socialism or autocracy/oligarchy/fascism.

"Accordingly, by now persecuting as Socialist what formerly it had celebrated as Liberal the bourgeoisie admits that its own interest orders it to raise itself above the danger of self government...." Western Liberal Democracy is not a resolution to class warfare, like Socialist Democracy aims to be, but the permanent institution of class warfare with the express goal of governance by the elite.

"The parliamentary regime leaves everything to the decision of majorities (within Parliament) - *how can the large majorities beyond the parliament be expected not to wish to decide?"* The parliamentarianism of Western Liberal Democracy is false and unrepresentative, culminating in rule by parties which are controlled by the elite. This is unlike the parliaments in Socialist Democracy, where cobblers become parliamentarians, as in Cuba's 2018 legislative vote.

No wonder Western schools don't want to discuss this era!

By examining the era of 1848-52 we see that Western Liberal Democracy totally discredited itself out of the gate, and also that we have the same problems as we did 175 years ago: it is autocracy improved into aristocratic rule, but never popular rule. Western Liberal Democracy is so undemocratic that it is not even worthy of the moniker Western "Liberal Democracy"!

Thus the Revolution of 1848 in France was a success. It culminated in the 1852 referendum on Louis-Napoleon Bonaparte's "self-coup" against an oligarchical and usurping parliament, and the replacement of the 2nd Republic with the 2nd Empire, to be headed by the new "Napoleon III". It was approved by 97% of voters with 80% turnout. Over 8 million Frenchmen wanted to vote, and they only could in 19th century France by agreeing that the Bonapartist vision of the French Revolution was the only way to maintain the gains of the French Revolution amid a continent full of absolute monarchy and failed revolutionaries AND by rejecting the Western Liberal Democracy of the 2nd Republic.

1848 succeed in France precisely because voters rejected Western Liberal Democracy entirely. Four years to figure it out is not so bad at all?

Thus the period between the 2nd and 3rd Republics is falsely slandered as being equivalent to all the other absolute monarchies of the time. We have been through this before: we are talking about an elected Bonaparte, who naturally was slandered by his autocratic and oligarchic contemporaries everywhere else in the region.

Without embracing the will of the inherently progressive French electorate - inherent because there was no other mass electorate at this time - and their eventual selection of the Bonapartes, we are stuck with siding with awful absolute monarchs or awful Liberal Democrat oligarchs.

The rebuffed Western Liberal Democrat, with all their arrogance, remained non-plussed, as Marx noted: *"At all events the* (social) *democrat comes out of the disgraceful defeat as immaculate as he innocently went into it...."*

However, in 2022 we must reject Marx's total condemnation and consider the Revolutions of 1848 a success in France: The preservation of universal male suffrage was a spectacular advance from the rest of Europe. This advance alone allows us to clearly see that the ideals of 1789 and the movement away from autocracy still progressed, even if slowly.

But 1848 was an advance for another reason: it allowed the first implementation of modern Western Liberal Democracy... and its endemic flaws were immediately revealed. It became clear that Socialist Democracy was the only true solution if one wants broad prosperity, stability and equality for the average person - thus the Paris Commune. Those who don't realise that are stuck in a useless doom loop of 1849-52.

The rise of Louis-Napoleon Bonaparte is not as thrilling as that of his uncle. He is a modern politician, with plenty of flaws, but the French at the time knew he was a progressive option compared to absolute monarchy or Western Liberal Democracy.

Algeria: Modern France's original sin keeps returning to ruin French democracy

Before we get into Marx's failure to appreciate the achievements of France's 1848 Revolution and the rule of Louis-Napoleon Bonaparte in opposition to Western Liberal Democracy, we must briefly analyse Marx's failure to take account of the role the conquest of Algeria played on the French mainland's politics in 1848.

Marx's focus was more on financial and industrial systems, instead of imperialism. It's a significant omission: the treasures, resources and stolen wages of imperialism are enormous - we are talking of the gains of impoverishing an entire country. But where Marx really failed was in not noting the enormous political-cultural impact of being a coloniser.

What the events of 1848 proved, and which Marx failed to note, was how Western Liberal Democracy works hand in hand with militaristic imperialism to repress their nation's own masses. This is an incredibly important analysis to take from 1848 because the French army went from being a Revolutionary Army in 1789 to an imperialist army in 1830, and with devastating domestic political consequences.

The colonisation of Algeria was of an entirely different order than the colonisation of the New World, and we must delineate this difference: the colonisation of a Mediterranean space which saw Marseilles and Algiers socially interact for over two millennia is not at all the same thing as a (ignorant) Western perception of heathen savages who need to be converted. Yes, France had other imperialist domains but we cannot underestimate the power of French Algeria in French history from 1830 until today.

Algeria was invaded in 1830 to try and divert public dissatisfaction and to forestall a royal coup by the House of Orleans, which would end the Bourbon Restoration. This takeover happened at the same time as the fall of Algiers - less than three weeks apart in July 1830. The finances and prestige of Louis Philippe I among the elite was enormously supplemented by turning what started as a punitive expedition into the 132-year occupation of Algeria. This new "imperialist class" was too ignored by Marx in the French events of 1848.

A proof of the political-cultural impact of this new "imperialist class" is found in the person of Louis-Eugène Cavaignac, who went directly from being governor of Algeria to quelling the June 1848 uprising. He was as vital a player in 1848 and beyond as anyone save Louis-Napoleon Bonaparte, to whom he finished second in the 1848 presidential election. As Marx noted: *"Cavaignac, the General of the bourgeois republican party, who commanded at the battle of June* (Days), *stepped into the place of the Executive Committee with a sort of dictatorial power."* The election of Louis-Napoleon Bonaparte in December would end this dictatorship, but not before the imperialist Cavaignac ruled over the drafting of the November constitution which gave the elite class ruling power over France. This is not a small thing!

The person of Cavaignac thus represents the new capitalist-imperialist rot which would turn against its own people, like a CRS riot cop who aims his or her rubber bullet gun at the faces of Yellow Vests. Marx fails to emphasise that it is the imperialism against Muslim Algeria which provided this muscle to topple 1848. Or that the beloved National Guard was sapped by this imperialist deployment. Or that French culture had certainly become hardened by a war which was not waged at all for progressive revolution.

Romaric Godin, economics reporter at top French media

Mediapart, in his book The Social War in France (*La guerre social en France* - 2019) recognised Cavaignac's import (even if Godin does not recognise the importance of imperialism) as both a new type of politician and its clear parallel with Emmanuel Macron. Godin wrote: *"Democratic authoritarianism is that of Cavaignac in 1848 and Adolphe Thiers* (the future president of the 3rd Republic who colluded with Bismarck to siege the Paris Commune) *of 1871: that which uses the entire legislative capacity to repress opposition. This sort of abuse is sanctioned by the law and thus is perfectly legal."*

Western Liberal Democracy actually begins with Cavaignac, who suppressed those calling for Socialist Democracy, the National Workshops and a role for the peasants and the proletariat in politics in June 1848. We can draw a straight line from him to Macron's crushing of the Yellow Vests, and both men are garlanded by Western Liberal "Democracy".

Indeed, more and more seem willing to call 21st century France "*democratic authoritarianism*". Muslim Algerians knew it back in 1830, and by 1848 everyone knew that authoritarianism is what Western Liberal Democracy has always truly been.

<—>

5

Louis-Napoleon: The revolutionary difference between Bonapartism & Western Liberal Democracy

For Marx all of society was divided into classes - classes which played political roles. What's unfortunate is that he fundamentally believed that the average rural person - 85% of mid-19th century France - was incapable of playing a political role. It's a major blind spot, but it was actually a common mistake back then.

It's a common mistake even now: Rejecting the part played by the rural voters continues to be a 175-year problem for Western leftists.

Yes, in 1848 Marx was a working socialist who was going to fight, write and lobby for Socialism - and denigrate all the other parties vying for influence in the new 2nd Republic (1848-52) - but in 2022 we can see that his disregard for the rural masses was also a major factor in his rejection (and rather slandering) of Louis-Napoleon Bonaparte, who was elected France's to be first president in 1848.

In the previous chapter I noted how two crucial facts are always left out of any discussion of the 2nd Republic and Louis-Napoleon Bonaparte's coup against the legislative branch (and subsequent establishment of the 2nd Empire: 1852-70):

1) the legislative branch voted to subordinate the 1848 constitution

to the majority will of parliament - thus they made a coup against the people's constitution, and 2) the legislative branch gutted 1848's progressive advance of instituting universal male suffrage, thus they made a coup against the people and millions of new voters. Thus, it is the oligarchical parliament which made the first coup - the Bonapartist coup was a reaction to these outrages. Critically, it was approved in a referendum so large it was then the world's largest referendum.

The simplest definition of "Bonapartism" is accepted as, "A political movement associated with authoritarian rule, usually by a military leader, supported by a popular mandate." Of course I am not arguing for Bonapartism being progressive in the 21st century, but from 1799-1870 the Bonapartes were the only elected chief executives in Europe, and that certainly was progressive! The failure is in obscuring the Bonapartes' historical context and judging solely by 21st century standards - which is ludicrous and dooms us to never understanding history and repeating the same mistakes.

Without embracing the will of a mainly rural French electorate intent on keeping the spirits of 1848 and 1789 not just alive but actually partially implemented via their election of the Bonapartes, we are stuck with siding with awful absolute monarchs or awful Liberal Democrats.

By denigrating both Bonapartes leftists agree with conservatives that not only was 1848 a failure everywhere including the one place it reportedly succeeded - France - but that the French Revolution was a failure as well. This forces us to lose the thread of political history: moving away from unelected, theocratic autocracy and towards greater self-empowerment and democracy.

So, Marx got Louis-Bonaparte all wrong. He's not as thrilling as his uncle, but he should no longer be portrayed as the "farce" in Marx's famous history repeated as farce idea from his essay *The Eighteenth Brumaire of Louis Bonaparte.*

What's farcical is that people keep championing ruinous, repugnant

Western Liberal Democracy even though it was voted out after just three years in France.

From Burke to Marx to 'deplorable' Brexiteers & Yellow Vests - both left and right have been biased against rural people

Marx's *Brumaire* clearly tried to obscure crucial truths: He waited until the absolute end of his famous essay to explain that Louis-Napoleon Bonaparte's elevation to emperor was democratically approved and justifiably rests on his insistence on 1848's unprecedented implementation of universal male suffrage.

"(Louis-Napoleon) *Bonaparte represents an economic class, and that most numerous in the commonweal of France - the Allotment Farmer. As the Bourbons are the dynasty of large landed property, as the Orleans are the dynasty of money, so are the Bonapartes the dynasty of the farmer, i.e. of the French masses. Not the Bonaparte who threw himself at the feet of the bourgeois parliament* (as Marx notes Louis-Napoleon did repeatedly from his election in 1848), *but the Bonaparte who swept away the bourgeois parliament is the elect of this farmer class. For three years the cities had succeeded in falsifying the meaning of the election of December 10* (1848, Louis-Napoleon's election as president), *and in cheating the former out of the restoration of the Empire. The election of December 10, 1848, is not carried out until the 'coup d'etat' of December 2, 1851.*"

Marx asserts what the Yellow Vests assert and what this book asserts: the parliaments of Western Liberal Democracy refuse to implement the will of the average voter, and we have known this since at least 1848.

Marx's vital analysis of democratic denial by Western Liberal Democratic parliament only comes after scores of pages of denigrating Louis-Napoleon Bonaparte as personally unfit for office. However, 175 years later, we can see it clearly right there: Louis-Napoleon Bonaparte partially confirmed the people's victory of 1848 just as Napoleon Bonaparte partially confirmed the people's victory of 1789 - both upheld the democratic will, opposed oligarchs and valued the nation's esteem over mere power or money.

The "*Allotment Farmer*" referred to by Marx is the rural proletariat, whether they own their own small holdings or are sharecroppers. 1789 broke up the large estates of the church and created these small holdings, which was really the main economic blow to end French feudalism. It is incorrect to falsely slander the land redistribution post-1789 as something which only profited the richer peasants and professionals, because as the Revolution went on poor peasants were undoubtedly buying land. By the turn of the century 70% of land buyers were peasants and only 30% were noblemen, dealers, merchants and lawyers, per Tulard. Even if the poorest peasants could never afford their own land the French Revolution's ending of tithe, seigniorial dues and primogeniture represented an enormous leftist leap for the lives of all peasants. One shouldn't have to be a Maoist to grasp that finally giving peasants property and economic freedoms at the expense of the elite and an elite-infested clergy was a spectacular advance in its day. To not see all this as historical progress - even if not ideal - from feudalism is to lose the thread completely. In order to maintain these advances French farmers used arms, then the guillotine, then votes. The fear of a return to feudalism - especially in the context of a total failure of the 1848 Revolutions everywhere else across Europe - was a real, regular fear for the French peasant in the 2nd Republic, and it is preposterous to understate this reality.

Marx continues, and it's clear that he sees the formally feudal masses of this era as being incapable of embracing Socialism; of a need for an urban vanguard party; that he could be describing the Yellow Vests 170 years later:

"The allotment farmers are an immense mass, whose individual

members live in identical conditions, without, however, entering into manifold relations of one another. Their method of production isolates them from one another, instead of drawing them into mutual intercourse. In so far as millions of families live under economic conditions that separate their mode of life, their interests and their culture from those of the other classes, and that place them in an attitude hostile toward the latter, they constitute a class; in so far as there exists only a local connection among these farmers, a connection which the individuality and exclusiveness of their interests prevent from generating among them any unity of interest, national connections and political organisation, they do not constitute a class."

If rural farmers - in the breadbasket of Western Europe and in Europe's then-richest and most politically advanced country - cannot constitute a political class (even with a vote for the males which clearly levelled and united them, even!) then Marx necessarily sees French politics as limited to urbanites and non-farmers. It's an incredibly English-influenced view of politics: suffrage would be excluded for Britain's agricultural workers until as late as 1884, until the Representation of the People Act. Thus, we see that the rural-urban divide in the Anglophone world, and their view that ruralites are second-class citizens who should be excluded from politics, is not since Brexit or the Yellow Vests but extends deep into the roots of even Socialists.

Yellow Vest: "What we have in common is that we share a feeling of injustice, about climate, about fiscal policies, about work. They are making laws about retirement, unemployed people, everything – so there is a lot of different people here today, but what we all have in common is a feeling of injustice."

Marx continues: *"Consequently, they are unable to assert their class interests in their own name, be it by a parliament or by convention. They cannot represent one another, they must be represented. Their representative must at the same time appear as their master, as an authority over them, as an unlimited governmental power, that protects them from above, bestows rain and sunshine upon them. Accordingly, the political influence of the allotment farmer finds its ultimate expression in an Executive power that subjugates the commonweal to its own autocratic will."*

Marx almost sounds like French farmers want to return to feudalism's domination by a master?

Because around 85% of France is incapable of political action for Marx (even with a vote for males!), and only appreciates absolute autocrats (Then why did they fight for the French Revolution!), then the only alternative is for political life to be limited to a vanguard party drawn from urban classes. This urban snobbery, conscious or not, is still rampant today across both sides of the spectrum, but the left rarely examines this "acceptable" prejudice they often display.

However, we need to stress that Marx was not at all alone. Edmund Burke shared the same incorrectly dim view of rural political capabilities as Marx. Interestingly, Burke also wrote in his *Reflections on the Revolution in France* that this new Western Liberal Democracy would perpetually depend on those classes which oppress the rural masses. He notes that it would be dominated by what I have often written about: not a vanguard class inspired by Socialist Democracy but Bankocracy.

> *"The whole of the power obtained by this* (France's 1789) *revolution will settle in the towns among the burghers and the monied director who lead them. The landed gentleman, the yeoman, and the peasant have, none of them, habits or inclinations or experience which can lead them to any share in this sole source of power and influence now left in France. The very nature of a country life, the very nature of landed property, in all the occupations, and all the pleasures they afford, render combination and arrangement (the sole way of*

procuring and exerting influence) in a manner impossible amongst country people. Combine them by all the art you can, and all the industry, they are always dissolving into individuality. Anything in the nature of incorporation is almost impracticable amongst them. Hope, fear, alarm, jealousy, the ephemerous tale that does its business and dies in a day - all these things which are the reins and spurs by which leaders check or urge the minds of followers are not easily employed, or hardly at all, amongst scattered people. They assemble, they are, they act with the utmost difficulty and at the greatest charge. Their efforts, if they can be commenced, cannot be sustained. They cannot proceed systematically.

It is obvious that in the towns all things which conspire against the country gentleman come in favor of the money managers and director. In towns combination is natural. The habits of burghers, their occupations, their diversion, their business, their idleness continually brings them into mutual contact. Their virtues and their vices are sociable; they are always in garrison; and they come embodied and half disciplined into the hands of those who mean to form them for civil or military action.

All these considerations leave no doubt on my mind that, if this monster of a constitution can continue, France will be wholly governed by the agitators in corporations, by societies in the towns, formed of directors of assignats, *and trustees for the sale of church lands, attorneys, agents, money jobbers, speculators and adventurers, composing an ignoble oligarchy founded on the destruction of the the crown, the nobility and the people. Here are all the deceitful dreams and lies of the equality and rights of men."*

"*They are always in garrison*"... a sycophant, yes, but Burke was also a great writer. He also foresaw that Western Liberal Democracy was going to culminate in an "*ignoble oligarchy*" formed of "*agitators in corporations*", land speculators, "*attorneys, agents, money jobbers, speculators and adventurers*". Who today would not admit that this has turned out to be correct?

What Burke failed to foresee is that Marx, Lenin, Russia, China, Cuba, Iran and others would create new systems which would wrest control from both the monarchs and from this group - which rules along with monarchs in Western Liberal Democracies - and give it to the masses.

So Marx was not alone in thinking that the rural masses are difficult to wrangle into politics, but the weekly roundabout protest and the Facebook page - where freedom of assembly and speech/writing are enjoyed (or at least sometimes) - has definitely ended the isolation of the rural class. This enormous class of free farmers, which was only created by 1789 let's recall, had to wait a very long time to challenge the capital's death-grip on governance. What is the capital's 21st century response? To both accuse this rural class of racism while at the same time promoting mainstream politicians who have explicitly pushed imperialist racism.

In 1852 socialism was not sufficiently developed. Ruralites understandably turned to Louis-Napoleon Bonaparte after just 3 years of trying out bourgeois Western Liberal Democracy - the alternative was a return to feudalism, autocracy and the total death of 1789.

> "*The rooted thought of the Nephew becomes a reality because it coincided with the rooted thought of the most numerous class among the French,*" wrote Marx.

Marx was right to champion Socialism, but 175 years later we can champion Louis-Napoleon Bonaparte for his popular democratic legitimacy, something which Marx knew, but grudgingly refused to champion.

If the bourgeois have no values at all, then not only does liberalism have no values but neither does the first years after 1789

Also coming at the end of his analysis, Marx has rather tossed in this defense of half the country:

> *"But this should be well understood: The Bonaparte dynasty does not represent the revolutionary, it represents the conservative farmer; it does not represent the farmer who presses beyond his own economic conditions, his little allotment of land, it represents him rather who would confirm these conditions; it does not represent the rural population, that, thanks to its own inherent energy, wishes, jointly with the cities to overthrow the old older. It represents, on the contrary, the rural population that, hide-bound in the old order, seeks to see itself, together with its allotments, saved and favoured by the ghost of the Empire."*

Yet Marx is wrong all over the place, in this effort to portray Louis-Napoleon Bonaparte as the candidate of only the far-right farmer. Marx is wrong about who was a "*conservative*" "*hide-bound in the old order*": Louis-Napoleon Bonaparte was elected at a time when royalism was dominant across Europe and still a major part of France's own political spectrum. To imagine that in 1848 all of France's farmers had been converted to republicanism/anti-monarchism is certainly false - there were still plenty of royalist farmers (such as those who rebelled for years after 1789 and who tried to assassinate Napoleon Bonaparte), and they are the true "*conservative farmer*". Furthermore, Marx is implying that farmers who want to preserve the gains of 1789 (which is hardly an "*old order*") but are skeptical of 1848 are hidebound reactionaries *even though this farmer and his family* are the only ones to have thrown off the chains of autocratic feudalism in all of Europe! It's tortuous logic, indeed.

What Marx failed to admit here is that the desire to hold on to a little allotment, at a time when Anglo-Germanic-Russian autocracy offered only continued feudalism, contains plenty of Socialist revolutionary sentiment. It's surprising that Marx fails to admit this, because in the *Communist Manifesto* Marx is clearly not against the property of the allotment farmer: "*The distinguishing feature of Communism is not the abolition of property generally, but the abolition of bourgeois property. ... Communism deprives no man of the power to appropriate the products of society; all that it does is to deprive him of the power to subjugate the labour of others by means of such appropriations.*"

Yet it's clear: upholding 1789 was still a revolutionary act in 1848 Europe. I believe Marx was playing politics - he could not make a tactical support of Louis-Napoleon because he wanted the Socialists to win.

> *Yellow Vest: "The Yellow Vests won't stop until we get citizen-initiated referendums. We need some real democracy in our system, but the Yellow Vests can't do it alone. I'm glad more help from other sectors is on the way next week."*

As in the previous chapter, Marx proves that Liberal Democracy does not even offer or defend the bourgeois rights of mere Liberalism, but Marx goes too far in saying that the bourgeois have no virtues at all *when compared to monarchists.*

Marx differentiated between royal & bourgeois money and classes, but not between the differences between royal & bourgeois virtues

Marx views the rule of the bourgeois in the 2nd Republic as absolutely terrible, but it's not really clear if he views them to be as absolutely terrible as monarchy: he truly hates them both. He also truly hates Louis-Napoleon Bonaparte. Marx is only on the side of Socialism, which is fine, but he underestimates the non-royalists in how they reject the social order of the royalists, which is a vital progression of history:

> *"All classes and parties joined hands in the* (1848 uprising) *June Days in a 'Party of Order' against the class of the proletariat, which was designated the 'Party of Anarchy', of Socialism, of Communism. They claimed to have 'saved' society against the 'enemies of society'. They gave out the slogans of the old social order - 'Property, family, religion, order' - as the passwords for their army, and cried out to the counter-revolutionary crusaders: 'In this sign thou wilt conquer!'"*

I think we all get where Marx is coming from. He is also describing what the last chapter focused on: The February Revolution of 1848 was sold out over and over, culminating in the exclusion from power of all classes but the royalists, bourgeois wealth and the upper professionals.

But if we take a longer view of history we see that those were actually new slogans, as they come from a new Liberalist republican mindset - those slogans are not the slogans of monarchy at all!

Autocratic monarchy doesn't respect "*property*": they confiscate and bestow at will. They don't respect "*family*": they enslaved your family, forced you to work in their self-glorifying projects and some had the right to rape your wife on your wedding night. They don't respect righteous "*religion*" and good works: they conflate religion with praise of their person and total obedience to them, not to God. They don't respect "*order*": the "order" in the mind of one king or queen, i.e. their despotism, is "disorder" to everyone else, as they live in fear of that one mind in charge.

Marx does not see that these 2nd Republic slogans have an actual force among which was new in human history, even if their definition was misused by the ousted royalists and Liberalist republicans. Marx is making politics and thus was, fairly, more concerned with Socialism winning power than delineating a progression of history.

In 2022 no socialist-inspired country is against "*property*": it certainly expropriates from the appropriator those goods which the public needs (i.e. electricity, transport, schools, hospitals, etc.). Socialism does not break up the "*family*": it undoubtedly promotes the family with tax breaks for children, state-run nurseries, maternal and paternal leave, etc. Socialism is not against "*religion*": the USSR proved that this was an immoral failure, and thus religion and the state and different religions coexist peacefully in places like Cuba, Vietnam, Iran, etc. Socialism is not against "*order*": it enforces an order based around equality, whereas the order of Western Liberal Democracy is based around the violence required to prop up an oligarchy.

So the problem with the "*Property, family, religion, order*" upheld by Western Liberal Democracy is that these four things are of the conception held by a 1% who either champions or is still a part of the monarchical legacy, and not for and of the masses. Losing property to the 1%'s usury, losing family to the 1%'s hospital bills, losing religion to the 1%'s worship of individualistic sensation, losing order to the 1%'s idea of "slightly less despotism is offered by rule by our class" - this is not Socialism, but it clearly is Western Liberal Democracy.

What the Party of Order did was subvert these ideals which Liberalism and Socialism, both born in 1789, agree are necessary. What they disagree is in the conception of them.

It's notable that Louis-Napoleon Bonaparte is so contemptible to Marx yet Louis-Napoleon's enemies (François Guizot) said of his coup: "*This is the complete and definitive triumph of socialism.*" A reassessment of Marx's animus is clearly needed to clearly understand "the nephew".

Marx disliked Louis-Napoleon the way a working Socialist politician today dislikes Donald Trump

Marx spends an inordinate amount of *Brumaire* both suppressing the role of the rural masses and elevating the importance of the urban areas, as I have noted. He also repeatedly condemns Louis-Napoleon Bonaparte as the president of the slum-proletariat/lumpenproletariat, or what he calls the "La Boheme" social classes: people without merit and without any desire to acquire work skills, combined with pseudo-artistic types, outright criminals and addicts.

And yet Louis-Napoleon seemed to be a man after Marx's own leftist-writer heart? Sadly, he had the fortune/misfortune of being a Bonaparte, to Marx.

Louis-Napoleon clearly saw his political ideology as perpetuating the middle-of-the-road revolutionary path of Napoleon Bonaparte, which is based around ideas that government exists to serve the masses, stability while implementing progressive political changes, and a healthy and not jingoistic patriotism. A fuller definition is: A popular national leader confirmed by popular election, above party politics, promoting equality, progress, and social change, with a belief in religion as an adjunct to the State, a belief that the central authority can transform society, a belief in the "nation" and its glory and a fundamental belief in national unity. I note that Iran's revolutionary concept of what I term a "supreme leader branch of government" shares a lot of these characteristics.

Louis-Napoleon Bonaparte's path was quite similar to his uncle's, and with similar conflicts - he started as a revolutionary republican, fighting Teutonic autocracy in Italy. But his personal attempts at revolution - himself at the head of a Bonapartist revolt - landed him in prison. It's there that he starts to be much like a Marx - a widely-read socio-economic historian of the leftist variety, in stark contrast with the royalists and elite who will be seated in the 2nd Republic's first

National Assembly in 1849. His philosophy is ultimately not socialism but Bonapartism, with himself obviously at the head - and for this Marx cannot ally with him. Safely in the third millenium, we have a much easier choice than Marx to make, of course.

However, equating Bonapartism with absolute monarchism or unelected authoritarianism is as foolish as it was in the era of Napoleon Bonaparte. It also cannot be equated with Western Liberal Democracy.

I would like to ask Marx: How bad can Louis-Napoleon Bonaparte be when on October 10, 1851, he announces plans to restore universal suffrage and on October 16 his executive cabinet resigns over it?

Marx quotes Louis-Napoleon, who concludes with a perfect analysis of the 1849-51 rule of Western Liberal Democracy, but still with no credit from Marx. I think it's precisely because he, like so many Western leftists and unlike so many modern Muslim leftists, totally forgets the pernicious influence of monarchism:

> *"With such unhoped for successes, I am justified to repeat how great the French republic would be if she were only allowed to pursue her real interests and reform her institutions, instead of being* ***constantly disturbed*** *in this by demagogues, on one side, and on the other,* ***by monarchic hallucinations****. The monarchic hallucinations hamper all progress and all serious departments of industry. Instead of progress we have struggle only. Men, formerly the most zealous supporters of royal authority and prerogative become the partisans of a convention* (the National Assembly) *that has no purpose other than to weaken an authority that is born of universal suffrage. We see men who have suffered most from the* (1848) *revolution and complained bitterest of it proving a new one for the sole purpose of putting fetters on the will of the nation."* (emphasis mine)

Modern Iranians certainly know what it means to still be disturbed by those insanely pushing *"monarchic hallucinations"*. Marx failed to appreciate Louis-Napoleon's railing against the royalist threat even though that is exactly what the average voter in France (a farmer) wanted to hear, because a return to feudalism was horrible to them and quite a real danger. Nor did he appreciate the average voter's brand-new goal: ending the self-interested oligarchy which is Western Liberal Democracy.

Louis-Napoleon Bonaparte is an advance in global political history because he is against the new, total domination of the bourgeois, here in the form of a parliamentary republic, which ended universal suffrage and which dominated in many ways more thoroughly than in the previous monarchy, as Marx himself wrote.

Like his uncle, Louis-Napoleon is far from a perfect political hero, but he is no Western Liberal Democrat, nor is he an absolute monarch, nor does he disbelieve in the ideals of 1789 or of 1848 - for that they elected them emperor.

What's needed in 2022 is not a new emperor, but the reforms which make representative democracy truly representative across the West, and an ousting of all royal/aristocratic/technocratic "hallucinations" of their supposed superiority over people like the Yellow Vests.

> *Yellow Vests: "Yes, there are many Yellow Vests who are poor and unemployed, but there are countless Yellow Vests who have stable jobs. We are all together regardless of our ethnic or religious background, because the Yellow Vests are the true representative of a united France."*

Appreciating Bonapartism over Western Liberal Democracy isn't being blind to its failures

Marx's recap of the historic vote approving Louis-Napoleon Bonaparte's self-coup here, which admits that his primary electoral support was the democratic mass:

> *"Suffice it here to say that it was a reaction of the farmers' class, who had been expected to pay the costs of the February* (1848) *revolution against the other classes of the nation: it was a reaction of the country against the city. It met with great favor among the soldiers, to whom the republicans of the 'National'* (a bourgeois republican newspaper - started by Adolphe Thiers) *had brought neither fame nor funds; among the great bourgeoisie who hailed Bonaparte as a bridge to the monarchy; and among the proletarians and small traders, who hailed him as a scourge to Cavaignac. I shall later have occasion to enter closer into the relation of the farmers to the French revolution."*

I began this chapter where Marx concluded - the relation of the farmers to French politics.

At the end of the previous chapter I stressed the importance of Western Liberal Democracy's very first "liberal strongman", Louis-Eugène Cavaignac. He went from being the governor of Algeria to leading the repression of urbanites ("*proletarians*") in the June Days of 1848, and thus was despised. The army's rank and file was full of lower-class men who lacked better job offers precisely because the elites who would staff the 2nd Republic's unicameral parliament abolished the National Workshops, a fundamental demand of the the revolution, which is what then set off the June Days uprising. So of course they approved of Louis-Napoleon Bonaparte and opposed the imperialist Cavaignac, probably just as many rank-and-file Western soldiers probably opposed Afghanistan, Iraq, Mali, Indochine, Korea, the Falklands, etc. and etc., or at least after they actually realised what they were fighting for.

What Marx wants to stress, necessarily, is that Louis-Napoleon

Bonaparte was allied with both the rural masses as well as the new rich bourgeois. It's the same failing of "the uncle": neither were committed Jacobins, i.e. Socialists; it's also the same virtues - opposing the royalists and restraining a dictatorship of the Liberalist bourgeois.

> *"I have already indicated that, since the entry of Fould* (a banker representing the stock exchange) *in the Ministry that portion of the commercial bourgeoisie that had enjoyed the lion's share in Louis Philippe's reign, to wit, the aristocracy of finance, had become Bonapartist. Fould not only represented Bonaparte's interests at the Bourse, he represented also the interests of the Bourse with Bonaparte."*

Marx also relates that this new *"aristocracy of finance"* had also grown to include government bonds, which remain the lynchpin of the Western economic capitalist system today. The French central bank and modern stock exchange were created by Napoleon Bonaparte - it was a new and slowly growing leviathan, but by 1848 it was able to leave the Bourbons and Orleanists behind.

Marx is relating how by 1851 the financial-industrial-imperialist wealth which had backed the House of Orleans coup in the 1830 Revolution (commonly referred to as the July Revolution) had continued to grow in power to the point where many broke free from the Orleanists to back Louis-Napoleon Bonaparte. These two groups worked together, with the rural masses, to push out the Bourbons and the Orleanist monarchical autocrats out of power once and for all.

(I did not cover it in this book, but the July Revolution of 1830 is often called the *Trois Glorieuses* in French ("Three Glorious [Days]"). Both terms are less descriptive and more purposely opaque than a contemporary term: the Second French Revolution, as it inspired revolutions in Italy, Poland, the Netherlands and led to the independence of Belgium. Popular dissatisfaction was constant with the "July

Monarchy" (the House of Orleans and Louis Philippe I), producing a week of revolution in 1832 (the June Rebellion of 1832/Paris Uprising of 1832), which was the subject of Hugo's *Les Miserables*, and then finally the Revolution of 1848. Louis Philippe I was notable for coopting Bonapartiste discourse, appointing Bonapartists to high positions and publicly venerating Napoleon Bonaparte. The political advance of the July Revolution was slight: replacing the ultra-royalist Charter of 1814, which provided a short bill of rights within a strong monarchy, similar to the UK, with the Charter of 1830, which barely expanded suffrage and loosened press controls.)

Vitally, Marx believes the experience of the 2nd Republic proved to one and all that Western Liberal Democracy was a total failure, and thus even France's elite approved of the self-coup. This is an entirely rational conclusion drawn from his experiences of the time, and in concordance with class warfare - the royalists and bourgeoisie simply wanted to get back to business, and Western Liberal Democracy was not yet skilled enough to efficiently aid the oligarchy:

"It (the leaders of the "bourgeois republic") *declared unmistakably that it longed to be rid of its own political rule, in order to escape the troubles and dangers of ruling."*

Thus Marx's explanation of why Western Liberal Democracy went down without a fight - it is not worth fighting for.

Marx quotes *The Economist* from Feb 1851 on Louis-Napoleon's coup:

> *"Now we have it stated from numerous quarters that France wishes above all things for repose. The president declares it in his message to the Legislative* (National) *Assembly; it is echoed from the tribune; it is asserted in the journals; it is announced from the pulpit; it is demonstrated by* ***the sensitiveness of the public funds*** *at the least prospect of disturbance, and their firmness the instant it is made manifest that the Executive is far superior in wisdom*

and power to the factious ex-officials of all former governments." (emphasis mine)

France was becoming a modern Bankocracy, but royalist hallucinations were slowing this down.

From *The Economist* in November 1851: *"The President is now recognised as the guardian of order on every Stock Exchange of Europe."*

Like in 1799 a Bonaparte was going to win democratic approval by finding a propertied ally against the royalists. In 1799 it was those whose profited from the sale of the *assignats* - in 1851 it was those who profited from industrial-financial-imperialist wealth. In both cases the peasants and proletariat supported the Bonapartists, even if Marx claims that only the slum-proletariat (and thus not the honest workers and artisans) supported "the nephew".

Thus the essence of Louis-Napoleon is similar to his uncle's: A France advancing politically too far ahead of the rest of Europe in 1848 and garnering total enmity, thus acquiescing to only a moderate revolution by 1852. The compromise gives the average Frenchmen unparalleled rights but with a price of not neutering a new, usurious aristocracy. One half is the righteous rejector of Western Liberal Democracy (a bourgeois parliamentary republic) and unelected monarchy in favor of universal suffrage, but the other half is a refusal to tax the wealthy, prohibit the usurious methods of the new financial class against the recently-propertied allotment farmers, resume the National Workshops (which would have reduced the power of the industrial class), or confiscate the wealth of the landed royalists - all the things which 1917, 1949, 1959 and 1979 would do.

Because Louis-Napoleon Bonaparte did not stop the financial oligarchy this happened, Marx wrote in 1871:

"The Second Empire had more than doubled the national debt, and plunged all the large towns into heavy municipal debts. The

war had fearfully swelled the liabilities, and mercilessly ravaged the resources of the nation. To complete the ruin, the Prussian Shylock was there with his bond for the keep of half a million of his solders on French soil, his indemnity for 5 billions, and interest at 5 percent on the unpaid instalments thereof. Who was to pay the bill? It was only by the violent overthrow of the (Paris Commune) *republic that the appropriators of wealth could hope to shift on to the shoulders of its producers the cost of a war which they, the appropriators, had themselves originated. Thus, the immense ruin of France spurred on these patriotic representatives of land and capital, under the very eyes and patronage of the invader, to graft upon the foreign war a civil war - a slaveholders' rebellion."*

That is a stunning historical passage which sums up much in 1871, and is addressed in the next chapter on the Paris Commune.

It's about knowing the real enemies - it is not the Bonapartes

This chapter requires so much Marx because the birth of Western Liberal Democracy was such a rapid failure that it appears complicated. With Marx's tremendous journalism its lifecycle was made clear.

Facing a reign of Louis-Napoleon Bonaparte and the rural will, the socialist Marx writes:

"All the same, the revolution is thoroughgoing. It still is on its passage through purgatory. It does its work methodically. Down to December 2, 1851, it (the revolution) *had fulfilled one-half of its programme, it now fulfils the other half. It first ripens the power of the Legislature into fullest maturity in order to be able to overthrow it. Now that it has accomplished that, the revolution*

proceeds to ripen the power of the Executive into equal maturity; it reduces this power to its purest expression; isolates it; places it before itself as the sole subject for reproof in order to concentrate against it all the revolutionary forces of destruction."

Marx understood what many have covered up: Louis-Napoleon Bonaparte expressed and achieved the total failure of the legislative branch in Western Liberal Democracy - your faith in Congress or the National Assembly or the Parliament of the United Kingdom is a total waste.

We see the reasons why Western Liberal Democracy does not wish to remember the 2nd Republic - it was a total failure which saw parliament commit coups agains the constitution and the voters. Western Liberal Democracy hasn't politically allied with the average person from its very beginning. It took an elected emperor to preserve the progressive idea of expanding democracy.

That passage also reveals Marx's slandering of Louis-Napoleon Bonaparte - he is "*the sole subject for reproof*" remaining. For Marx elite English parliamentarianism had been totally discredited - all that was left to do was to discredit the monarchical executive.

Yellow Vests: "People are angry because Macron has only represented just the interests of the rich class, billionaires and the bankers. Last year alone 500,000 more people fell under the poverty line in France, which is a direct result of Macron's policies."

Marx, as we will see with Trotsky, believed passionately that both monarchy and Liberal Democracy had discredited itself - they were both right, but not enough agree, still.

It would take nearly 20 years, not just 3, for Louis-Napoleon Bonaparte to discredit himself and to be replaced by the Socialist Democracy of the Paris Commune.

Louis-Napoleon Bonaparte's real virtue is that he was fighting with the people against the most dominant part of the oligarchy - the Bourbons and Orleanists, with all their accumulated wealth and influence. This is the group which wanted a disastrous, reactionary return to feudalism, and failing to realise that Bonapartism was not the biggest democratic threat is to misunderstand a century of French history.

Emmanuel Macron is thus not like Louis-Napoleon Bonaparte, and surely he never aimed to be such a populist. Macron more resembles the key figure from 1871, Adolphe Thiers, who also colluded with foreign powers to weaken France. But that is for the next chapter.

<—>

6

The Paris Commune: The true birth of neoliberalism and EU neo-imperialism

One hundred and fifty years later it's clear that the Paris Commune of 1871 was four things, and only one - the last on this list - is widely understood in 2022.

1. A reverse of the American Civil War: In France it was the slaveowners and slave traders who - as opposed to initiating it - forbid and fought down a rebellious secession. I think Marx would have been more effective in his description if he had compared France with the situation in the US, as it's an interesting reverse parallel.
2. For rightists: It's interesting that they never look at how their victory over the Paris Commune furthered the right's ideology and goals. It's almost as if the champions of Liberalism don't want to admit that armed treason with Bismarck was the reason for their victory in France?

   Too bad for them - there's no doubt that's what it was. 1871 marks the restoration of Liberalism after the voter-approved coup of Louis-Napoleon Bonaparte in 1852. But the Third Republic created in 1871 is no longer a "French" government based on Liberalism - as in 1848-52 - but a new type of Liberalism based on collusion among the international elite: thus, it is truly "neoliberalism". If we're going to call anything "neoliberalism" - even though it's all fundamentally just the same old "Liberalism" - this is the most accurate place in history to add that prefix. Most add it over a century later, incorrectly.

3. If the Commune represents such a major advance in global leftism because it's the first sustained example of the dictatorship of the proletariat - for two months -, then the armed victory of an international elite class over such a major advance must herald something equally significant, no? It does: The Commune represents the very neo-imperialist dictates, with their first troops, of what would eventually be instituted as the European Union.

   The definition of neo-imperialism is not simply the replacement of direct rule by Western colonisers with Westerners' indirect rule via local Brown puppets - neo-imperialism also includes Westerners waging imperialist war on their own Western people for the benefit of an international 1%. The first modern example of this intra-European class warfare (not merely feudal class warfare) started with the Commune. The European Union is the bureaucratic expression of these forces which defeated The Commune.

4. Lastly, there is total understanding that, for leftists, all we need is Frederich Engels' famous concluding remarks on the 20th anniversary of the Commune: *"Well and good, gentlemen, do you want to know what this dictatorship looks like? Look at the Paris Commune. That was the Dictatorship of the Proletariat."* This is the most widely understood understood of the four assertions.

   The Commune is a big deal, but we need to make it a big deal for the victors, because they - rightly - are ashamed of it.

The objective history: The Commune was defeated by the armed collusion of the French 1% with the German 1%

Marx's writings on the Paris Commune came in truly real-time. It's incredible journalism that he got it so right but also so quickly, but what's more shocking is what actually transpired:

The Paris Commune came after the capture of Louis-Napoleon Bonaparte in the Franco-Prussian war of 1870. The average person was fine with this ignominious end to the Bonapartist imperial era - the modern executive branch had been discredited. In 1852 France had democratically sanctioned the self-coup of the executive branch against the usurping, unrepresentative and already disgraced legislative branch of Western Liberal Democracy, and by 1870 France was ready to let go of the world's most progressive monarchy. They wanted something new - Socialist Democracy - but the Western Liberal Democratic elite was happy to push aside Bonaparte and re-usurp power, exactly as they did from 1849-51, when the National Assembly subverted the 1848 constitution to the majority will of parliament and gutted universal male suffrage. To achieve this re-conquering of the French people it took German troops to put them back into power; it took months of starvation, 30,000 innocent deaths, censorship and totalitarian controls around Paris; it took the total rejection of any democratic will… but this is "neoliberalism" - should we be surprised?

A hastily-assembled French government of the rich colluding with Bismarck's occupying Germans to bombard and siege Paris, what?

> *"The conspiracy of the ruling class to break down the revolution by a civil war carried on under the patronage of the foreign invader… culminated in the carnage of Paris."*

That's from Marx, but it's not a "a history" - it's "the history".

How can this be anything other than treason? How can this be anything other than forcing political regression onto France? How can the success of such a faction be anything other than ultimately anti-France?

These unanswered questions from supporters of the West add up to a major theme of Western history: the covering up of the early crimes of Western Liberal Democracy, which hypocritically loves to endlessly focus on the early errors of a far more moral and democratic movement - Socialism.

It's truly accurate to call these post-1871 war French legislators the "anti-Resistance" of French history, because instead of fighting against autocratic Teutons they colluded with occupying Prussia to subvert the democratic will of Paris and, above all, to ring-fence them from the rest of the nation to keep Paris' victory of Socialist Democracy from spreading.

> *Yellow Vest: "We didn't score very well in last month's European elections, but remember that we had only a few months to get everything organised, unlike all the other parties. What the Yellow Vests have hammered into people's heads is the reality that, our purchasing power is never going to rise, our debt to high finance can only keep rising, and that tax evasion will only continue to rise unless voters fight for our cause."*

You likely have no idea whose these legislators are, and nor does the average Frenchman. The treasons of Western Liberal Democracy are as hushed up as they are rewarded - the head collaborator, Adolphe Thiers, became the first president of France's Third Republic.

A major difference between the French Revolution of 1789 and the Commune is the lack of violence in Paris - until, that is, the forces of liberal democracy showed up and slaughtered as many in Paris as had died in the entire nation during "the Terror" (1793-4). Of course, all one hears about is the Terror of 1793-4 and never this far worse Terror

- it's far worse because the victims included far more women, children, poor and innocent, who were all executed without trial, as opposed to the many unrepentant elite of 1793-4. The Terror in the Western world is that rich people got tried and sentenced to death - poor people executed without a trial is no problem for Western Liberal Democrats, of course. This false reality is because the winners write the history books, but there's no doubt that as Socialism prevails over Western Liberal Democracy the true terror will be rightly named more and more.

Not a 'slaveowners rebellion' but a true reversal of the US Civil War

Marx, in his writings on the Paris Commune, repeatedly dubs it a "*slaveowners rebellion*", but it's actually the inverse - Paris rebelled, not the ruling slaveowners, and after months of siege Parisians called to secede and to establish a new republic.

France had banned slavery, again, in 1848, but the Western Liberal Democrats conniving with Bismarck to establish their mutual control over the masses of Paris contained many former slave-traders; contained families whose wealth was based on centuries of slave trading; contained members had financial dealings with countries who had not yet banned slavery, thus Marx is entirely justified to call them "*slaveowners*".

There is also major significance that the opposition to the Paris Commune was first landed at an assembly in Bordeaux: it's a port city built on the slave trade. The elite of Bordeaux, which is located within the department of Gironde, were consistently among the most reactionary, pro-slavery, anti-democracy elite in France (even more than almost English-sighting Brittany, the only region which sent troops to conquer The Commune).

Thus "slaveholders" did not secede against France, like in the US in

1861, but instead colluded with foreign occupiers and the slaughterers of French soldiers in order to contain a rebellious attempt at a new governmental structure. *The Civil War in* France, the name of Marx's famed pamphlet on the Commune, was caused by the restoration of popularly-rejected Western Liberal Democracy, and only via a treasonous siege did it remain a "Paris Commune" and not a true "Second French Revolution".

Having established what transpired and the unpopular role and ideology of the slave-traders/Western Liberal Democrats who prevailed, we can move on to what these colluding traitors of the nation's largest city established.

The restoration of liberalism = neoliberalism = anti-democracy, censorship & oligarchy

Even if the people of France were done with monarchy and empire, aristocracy and autocracy, false meritocracy and unrepresentative faux-technocracy, their Liberalists, constitutional monarchists and autocrats alike were not.

The elections for the first legislature of the new Third Republic were with Prussians in half the country - should we be surprised that neoliberalism's birth came under totally undemocratic voting conditions? Two-thirds of its members were either Orleanists or Bourbonists - yes, royalism and autocracy has prevailed in an alleged "Third Republic" built on mass murder in the capital.

> *Yellow Vests: "There has been so much police brutality today and in recent months. It's clear that the 5th Republic is dead, and that we must change not only the Macron regime, but our entire system. The French people are being ruled by thieves."*

It cannot be stressed enough how the Paris Commune relates to the overall historical trend of fighting monarchy and autocratic mindsets: 100 years after the French Revolution the Third Republic was a "republic" mainly run by royalists! This is no longer a "French" government based on Liberalism - as in 1849-52 - but a new type of Liberalism based on collusion among the international elite: it's neoliberalism.

As the years passed in the Third Republic these royalists would have to renounce their royalism - seeing that it was totally rejected by the French people - and thus they would switch their allegiance to the new neoliberalism. The result was clear to much of the new "Third World": With the fig leaf of republican and democratic institutions France's overseas empire would now become the world's second-largest. The idea that Louis-Napoleon Bonaparte or his uncle represented an "empire" more venal than that of the Third Republic is a totally unsupportable fiction.

Marx notes how the Commune differed from the 1%-er desires of Western Liberal Democrats: in The Commune the worker and lower classes were joined by the petty bourgeois, just like with the Yellow Vests. What united them was the debt-producing and rent-seeking of Liberalists.

> *"And yet, this was the first revolution in which the working class was openly acknowledged as the only class capable of social initiative, even by the great bulk of the Paris middle class - shopkeepers, tradesmen, merchants - the wealthy capitalist alone excepted. The Commune had saved them by a sagacious settlement of that ever recurring cause of dispute among the middle class themselves - the debtor and creditor accounts* (via the postponing of debts for 2-3 years). *The same portion of the middle class, after they had assisted in putting down the working men's insurrection of June 1848 had been at once unceremoniously sacrificed to the creditors by the then Constituent Assembly. But this was not their only motive*

> *for now rallying around the working class. They felt there was but one alternative - the Commune, or the empire - under whatever name it might reappear. The* (2nd) *empire* (of Louis-Napoleon Bonaparte), *had ruined them economically by the havoc it made of public wealth, by the wholesale financial swindling it fostered, by the props it lent to the artificially accelerated centralisation of capital, and the concomitant expropriation of their own ranks."*

To champion Louis-Napoleon Bonaparte over the first class of Western Liberal Democratic politicians is one thing, but we should see here why our modern leftist support must be limited for Louis-Napoleon Bonaparte: He failed to stop, as president or as elected emperor, the modern home-based debt-slavery which remains rampant in the West today:

> *"In the eyes of the French peasant the very existence of a great landed proprietor is itself an encroachment on his conquests of 1789. The bourgeois, in 1848, had burdened his plot of land with the additional tax of 45 cents, in the franc; but then he did so in the name of the revolution; while now he had foment a civil war against revolution; to shift on to the peasant's shoulders the chief load of the 5 billion of indemnity to be paid to the Prussian. The Commune, on the other hand, in one of its first proclamations, declared that the true originators of the war would be made to pay its cost."*

So we see the roots of neoliberalism both politically and economically: multinational autocrats and elite bourgeois against all workers and the modern, essentially precarious middle class.

(In a parenthetical from the larger point of the shift from serfdom to debt-serfdom in France: Here we see the cause of the reparations which France demanded after World War I. These reparations are always historically portrayed as unjustified and as a major cause of Germany's hyper-inflation and the rise of the Nazis. Again, we see how the refusal of Western Liberal Democracy to honestly examine its formative years from 1848-1914 has led to total historical ignorance. Germanic people will also point out that this debt load reflected the same debt load Napoleon put onto Germany, but the differences are enormous: France fought defensive war after defensive war from Prussian-Austrian-Hungarian aggression, and France was also received as liberators from feudalism - 1871 is not liberation at all!)

1871 is popularly portrayed as a localised and extremely radicalised movement, and even immoral: from Wikipedia, and without explanation or justification - "*The principles underpinning the Commune were viewed as morally degenerate....*" It's not portrayed as the "French Civil War of 1871" only because of the vast censorship tactics used against it.

> "*The Rurals* (i.e. the Bordeaux Assembly) *- this was, in fact, their chief apprehension - knew that three months' free communication of Communal Paris with the provinces would bring about a general rising of the peasants, and hence their anxiety to establish a police blockade around Paris, so as to stop the spread of the rinderpest.*"

In the 21st century we see how Western Liberal Democracy, after realising what devolving the "power of writing" via digital social media can do, has responded with vast censorship against their "*rinderpest*" classes of today. Of course, Western Liberal Democracy has brutally repressed Socialist thought for nearly two centuries.

> "*While the Versailles government* (the Bordeaux Assembly would relocate to Versailles, the longtime seat of autocracy, in March 1871), *as soon as it had recovered some spirit and strength, used the most violent means against the Commune; while it put down the free expression of opinion all over France, even to the forbidding*

of meetings of delegates from the large towns; while it subjected Versailles and the rest of France to an espionage far surpassing that of the Second Empire; while it burned, by its gendarme inquisitors, all papers printed at Paris, and sifted all correspondence from and to Paris; while in the National Assembly the most timid attempts to put in a word for Paris were howled down in a manner unknown even to the Chambre introuvable of 1816 (The ultra-royalist and uber-reactionary Chamber of Deputies of the Bourbon Restoration)*; with the savage warfare of Versailles outside, and its attempts and corruption and conspiracy inside Paris - would the Commune not have shamefully betrayed its trust by affecting to keep all the decencies and appearances of liberalism as in a time of profound peace?"*

It's the same problem as in 1849: Western Liberal Democracy does not even protect the democratic freedoms described in Liberalist thought. There is never a free marketplace of ideas if the ideas discuss eliminating the oligarchic parliamentary style of government which dominates the West. Similarly, Iran, Cuba, China and other Socialist-style democracies censor calls to counter their popular revolutions, but there are two key differences: Western Liberal Democracy hypocritically claims to be more tolerant when they are not, and the notion of Western Liberal Democracy's popular support is a false construction.

Because of the cutting off of communications - as well as because of the massive bloodletting when the siege was broken - the French Civil War remained a limited affair: it was the working people of Paris, and the politically progressive there, against the nation-wide banker-lawyer-landlord-aristocrat elite who were colluding with occupying Germans. It could have been the fourth major progressive national revolution in 82 years, but it was massacred before it reached that level.

Yellow Vest: "They are using even harsher tear gas on us, and people are dropping to the ground left and right. Our demand is for a more equal and more democratic society, and this does not merit such inadmissible violence. The government must listen to the people of France."

It remains clearly a class war, and an international one, and that's why the Commune is so vital. Whereas a century earlier it was royals colluding against their own people the Commune saw foreign-backed Liberalist politicians doing that.

It's truly the birth of the principles of the European Union.

The Commune as the birth of EU neo-imperialism

Returning to the theme of European political history I set out in the Introduction, 1871 represents a vital step beyond Europe's original imperialism, which started with the Columbian era of Old versus New World, and then also a step beyond France's occupation of Algeria in 1830: The refusal of a huge proportion of France to refuse support for armed war on Paris forced Bismarck to release hundreds of thousands of prisoners of war, who were then used to reconquer Paris.

"This army, however, would have been ridiculously ineffective without the instalments of imperialist war prisoners, which Bismarck granted in numbers just sufficient to keep the civil war going, and keep the Versailles government in abject dependence on Prussia," Marx wrote.

These represent the first-ever shock troops of European neo-imperialism. If Western Liberal Democracy was truly honest about its elitist individualism these men would be lionised as the first neo-imperial EU foot soldiers. Should we see a "Frexit" similar troops might be mustered if financial war fails to force them back into the EU neoliberal empire.

The Third Republic was formed amid German occupation, in the hastiest of a wartime vote, in order to approve a peace plan with Germany, but also - critically - to put the most unfit, unpatriotic, pro-neoliberal 1% people into power. It's a hallmark criticism of Western Liberal Democracy that their politicians are incredibly distrusted and the puppets of big money - the same goes for the first representatives of neoliberals, per Marx.

> *"The population could not but feel that the terms of the armistice rendered the continuation of the war impossible, and that for sanctioning the peace imposed by Bismarck the worst men in France were the best. .... There is but this difference: that the Romans had no mitrailleuses* (volley machine guns) *for the despatch, in the lump* (sum), *of the proscribed, and that they had not 'the law in their hands' nor on their lips the cry of 'civilisation'."*

We see here that the faux-moralism of Western Liberal Democracy truly began in 1871 as well.

> *"That, after the most tremendous war of modern times, the conquered and conquering hosts should fraternise for the common massacre of the proletariat - this unparalleled event does indicate, not, as Bismarck thinks, the final repression of a new society up heaving, but the crumbling into dust of bourgeois society."*

What Marx misses is that - by his own analysis - the petty bourgeois/small traders/true middle class was also massacred in 1871. The Yellow Vests alliance with this class - as opposed to the general leftist contempt for even the most near-bankrupt shop-keeper - is thus a significant broadening of leftism and also a return to what actually worked.

Yellow Vest: "The G7 is spending 30 million euros over one weekend to give rich ministers champagne, caviar and lobsters, while people in France don't have money for food or electricity. They talk about saving the environment, but only after flying here in their private, first-class planes. France's billionaires see their fortunes rise every year, whereas the minimum salary France is forced to stretch more and more. We need a real redistribution of wealth."

The Socialist Paris Commune lost. What up-heaved was not socialist society but a new form of Liberalism - one where Western elitist-imperialists turned on Westerners themselves in massacres formerly reserved for Brown peoples. It also marks the start of where Liberalism began its war to eradicate Socialist-inspired societies, a war of eradication which was as brutal and as highly-censored as the monarchical war against Liberalism was before the two began colluding in 1871.

Paris Commune: The start of what 1917, 1949, 1959 and 1979 carried

To summarise simply:

"It was essentially a working class government, the product of the struggle of the producing against the appropriating class, the political form at last under which to work out the emancipation of labor. … The Commune was therefore to serve as a lever for uprooting the economical foundation upon which rests the existence of classes, and therefore of class rule."

And if we aren't working for a classless society, then why are you reading this? Go out and rob, cheat and steal to join the upper class, and then join in their suppression of the working, middle, pensioner, student, youth, female, minority, etc. classes.

There's a lot of nonsense emanating from France on the Commune - four months of siege will do that to you, perhaps - and it's on the side of the anarchists.

The Commune is considered by anarchists to be their heyday - a day when the stages of Socialism and communism were leapfrogged (who needs development?) - and the immediate repression didn't give a chance to push aside these deluded bores. The only thing duller than the founder of collective anarchism, Mikhail Bakunin, and his self-referential writings on the Commune are his metaphysical thoughts. The certainties of the Commune's anarchists are as full of false "universal values" as much as any Western Liberal Democrat. Marx and Trotsky detested their generations's anarchists as much as the Yellow Vests refused to hand any sort of political leadership to Black Bloc or Antifa.

Western Liberal Democrats love to focus on the most individualistic, fantastic and nonsensical ideas espoused during The Commune - again, four months of siege will produce some of that - because it avoids any talk of the actual politics which was discussed, and allows for caricatures such as "*morally degenerate*". They want to make The Commune like May 1968, but the former was not just a movement for individual rights but about the political right to form a new type of government. As time goes on the unity of the Yellow Vests and their political goals became more apparent - not *68ard* individualism but 1789 class and cultural warfare. The Yellow Vest are a class warfare group.

But the biggest problem leftists must unlearn from the Commune's legacy is that it was totally Parisian. It's led to a veneration of urbanites as outdated as the veneration of factory proletariat - rural people, cubicle dwellers, pensioners and other groups must be in the vanguard, too.

Here's an interesting thought: if we are to accept that - at 1871's time of rural domination - that the urban areas were the political vanguard, then perhaps we should consider that today, when most societies are urbanised, that rural areas are now the political vanguard? With the Yellow Vests this generalisation appears to hold generally true.

What's interesting is that the Paris Commune proved Edmund Burke correct regarding the way Western Liberal Democracy, in its ultimate goal of federalism (seen in the US, Canada, Germany, Australia and in many Western monarchies which are allegedly just "unitary"), centers everything around the capital and thus ultimately creates fragmentation and disunity. Federalism is opposed in Socialist democracy because Western Liberal Democratic federalism serves to weaken society by weakening the power of government and thus increasing the power of the rich individual - it allows for capitalists to "divide and conquer".

> Burke foresaw this: *"You cannot but perceive in this scheme that it has a direct and immediate tendency to sever France into a variety of republics, and to render them totally independent of each other without any constitutional means of coherence, connection or subordination, except what may be derived from the acquiescence in the determinations of the general congress of the ambassadors from each independent republic."*

More importantly, Burke would't have been surprised one bit by the elite's response in 1871 to the democratic rejection of Western Liberal Democracy:

> *"Neither they have left any principle by which any of their municipalities can be bound to obedience, or even conscientiously obliged not to separate from the whole to become independent, or to connect itself with some other state. … To this the answer is: We will send troops. The last reason of kings is always the first with your Assembly."*

Indeed: become Western Liberal Democratic or die, be sanctioned, etc.

Burke sees a more modern Western problem - capital domination - but agrees that Western Liberal Democrats must control the capital above all.

> *"All you have got for the present is a paper circulation and a stock-jobbing constitution; and, as to the future, do you seriously think that the territory of France, upon the republican system of eighty-three independent municipalities (to say nothing of the parts that compose them), can ever be governed as one body or can ever be set in motion by the impulse of one mind? When the National Assembly has completed its work, it will have accomplished its ruin. These commonwealths will not long bear a state of subjection to the republic of Paris."*

Because the "republic of Paris" in 1871 was Socialist the rest of France had nothing to fear from the capital - quite the reverse in modern Western Liberal Democracy. The smothering of local cultures via an ethnocentric capital is something expressly opposed in Socialist Democracy.

In order to forestall incorrect anarchists about Marx, we should note his recognition of the need for centralisation. *"The centralisation of government,* ***required by modern society****, rises only upon the ruins of the military and bureaucratic governmental machinery that was forged in contrast to feudalism."* (emphasis mine)

Above all the Commune represents what neoliberalism requires: armed rule is what keeps Western Liberal Democracy going.

We would do well to remember that Engels believed the biggest mistake of The Commune was to not attack the real heart of Western Liberal Democracy: its Bankocracy.

"The hardest thing to understand is certainly the holy awe with which they remained standing respectfully outside the gates of the Bank of France. This was also a serious political mistake. The bank in the hands of the Commune - this would have been worth more than 10,000 hostages. It would have meant the pressure of the whole of the French bourgeoisie on the Versailles government in favor of peace with the Commune."

At Tahrir Square in Egypt I reported that the first place protesters went to was the television media centre: The main problem is not persuasion, but financial - the people will always admit that Western Liberal Democracy has failed. They should have taken over the banks, just as the Western invaders of Libya knew - they looted the authoritarian form of Islamic Socialism of so much gold that it's been called the "biggest heist in the world".

The Commune ends nearly 100 years of French leadership of progressive politics, as Russia and Eastern Europe would take the reins in the next generation.

What started with the Paris Commune would be bookended in 1936 with the Spanish Civil War. Spain was a non-wartime, legal and national Paris Commune, but neoliberal and neo-imperial Western Liberal Democracy chose war just like in 1871.

<—>

7

Where the West is stuck: The Fascism of the 1930s and the 'Fascism' of the 2020s

Starting in 1917 the same reactionary European nations which attacked in the 7 European Wars Against the French Revolution now transferred this same refusal to make peace with the Soviet Union. The problem has always been an idea - anti-autocracy, the idea from which Socialist Democracy flows (and the Yellow Vests) - and not a particular nation.

There is a clear moment when France definitively handed over its longtime leadership of European progressive politics. It is not 1914, when, unlike the Soviet Bolsheviks, French socialists went along with World War I: it is the creation of the Popular Front (*Front Populaire*) following the death of 15 people in a right-wing riot in 1934. The idea that committed socialists must be united with everyone from fake-leftists to right-wingers in order to fight Fascism proved to be a total catastrophe.

Yet this idea remains the policy of Western leftism today, and it is still producing catastrophes.

The European lesson of the 1930s is that the working and middle class handed power to the socialists and communists - who immediately gave power back to the bourgeois!

Ever since the Brexit vote against the neoliberal and neo-imperial European Union Western democracies are perpetually stuck in 1936: constantly warning of "Fascism" and constantly producing failures as bad as the original Popular Front in France.

However, because there is a total misunderstanding of what Fascism is it is critical for us to end the Western propaganda on the rise of Germanic National Socialism in order to properly understand European history then and now. It is "Germanic" and not just "German" because their adherents were from Austria, Hungary, Prussia and other longtime German language/culture areas.

Germanic National Socialism had something vital in common with Socialism: a clear rejection of Western Liberal Democracy. Without elucidating the common thread of post 1789 political history - that Western Liberal Democracy is an oligarchy which has been barely modified from autocracy - European history makes no sense in 1936 or after. We may as well say Napoleon Bonaparte wasn't a leftist revolutionary!

We move from the Paris Commune to 1936 because what occurred in 1936 was extremely similar: In February 1936 the electoral victory of a Popular Front coalition in Spain led to a legal take-over by socialists and anti-monarchists, only to see an international coalition of reactionaries arise - to prop up the dictator General Francisco Franco - and to foment civil and international war.

The Popular Front in France actually created the disastrous policy of "nonintervention" - the French left created it order to not intervene in the neighbouring Spanish Civil War. Nearly all of Europe signed up to diplomatically isolate and economically blockade the Spanish Republic. Indeed, Western Liberal Democracy wants to talk honestly about the Spanish Civil War as much as they want to they want to talk honestly about the Paris Commune, 1848 or the 7 European Wars Against the French Revolution.

In May 1936 what would become the final elections of the French 3rd Republic were held. Amid the Great Depression the centre-left and left finally won control of the government, with 60% of the vote, and via campaigns expressly against the unprecedented power of the historically-recent banking oligarchy. In July the Spanish Civil War began, and despite massive French support for the Republican leftists France's allegedly left-wing government colluded with the British on the policy of non-intervention. Viewed from the new center of progressive politics - Moscow - the Popular Front's non-intervention confirmed to the USSR that Western Europe was never going to have a Socialist revolution; that such an idea had been a fool's errand for decades; that Western Europe was going to side with fascism and go over to it, as Vichy France soon would. The USSR and Mexico would be the only nations to provide armed support to the Spanish Republic.

The Popular Front and Leon Blum, the first Socialist to be Prime Minister in France, would do a U-turn on the promised domestic reforms he was elected to implement. This is exactly what the Socialists François Mitterrand and François Hollande would do in 1983 and 2012, respectively, when they were handed power and mandate to implement leftist reforms. 1936 marks the point when Western leftists indisputably proved that they have abandoned Socialist Democracy in favor of Western Liberal Democracy - a fundamentally right-wing ideology rooted in monarchism, autocracy and oligarchy - and are thus right-wingers on the global political spectrum.

In April 1938 France's Popular Front collapsed after failure in almost every sense. Its colossal disappointment after such huge progressive excitement caused massive disillusionment and directly led to the establishment of Fascism in France two years later. The Popular Front provided the death knell for Western Liberal Democracy. Rather it should have, but by 1946 fascists, royalists and Western Liberal

Democrats would - to steal a phrase from Marx regarding a similar melding for all classes of wealth in the 19th century - "become bourgeois", i.e. all meld into one in order to stop Socialist Democracy.

This is where the West remains today.

They are totally against Socialist Democracy at home and abroad, and claiming Popular Fronts are needed to elect fake-leftist candidates who inevitably prove to be tools of long-running oligarchies. This will be discussed in later chapters.

In September 1938, now led by the Reformists (this is the most accurate term for the very misleadingly named "Radical Party" of France), the Munich Pact saw France stab the USSR in the back on the Franco-USSR pact of 1935, which stipulated joint military action against German belligerence. The Munich Betrayal, as it's also known, saw France and the United Kingdom collude with fascist Germany and Italy to hand a huge chunk of Czechoslovakia to Hitler. Instead of combatting Germany's war on Czechoslovakia the Popular Front preferred "appeasement" with Fascism.

The collusion would continue: France and the UK recognised Franco in February 1939, even though he held just two-thirds of the country and not Madrid.

(The army Franco originally led to start the war was the Spanish Army of Africa, based in Morocco. Much like France with Algeria in 1848 and beyond, we see the pernicious domestic political effects of Europe's Old World imperialism once again.)

Because we have located the start of neoliberalism and European neo-imperialism with the Paris Commune we see how these collusions make sense: these are Western Liberal Democratic countries, thus run by an oligarchical elite, thus opposed to any Socialist-inspired country. They will always wage war against Socialistic ideas which oppose oligarchical Western Liberalism which, thanks to the domination of the banker class by the start of the 20th century, is more "globalist" than inter-marrying monarchs ever were. Popular Fronts are inevitably proven to be useless - they are mere safety valves for genuine leftism.

By June 1939 national polls showed that 84% of Britain favored an Anglo-French-Soviet military alliance - Britain's Western Liberal Democratic politicians had no choice but to give the appearance of an effort. After six weeks of negotiations it became clear to Moscow that Britain's appallingly minor representations were not interested in any sort of alliance with Socialist Democracy.

Only two days after they left a German delegation arrived in Moscow and the Molotov-Ribbentrop Pact (a non-aggression pact and not any sort of alliance) was concluded precisely because the USSR saw that Western Liberal Democracies would never allow peaceful relations with socialist-inspired systems. Just as the revolutionary Napoleon Bonaparte wasted time in a burnt-down Moscow trying to make peace with an autocrat who never wanted it, so the USSR wasted time trying to make peace with autocrats and oligarchs.

> *Yellow Vest: "What I want for Christmas is for the Yellow Vests to join France's social movements to stop Macron's neoliberalism. But it would be even better if the whole world would become Yellow Vests to stop the ravages of high finance and globalisation."*

Western leftists (mostly Trotskyists) howled that the Molotov-Ribbentrop Pact was a betrayal of leftist ideals. That's a stunningly opportunistic and hollow claim, considering just how much France's Popular Front and Western Liberal Democracies failed to defend Spain, and also how Western nations refused make peace with Moscow. Moscow had waited for 19 years for any other European country to turn Socialist, but European progressive political thought was spent in Western Europe after 150 years.

Thus the USSR had given up, as it was clearly the eve of war. The Stalinists would certainly be proven right that Fascism would sweep

Germany, Austria, Spain and France - history clearly exonerates them, and indicts Western Liberal Democracy.

The USSR made a non-aggression pact with Germanic Socialism because at the time so many assumed that Fascism was going to fully replace totally re-discredited Western Liberal Democracies. That may seem hard to believe today, but the idea that Western Liberal Democracy was totally dead *was a fundamental assumption of leftists*, such as Trotsky, just as it also assumed by Marx in 1852.

It's vital to understand this proper timeline of European history leading up to the Molotov-Ribbentrop Pact because it is entirely in keeping with the overarching theme of European history since 1789: collusion by oligarchical elites to rule in autocratic fashion, and in order to suppress Socialist Democratic ideas.

Of course Western Liberal Democracy has always tried to obscure this history, and they still do: a resolution adopted by the European Union in 2019 stated that the Molotov-Ribbentrop Pact "*paved the way for the outbreak of World War II*", in a shameful rewriting of history. I don't expect the EU to pass resolutions for the 7 European Wars Against the French Revolution, the failed Revolutions of 1848 or the Paris Commune anytime soon....

The West's elite is fighting for Western Liberal Democracy, and thus they do not permit honest discussion and honest critiques of Western Liberal Democracy. This explains why there is no admission regarding the historical reality that Nazism and 1930s European fascism won power precisely because so many people grasped that Western Liberal Democracy was nothing but awful oligarchy.

Denying this historical reality is why Western politics has stopped making sense to the average Westerner: They simply cannot understand what Fascism was, what it is, or how it arose - it arose via Fascism's successful, popular condemnation of Western Liberal Democracy.

The problem is that Socialists don't stress this point enough, in their nonsensical fear of being seen as colluding with Fascism.

Knowing what 'Fascism' truly is, and why socialists shouldn't disavow it completely

Just as monarchy and feudalism was totally discredited to the average European by 1848, so Western Liberal Democracy and "debt feudalism/Bankocracy" was totally discredited by 1939.

This successful condemnation is why it's simply inaccurate and absurd to say things like the "Nazis had no Marxism". To do so is tremendously counterproductive and simply false. Mussolini was the editor of *Avanti!*, the official voice of the Italian Socialist Party, and was once a leading Italian Socialist. Socialists do not want to admit these things, but the failure caused by not explaining Fascism's relationship with Socialism is that we cannot understand Western political history if we relinquish the incredibly necessary democratic criticism of Western Liberal Democracy and "Capitalism With Western Characteristics" as evidenced by Fascism's rise.

Hitler, reader of Marx, summed it up the initial similarities himself in 1922: Without his alleged "*essential principle*" – race – Nazism "*would really do nothing more than compete with Marxism on its own ground*".

However, instead of dispossessing a noble class via class politics he dispossessed races to create a new noble class… and that is not really Socialism, nor anything advocated in Marxism.

Why should Socialists fear admitting the Marxism in Germanic socialism? If they do it's probably because they seek the approval of Western Liberal Democrats. It's clear that by including race – this is not truly Marxism or Socialism, but something different.

Or when Hitler rejected the class struggle, vital to Socialism, by saying: "*There are no such things as classes: They cannot be. Class means caste and caste means race.*" Well, Nazism may include some Marxist analyses of political and economic historical development but this is not really Socialism, but something different.

Making an alliance with corporate powers, instead of appropriating from the greedy expropriators this is not really Socialism, either.

Choosing central guidance instead of central majority ownership… this is not really Socialism.

Hitler was also the least internationalist politician you can think of - he totally rejected the internationalism of the class struggle and replaced it with a "community of the *volk*". He only wanted to protect Teutonic citizens in his all-Germanic nation.

We can go on and on pointing out these differences.

But the rejection of Western Liberal Democracy – due to its decades of failures by an oligarchical, corrupt, plutocratic leadership barely different from 18th century monarchy – that actually is the same as Socialism. The rejection of Western Liberal Democratic economics – due to the decades of failures by free market capitalism (i.e. the economic component of Liberalism) – that is the same as Socialism.

The Western Liberal Democrats of today simply do not want to talk about their often democratic rejection by people who feel its failures intimately.

Yellow Vest: "Our media have lost all credibility. Everything that you see on the mainstream media, and all of their reporters are under the boot of the government. For them the Yellow Vests don't even exist anymore, on both the private and public stations."

So what was German National Socialism and Italian Fascism? It is socialism minus the hopeful egalitarianism and the internationalism, and replaced with pessimistic Darwinian elitism and racism. It's a right-wing socialism whose only virtue is that it openly opposes the rich-are-smarter-and-should-rule ideology of Western Liberal Democracy, which opposed most of the French Revolution, Napoleon Bonaparte, won the counter-revolutions of 1848, laid the foundations of the neo-imperial European Union in 1871, colluded to create World

War I in order to forestall Socialist revolution and which was ruining society in the 1930s just as it does today.

But proponents of elites who rule through a Bankocracy don't want people to understand that Fascism and Germanic National Socialism came to power by opposing the domination of international high finance and Liberalism (whether "neo-", "ultra-" or *sans-préfixe* it's all the same: free markets, unregulated capitalism, rights only for those who can afford it), which forever is ultimately cover for an autocratic oligarchy.

So it can't be stressed enough: Socialism has nothing to fear from free, honest, patient examination of the Nazis' relationship with Socialism. What needs to be rectified is the total disavowal of Fascism which excludes its criticisms of Western Liberal Democracy.

However, Western Liberal Democracy has much to fear regarding true discussions of their relationship with the Nazis. They, over and over, allied with Fascism against Socialism in the 1930s; they colluded with the surviving Nazis and Fascists after 1945; they encouraged 3rd-generation Nazis in places like Ukraine in the 21st century. Thus since the 1930s Fascism and Western Liberal Democracy have been cooperating for more often than they have been fighting.

Where does Fascism fit in the course of European economic development since 1492?

The Fascists ultimately came to power by claiming they were different in their economic aims than Western Liberal Democrats.

By the turn of the 20th century industrialisation was no longer a novelty but the defining economic force. Landed wealth, Old World colonisation wealth, sea-trading wealth and mid-late 19th century industrial-financial wealth had been melded together into a banker-dominated financial system in which - of course - old money was predominant. The new banking system they created controlled the means of production and usuriously owned the land on which serfs recently lived. This is a clear timeline of economic history - it is not hard to understand, nor is it eternal.

Fascists promised to expropriate the wealth now held in the stewardship of banks and to do it via a new class - that of the magistrate; of individualist political power.

The word "Fascism" stems from "fasces", which is a bundle of sticks wrapped together topped by an ax. It's originally an Etruscan symbol which symbolised the power of - not the people wrapped together - the magistrate. What was the magistrate in Rome? He was a high-ranking officer with both executive and judicial powers. Whatever the wealth or justice which Roman magistrates allowed to "trickle-down" was entirely up to them. It was an elitist, 1%-centered system and Fascism's advance was (allegedly) making the 1% class open to competition (which they said begins in one's DNA) and cutting out the longtime aristocracy and the new bankers. The seal of the United States Senate, an aristocratic house of lords, features two crossed fasces.

Beyond autocratic powers for a non-monarchical elite, Western Liberal Democracy also mostly agreed with the key plank of the Fascist's economic program. "Central planning" does exist in modern Western countries - it is based around the military. For example, in the United States their economy is guided by the Pentagon, the world's largest employer. The Pentagon hands out the fruits of their taxpayer-funded research to private companies; enriches their native bourgeoisie with hugely corrupt contracts; provides jobs for the masses terribly ineffectively; but it very effectively enriches their 1%.

Fascism was never for the people but dedicated to the power of those in power; for the status quo; for submission to essentially autocratic magistrates and politicians; against the redistribution of wealth and political power. It is only Socialism which reduces the power of the magistrate, who makes him or her accountable and who improves the person of the magistrate by making sure he or she is not solely drawn from the elite, grasping class.

Fascism is different from the globalist class of Western Liberal Democracy by insisting on nationalist competition and national sovereignty. The arrival of the European Union, the euro and the Eurogroup, which will supersede national laws without any concern for ideals of democracy, will render these desires essentially irrelevant. The main sin of Donald Trump's "Make America Great Again" slogan, or of Marine Le Pen, is that these two Fascist politicians both seek to restore some aspects of national sovereignty.

Trotsky wrote: *"Fascism, as we know, is born between the union of the despair of the middle-classes and the terrorist policy of big capital."* Yet the West never takes a class view and elevates big capital to the status of demigods - this is why to them Fascism must always be solely race-related and never economic-related. It's simply a half-truth, and not understanding and combating this dooms Western politics - and their own history - to total misunderstanding.

The 1% and their lackeys immediately called the Yellow Vests Fascists in part because it was a union of the lower and middle classes - like in the Paris Commune it includes a union of the lower class and the proletariat with the petty bourgeois small shopkeeper.

> *Yellow Vest: "For 10 years we have only created instability. 75% of France has serious economic difficulties. We have closed hospitals, nurseries, schools - everything is being closed, and this can't go on!"*

Due to their insistence on elitism, Fascism could have only ever allied with Liberal Democracy - the Molotov-Ribbentrop non-aggression pact is as far as it ever could have gone. However, if they had somehow allied with the USSR against Liberal Democracy what would they have permanently smashed? Answer: the Bankocracy which rules today.

It's vital to recognise this, because the current usage of "fascist" completely lacks this historical-economic component.

The Fascism of the 2020s is even more right-wing than the Fascism of the 1930s

Due to the refusal to honestly talk about Fascism - on both the Western left and the Western right - Western politics today are simply a catastrophe of nonsense and misinformation.

Their lack of knowledge allows them to obscure the fact that modern Western "Fascists" are even more right-wing than Hitler, who was quite reliant on the Marxist explanation of 19th century history and economics. However, the modern far-right wing has expunged Marxism, and thus they cannot be actual Fascists. Racism and Fascism cannot be mere synonyms for each other - unless the goal is to neuter them of all meaning.

Being more right-wing than Hitler… that seems like something which should be understood, no? However, Western Liberal Democracy doesn't want anything but propaganda regarding other systems and to stay mute regarding its own failures and treasons.

The best term for today's alleged "Fascists" would be "*Nalis*" - Nationalist Liberalists: they have all the jingoism, militarism, authoritarianism and imperialism of 1930s Fascists but combine it with Liberalist political structures and historical analyses, as well as economic inequality and rabid competition.

It's a simple and accurate political description, but only Socialist-inspired countries which have fully rejected Western Liberal Democracy would ever apply the term "Nali": Just as uninformed Socialists don't want to admit any ideological similarities with Nazism, so uninformed Western Liberal Democrats don't want to admit that they are actually fighting internecine wars with their "National Liberalist" brethren.

And what do Western Liberal Democrats care if calling far-right Ukrainians "Nazis" in 2022 unfairly tarnishes Socialism and spreads misinformation? Both wings of Liberalists (one nationalist, the other globalist) are united in their anti-Socialism.

Donald Trump and Marine Le Pen are two example of open Nalis, but so are two enemies - Russia's Vladimir Putin and Ukraine's Volodymyr Zelensky. The Russian military operation in Ukraine has been a catastrophe of misinformation on both sides regarding who is a "Fascist" and who is a "Liberal", and precisely because neither can admit that Fascism and Liberalism coincide and almost always ally, historically. Thus this battle between two Nali states is either a historical anomaly or, as I predict, Russia's invasion will mark a step away from their Nalism since 1991 and back towards Socialist Democracy. If Russia continues to insist that "Russophobia" totally equates with "Nazism", then this will herald their failure to return the fold of progressive politics.

In France, by 2017 the Great Financial Crisis – just the latest periodic failure of Liberalism – had inflamed the masses too much for every single politician to ignore: Marine Le Pen thus dropped the Reaganism of her father and made it to the second round of the presidential election. She defended economic ideas which were both similar to the French left and to the Germanic National Socialists of the 1930s. However, in the 2022 campaign Le Pen reverted back to far-right economics, dropping all her promises for things like a "Frexit" vote within six months of election and for repudiating banker debt - yet the mainstream media called her "Fascist" throughout the entire time.

The modern French and Western model was essentially created from 1928-1945, and what it took from Fascism and Germanic National Socialism is that economic planning must be limited to the military, and that xenophobia, identity politics and security are spectacles just big enough to dominate the headlines, and thus to distract from Liberalism's failures. To put it in 2022 presidential candidate Eric

Zemmour's terms: France's economic problem is Muslim welfare, not banker welfare. It's a pathetic intellectual analysis. When the unrest in Ukraine began France immediately realised that and Zemmour's popularity quickly halved, and he could not even advance past the first round in the 2022 legislative elections.

> *Yellow Vest: "If you look around here you see people of all colours and religions. For me it goes beyond questions of origin - it's really a question of social justice, regardless of someone's ethnicity or religion."*

During the 2022 campaign the convicted racist Zemmour said he was, "*here to save the French people and France...not here to save the world.*" It's a telling, semi-messianic remark because it is truly straight out of Adolf Hitler's platform in the 1930s.

But such a comparison was never made by the mainstream media, and it could never be made. Many have heard of Godwin's Law, or the rule of Nazi analogies: an Internet adage asserting that as an online discussion grows longer (regardless of topic or scope), the probability of a comparison involving Nazis or Adolf Hitler approaches. However, an important corollary is that whenever someone compares someone or something to Nazism – that person has lost the argument and/or the argument is summarily over.

Essentially, the world is to accept that all discussions of Western politics cannot discuss the anti-Western Liberalism ideology which was Germanic Nazism.

Thus it was impossible for them to accurately describe a 2022 French election where four of the five top candidates were all on the far-right – either economically, politically, culturally or all three. In the two-week interim between their two rounds of voting any criticism of Emmanuel Macron's record was immediately shouted down in the mainstream media as "support for Fascism" - voters surely wondered which candidate they were referring to? The failure to delineate Fascism from Western Liberal Democracy means that we also cannot understand where they have reconciled a century later, just as how liberalism and monarchy eventually reconciled.

The Western right is stuck in falsely believing that the right of 2020 is the same as in the 1930s, despite all the anti-racist gains made since then; the Western left is stuck in falsely believing that their "Popular Front" tactic is actual leftism, despite being neutered of Marxism and Socialism. This is why Western versions of history and their political discourse today simply make no sense. It only makes sense if we remember that obscuring political truths is a hallmark of Western Liberal Democratic history, and thus their versions are not intended to be truthful nor complete.

Not wanting to accurately define Fascism or Liberalism, but certain in their rejection of Socialist Democracy, after the first round vote in 2022 all the losing presidential candidates (except Zemmour) immediately called for an unofficial Popular Front against Le Pen, just as they did in 2017. What's vital and new is that the Yellow Vests empathically refused this form of class-collaborationism. The People's Front tactic must be seen for what it is: not an effort to fight Fascism but as a way to cement fake-leftism.

> Trotsky wrote: *"The racists pillage the Marxist program, successfully transforming certain of its sections into an instrument of social demagogy. The 'Communists' (?) as a matter of fact refuse their own program, substituting for it the rotten refuse of reformism. Can one conceive of a more fraudulent bankruptcy?"*

Trotsky wrote that in 1935 but anyone can see that this is where the West is stuck, still. To reformulate for the 21st century:

Racists reject certain sections of Western Liberal Democrat economics in order to preserve White citizens from the united Bankocrats, while left-wingers hysterically prop up right-leaning moderates who only seek to refine Liberalism into an ever-more unequal system. Can you conceive of a more fraudulent ideological bankruptcy than modern Western politics?

If "Nali" ever did catch on one thing is certain: it would be a huge improvement.

<—>

8

On 'Leon Trotsky on France' in order to reclaim Trotsky from the Trotskyists

Turning to Trotsky to help analyse the Yellow Vests is indispensable not because I am a Trotskyist but because Trotsky is the foremost socialist architect, describer and critic of the actual waging of political revolution.

In October 1917 Trotsky was elected chairman of the Petrograd Soviet, the revolutionary centre of Russia. He directed the organisation of the October Revolution's uprising against the Provisional Government, which had followed after the monarchy's toppling in the February Revolution. Trotsky knew what he was talking about, and perhaps more than anyone of his era he could accurately say what a revolutionary group needs to do to actually seize power.

The problem with Trotsky is not Trotskyism. He rejected making his name synonymous with the actual waging of progressive revolution, almost bewilderingly lamenting: "*To reaction and its agents 'Trotskyism' is the international menace of the socialist revolution.*"

The two are not and must not be synonymous. Trotsky would surely berate his 21st century adherents for the primary complaint leftists make towards his followers: To modern Trotskyists it's not "revolution" or "Socialism" unless it's "Trotskyism" and only "Trotskyism".

The problem with Trotsky is not Trotskyism, it's Trotskyists.

If Trotskyism used to be synonymous with revolution but it no longer is - which is certainly the case - then who should be blamed more than the followers who take his name? French presidential elections inevitably feature multiple Trotskyist candidates - they even cannot get along with each other, much less other leftists.

Trotsky is different from his modern followers in that he saw conditions in the 1930s as ripe for revolution - even overripe - and he was shocked that others couldn't see that what he helped effectuate in Russia was actually possible elsewhere, and right then. From November 2018 until June 2019 the Yellow Vests undoubtedly agreed that conditions were - at a minimum - ripe for a major break with the mainstream practices of Western Liberal Democracy, and they were also shocked that French leftists couldn't see that.

> *Yellow Vest: "We have to bring France to its knees, because that is all that our governments understand. We will block the entire economy for as long as it takes. The fight against capitalism is heating up around the world, so the Yellow Vests are not the only ones demanding huge changes."*

A big reason for their absence from the most revolutionary situation in France since 1968 is that today's Trotskyists are so discredited that they wouldn't have been welcomed by the Yellow Vests.

Today's Trotskyists seemingly live in a state where it is perpetually September 1917 - they cannot possibly support the few global nations who have selfishly "jumped the gun" and taken power in their own country without the Trotskyists, and allegedly at the expense of the global revolution. If Trotskyists could realise that monarchy still plays a huge role in the world they would realise that living in a state where it is perpetually January 1917 would be far, far more useful in actually pushing Socialism (and not just Trotskyism) forward.

What I will call Trotsky's definition of a revolutionary country is concise and clear, and any country fulfilling these requirements obviously deserves the fullest support:

> "*Meanwhile the hypothetical government* (Trotsky is referring to a Western Liberal Democratic government which actually stood up to Fascism) *would give nothing either to the workers or to the petty-bourgeois masses because it would be unable to attack the foundations of private property; and without expropriation of the banks, the great commercial enterprises, the key branches of industry and transport, without a foreign trade monopoly, and without a series of other profound measures, there is no possible way of coming of the aid of the peasant, the artisan, the petty merchant.*"

Above is the most basic condition for Socialist-inspired revolution on behalf of the people, and yet Trotskyists all over France and the West perpetually condemn any country which has made this critical first step on the road to citizen empowerment. Please note that Iran has not given up the Iranian people's control over all the "*profound measures*" listed above. Please also note that today's French Trotskyist groups usually incorrectly lump small merchants in with CEOs, instead of with the proletariat and farmers, while the Yellow Vests do not make that mistake.

Perhaps the most common word with Trotsky is "*expropriation*". Without the expropriation of the private property of the 1% then there is no movement which can make any type of Socialism - or the barest amount of Socialist Democracy - possible.

This definition is so useful because it illustrates how the establishment of banking power fits into the economic history of Europe since 1492. By the 1930s "*the banks*" of oligarchical Western Liberal Democracy had become first on the list of Trotsky's opponents of progressive politics, and both the Socialists and the Fascists came to power by promising to gut their power.

Non-Socialist readers may be alarmed by Trotsky's phrase "*attack the foundations of private property*", as though they alone had a trade monopoly, a key branch of any industry or a great commercial enterprise. Such persons simply like to fancy themselves budding bourgeois, and thus don't want a ceiling to limit their all-but-certain rise, as bourgeois culture inculcates them to want to do. Giving the masses control of these key mega-economic entities in order to deprive the bourgeois of the ability to subjugate the labor of others - and not giving up control over your home and the objects inside, nor your small business - is what Socialism is, and it's also what it takes to win stability, control and peace for the masses.

Today's Trotskyists are not on the front lines, and they don't support any serious fronts anywhere

Trotsky today would surely demand a redefinition of what "Trotskyism" is because for modern Trotskyists it apparently doesn't include demanding control of the means of major production or armed anything. Trotskyism in the 21st century has become subsumed by Western Liberal Democracy because they now limit themselves to working within it, not against it.

More than any other aspect of his personal thought these remarks he made in 1935 when talking of France encapsulate what Trotsky was fundamentally all about:

> *"This is why the most immediate of all demands must be for the*

> ***expropriation of the capitalists and the nationalization (socialization) of the means of production.*** *But is not this demand unrealizable under the rule of the bourgeoisie? Quite so! That is why we must seize power."* (emphasis his)

Any discussion cannot gloss over that point or this one below, which today's Trotskyists certainly ignore, seeing as how they reject any country which has actually enacted Socialist-inspired revolution and nationalisations, such as China, Cuba, Iran, North Korea, Venezuela, etc.:

> *"How can one come to soviet* (workers' committees) *power without an armed insurrection? How can one come to an insurrection without arming the workers? How can one defend oneself against fascism without arms? How can we achieve armament, even partial, without propaganda for this slogan?"*

Trotskyist propaganda today is totally devoid of such propaganda, and this is even though Trotsky's writing is full of denigration for peaceniks who refuse to fight for their rights. Such militarism is, of course, very different from a militarism which clamours for invasion:

> ***"The more successful the anti-militarist agitation becomes, the more rapid will be the growth of the fascist danger.*** *Such is the actual and not fanciful dialectic of the struggle."* (emphasis his)

By the 1960s the Western left had adopted anti-militarism as an almost iron law. Such history-ignoring nonsense translated into political nonsense which ultimately amounted to: reformism of the status quo at a snail's pace and with the ephemeral quality of a flower's existence. Western "Flower Power" didn't change the social pyramid, and Trotsky would not have been surprised at the political impotence of switching away from anti-militarist agitation while trying to win Socialist-inspired changes.

A fundamental question which must be posed is: Why did Trotskyists never come out in favor of arming the Yellow Vests *for their own self-defense*? Every one know they were getting attacked every Saturday by police. If today's Trotskyists are merely content to be tiny, ineffectual parties within Western Liberal Democracies, can't they at least promote defensive measures to defend the mere rights of Liberalism, such as freedom of assembly? Surely this would be the bare minimum Trotsky would have promoted as regards to the Yellow Vests.

This is a question which requires far more reflection because it strikes at the hypocritical heart of Western Liberal Democracy. The Yellow Vests show how the West refuses to accept even the barest Liberal Democratic rights of 1789, and in addition to rejecting all the egalitarian measure promoted by Socialist Democracy. It will be discussed in the chapter *What the Yellow Vests can be: a group which can protect Liberalism's rights, at least.*

A perfect time for France's Trotskyists to provide defensive assistance was during the Yellow Vests attempted establishment of a permanent camp near the Eiffel Tower in March 2019. Of course, they also needed defensive help every Saturday for months, as well.

The primary propaganda organ of Trotskyism - the World Socialist Web Site - never made such calls to action even though they are based in the United States and thus out of the reach of French intimidation and repression! The WSWS did correctly stress the need of the Yellow Vests to remain apart from the totally-discredited political establishment, such as parties and unions, (though this point was already non-negotiable to the Yellow Vests) but only to finally insist that they needed to be led by a Trotskyist vanguard provided by the International Committee of the Fourth International. Reject everyone else but me - it's typical modern Trotskyism. The irony is how much the Yellow Vests and Trotsky have in common - both emphatically reject class-collaborationism.

Trotsky would have disavowed his namesakes for failing to seize the once-in-century moment provided by the Yellow Vests, and this is proven by his own writings.

For example, in 1936 Trotsky appeared to be apoplectic with France's leftists: 1.5 million out of 10 million French people voted communist and - to a guy who made a revolution with much less - that should have been enough to make a revolution in France.

> *"When one and a half million voters cast their ballots for the Communists, the majority of them mean to say thereby: 'We want you to do the same thing in France that the Russian Bolsheviks did in their country in October 1917.'"*

In the West the Yellow Vests are the first popular political force operating on essentially Socialist-inspired ideas since 1936. They are the first political force willing to operate under repressive and hotly-debated conditions since 1936. They are the first French progressive political force to have even more popular support than the combined leftists did in 1936: polls showed the Yellow Vests as having 75% approval rating and always - even after so much propaganda and repression - as having a majority approval rating in a country where such popularity was long considered unachievable.

In 1936 Trotsky dismissed the vote results for not only the Radicals (it's a misleading name - they were "Reformists" of Western Liberal Democracy) but the further left Socialist Party as well: he didn't care about their score because they were not a working class party in composition or policy like the Communists were. The Yellow Vests are working class in composition and policy, but where were/are the Trotskyists? The Yellow Vests' fault was not being openly Trotskyist, obviously.

Trotsky would diagnose the problem today as one of poor leadership, which was his most common refrain. However, the worst leadership among Western leftists is among the Trotskyists because they clearly do not even champion the essentials of Trotskyist thought.

> *Yellow Vest: "So many of these types have been bought off by Macron and are happy to stay in his pocket. Pensioners, the jobless and public workers have been marching for seven months and our so-called intellectuals spit on us! We are getting beaten and gassed, and they criticise us!"*

In 2022 I believe Trotsky would have backed countries like Iran because of to whom he pointed his vast criticism when discussing France: the proponents of Western Liberal Democratic measures, and those who seek appeasement via measures which fall short of expropriation. From the multiple French Trotskyist parties to the WSWS they spent more time boosting their own minuscule parties than the Yellow Vests, which is to say that they are actually totally committed to working within the framework of Western Liberal Democracy. It's really the exact opposite of what Trotsky suggested!

Western Trotskyists are not revolutionary - they are waiting for that laughable *"hypothetical government"* which Trotsky himself noted would fail even if ever installed, and he was proven right by the failure of France's 1936 Popular Front. Marxist-inspired analyses of history make it clear that the Western Liberal Democratic framework will never create permanent programs which guarantee a permanent redistribution of political power and wealth which aims at boosting the lower and middle classes - not in wartime, pandemic-time or any other hypothetical time.

The absurd contradictions and hypocrisies of the modern Trotskyist movement pale so enormously when held up with the actual achievements of Stalinist-inspired (i.e. USSR-inspired) movements which Trotsky famously rejected.

We should not blame heroic and committed Trotsky!

We should wrest him away from today's declared Trotskyists, as they refuse to actually put into practice his ideas while claiming his mantle, and we should redefine Trotskyism to describe more accurately what his necessary contributions were to Socialism.

Trotskyism: A line of Socialist thought which emphasised the need of a vanguard party to encourage demanding power from the Liberalist and monarchist elite, by force while always remaining in dialogue with the masses, in order to expropriate their political power and economic wealth for the benefit of the masses.

The above definition retains Trotsky's beloved notion of a vanguard party, but it can clearly include Cuba, China, Iran, Hezbollah and others - this is how Trotsky can be wrested from Trotskyists. Trotsky didn't want his name becoming synonymous with Socialist revolution, but he sure wouldn't want it affiliated with today's totally unTrotskyist Trotskyists!

As with Napoleon Bonaparte, the well-being and understanding which Socialist analysis has to offer insists on the political rehabilitation of a person whose adherents have misunderstood, distorted and often disgraced him. The revolution does not have to eat its young, as counter-revolutionaries insist. By first fully dispatching the oldest enemy of Socialist Democracy - the autocratic oligarchy embodied by monarchy, whose ideals have been subsumed by Western Liberal Democracy - we will clear the way to end arrogant imperialism and elitism, an indispensable first step towards demanding Socialism at home.

But we should wrest Trotsky not just from the adulation which he himself opposed but also from Trotsky himself. Consider the perspective of W.E.B. Du Bois, certainly the greatest African-American political writer of his era and maybe ever:

> *"He* (Stalin) *early saw through the flamboyance and exhibitionism of Trotsky, who fooled the world, and especially America. The whole ill-bred and insulting attitude of Liberals in the U.S. today began with our naive acceptance of Trotsky's magnificent lying propaganda, which he carried around the world. Against it, Stalin stood like a rock and moved neither right nor left, as he continued to advance toward a real socialism instead of the sham Trotsky offered."*

W.E.B. Du Bois probably didn't deal often with French Trotskyists, as I have. Some, even their very top leaders, have often been very polite. Others have been even more impolite to me than the Anglophone section of the World Socialist Web Site. In early 2018 the WSWS and I engaged in point-counterpoint articles regarding their support for protests in Iran, their total lack of support for the Socialist-inspired Iranian Revolution and their rather middling support for a nation under constant imperialist attacks. To be brief, the online articles culminated in their penning of a 3-part pamphlet titled, *The Struggle against Imperialism and For Workers' Power in Iran: A reply to a proponent of "Iranian Islamic Socialism.* I was - and am - that proponent. I'm sorry to say that it wasn't much to read because they did something which no Iranian person would ever do and expect to remain credible to any Iranian: they attempted to give the Tudeh communist party all the credit for 1979. Excising the role of the mosque, of religious leadership and of the combination of a revolutionary interpretation of Shia Islam combined with key aspects of Socialism is to spread a fabricated, self-serving history of how revolution finally came to sweep out 2,500 years of Iranian monarchism. As a response to the pamphlet I wrote the book *Socialism's Ignored Success: Iranian Islamic Socialism* to finally describe to a Western audience the countless Socialist-inspired roots, programs and policies of undoubtedly revolutionary Iran. In my point-counterpart articles with the WSWS I went out of my way to praise them where justified, whereas their articles were personally antagonistic. They called me an "*apologist*", a "*flunkie*" and made other remarks which were totally unnecessary and which only made themselves look "*insulting*" and "*ill-bred*", much as Du Bois noted. Again the problem is not Trotskyism, but... I'm glad their pamphlet kindly appreciated that, "*Mazaheri's compliments are generous.*"

Trotsky believed that Stalin had no sincere care for the working class, only for the "bureaucracy" - that's false. The Trotskyist blame towards Stalinism for abandoning Western workers/leftism totally ignores his and the USSR's decades of leftist agitation, as the previous chapter detailed. The blame goes towards the forces of autocracy and the oligarchy of Western Liberal Democracy, not fellow communists and socialists.

In his consternation that others were not as ardently revolutionary Trotsky rejected the comparatively minor - when compared with the demands of monarchism and oligarchy - intra-Socialist compromises which allowed for a continuing *"advance towards a real socialism"*, even if only in one country at a time. Trotsky's war on the USSR - on "Stalinism" - is often viewed as a betrayal of the Socialist movement, and today's Trotskyists make this same mistake as regards to China, Iran, Venezuela and - if they progressed further - probably the Yellow Vests, too.

What Socialism cannot lose from Trotsky is the idea that the threat of armed revolution in the face of the repeated denial of human rights is the only certain path to an actual revolution in the aristocratic elite's property holdings. What it can lose is "*flamboyance*", "*exhibitionism*", acting as though one is "*ill-bred*" and being "*insulting*". Trotskyism seduced the individualist West in large part because both over-rely on the individual singularity of a vanguard party. There is an anti-democracy inherent in Trotsky's most constant complaint - the poor leadership of the leftist movement - as though if only Trotsky were still in charge, then all of Europe would be Socialist today.

I have presented a balanced view of Leon Trotsky here because a history of leftist movements is not possible without Trotsky, but a leftist history where Marx, Engels and Trotsky are the only leftists is an ineffectual and distorting absurdity.

A history where Napoleon Bonaparte is not a leftist, where the 1848 Revolutions were not the Counter-Revolutions of 1848, where the rise of Fascism is both Socialism's fault and yet is nothing but distorted Marxism, and where the Yellow Vests are not French leftism reborn are ineffectual and distorting absurdities.

The parallels between France today and the 1930s is of vital importance, and thus recalling Trotsky's assessments of France provides us with a wealth of parallels which are necessary to make in order to show how the problems of Western Liberal Democracy today are unchanged since 90 years ago, just as re-reading Marx reminds us the problems are unchanged since 175 years ago.

Trotsky's failure to see Western Liberal Democracy as able to subsume the ideals of Fascism

Trotsky has so much right - above all, his refusal to concede anything to Western Liberal Democracy - but let's focus on the few things he got quite wrong.

Trotsky's writings unmistakably reveal that he really thought Western Liberal Democracy/parliamentarianism/free marketism was truly dead. To Trotsky the only fight remaining was against Fascism. It's a mistake many leftists have made since 1850 - incorrectly assuming that Western Liberal Democracy doesn't have tremendous resources to survive.

Apparently Trotsky thought Fascism really was a "third way" - it was neither autocratic Western Liberal Democracy nor Socialist Democracy - but in the 1930s no non-Westerner would agree that jingoism, racism, authoritarianism and the myriad petty dictatorships of their leader class is something which only came to the fore in the West during their Fascist era of the 1930s. Of course, they had been experiencing it in their own colonised countries! To non-Westerners the oligarchy of monarchism, Western Liberal Democracy and Fascism is distinguished only in style and not function.

The lack of emphasis on the socio-cultural effects of industrial-era imperialism caused Trotsky to underestimate the jingoism, racism, social and economic regimentation, oppression of dissent and "dictatorship of the leader class" (i.e. the five features of the commonly-accepted definition of Fascism) in Western Liberal Democracy, and to falsely assume these were only attributes of Fascism.

Another problem may have been that Socialists in the 1930s were aghast that Fascists were using Marxist tools to accurately critique Western Liberal Democracy - this unneeded concern was discussed in the previous chapter. Today we see that Socialists should have been lumping Fascism and Western Liberal Democracy in the same boat, and some did: Stalin correctly said that Fascism and Social Democracy (i.e. reformists of Western Liberal Democracy) were twins, and we are now correct to say that Fascism, Social Democracy and Western Liberal Democracy are triplets.

It's no facile exaggeration - all three of these political schools of thought clearly united themselves after World War II against Socialist Democracy. The squabble between Fascism and Western Liberal Democracy was even more short lived than the squabble between the houses of Bourbon and Orleans!

Western Liberal Democracy survives because it has monopolised so many resources, and also because of its ability to unite in adapting its right-wing solutions - its brutal version of class warfare - and in contrast with the left's inability to unite. They are much more effective at class warfare in large part because they have such fewer people to organise/collude. The only real squabble between Western Liberalists and

Fascists is between choosing a cosmopolitan globalist elite dominated by new money, or a sovereign national elite dominated by old money, and how much xenophobia to employ.

Proof that Trotsky didn't understand the existing similarities between Western Liberal Democracy and Fascism is encapsulated in his complaint about Stalinist/Comintern Communism in 1936. I think every reader will be shocked at either his naiveté or his impossible demands upon the USSR: *"If the Soviet trade unions had given a timely example by boycotting Italy* (for invading Ethiopia), *the movement would, like a prairie fire, have inevitably embraced all of Europe and the whole world, and at once become menacing to the imperialists of all countries."*

The entire world was going to get set alight over Ethiopia, really?

Again, we cannot blame Trotsky: he is truly personally alight over the invasion of Ethiopia. But Trotsky is a progressive humanitarian and politically-active person - nobody else really cared about Ethiopia. Today neither Palestine, nor chemical weapons used against Iranians in the 1980s, nor the ongoing starvation of Yemen, nor any other blatant Western imperialist violence is setting the world alight. As the incredibly hypocritical double-standards regrading the 2022 refugees from Ukraine proves - the West only cares about White people, and even then only when either useful or of the proper class.

From 1789 to 2022 non-Europeans see the same racism, deadly abuse of power and privilege, haughty disregard and disinterest, and closed opportunities in both Western Liberal Democracy and Fascism. Trotsky goes on to complain, as usual, that this is a proof of failure in revolutionary leadership - but the leaders are not the problem but the people: the good people of the West have been governed by Western Liberal Democracy for too long, and thus by its false, elitist, over-competitive and bigoted precepts.

Trotsky also failed to foresee the monarchical-like expansion of the 21st century Western executive branch (justified at the start of the 21st century, as in 1830, by a need to dominate Muslims), which makes it even more similar to authoritarian Fascism.

It was perhaps myopia - being too deeply within Western culture and too unexposed to the non-Western viewpoints of the colonised. A Third Worlder didn't feel any real change in policy before, during or after the Western Fascist era - the violence is less brutal in its cultural presentation, but the violence is still brutal. A Syrian heard about the victory over Fascism in Europe on May 8,1945, but he certainly more deeply felt the shells which Charles de Gaulle dropped on him on May 29, in order to forestall any independence (human rights) movements. The French waged the Sétif and Guelma massacres in Algeria on V-E Day (Victory in Europe Day - May 8, 1945), and aided by the American army. How is this morally superior to Italy's invasion of Ethiopia?

"Is it not too late? No, everything shows that it is not too late. In France there is no powerful fascist party. Indeed, in France there will not be an organisation as large as Hitler's party even before the conquest of power: it is against the traditions and customs of the country." That was not a Western Liberal Democrat talking about the West's superior values - that was Trotsky in 1935, and he would quite soon be wrong about 60% the country, i.e. Vichy France.

Trotsky was especially wrong in the first part - how can a country occupying Algeria (even making it "France") not have a powerful Fascist force? Is it not "Fascism" because it's happening to non-Europeans? He was also wrong in the second part: there is no Fascist party in France, the UK and the US because their Western Liberal Democracies were already quite Fascistic. The idea that their traditions of elitism and oligarchy are anti-Fascist is nonsense to those they were currently colonising.

That quote is not Trotsky being racist, because of course he was not, but merely of Trotsky both succumbing to European ethnocentrism and of forgetting that France's traditions and customs also included the thwarting of progressive politics over and over. Trotsky was quite disproven by the extent of Vichy France, and almost a century later our goal is to explain why: He did not realise that France's impressive but relatively minor experiences with Socialist revolution have been drastically outweighed by the Fascism inherent in the *"traditions and customs"* of monarchy and, after 1848, Western Liberal Democracy.

As coming chapters will demonstrate, the rights and redistributions won by the Western masses in the postwar period (1945-1975) have been under constant attack in the third restoration of Liberalism (1975-today) and thus serve as an exceptional era in the anti-worker history of Western Liberal Democracy.

The idea that there has been neither revolution nor Fascism is a trick of Western Liberal Democracy, which openly allied with Fascism's supporters against Socialism immediately upon the cessation of WWII hostilities in order to fight Socialist Democracy around the world. It was absurd - Jim Crow-era United States assumed leadership of the "free world" while also being an Apartheid state - but imperialist Western Liberal Democracy controls the means, therefore they have the tools to employ and pay for the massive propaganda to uphold this idea.

How can Trotsky's great leaders lead a leaderless movement?

What's certain is that Trotsky would be somewhat at a loss with what to do with the leaderless Yellow Vests because he did not live in a leaderless time.

The Yellow Vests insist that they could not have sprouted successfully if they had acclaimed a leader precisely because all of France's leadership (Trotskyists included) are so discredited. However, this did not necessarily preclude France's Trotskyist parties nor the Trotskyist partisans in their several other prominent leftist parties from attempting to humbly, patiently and methodically forming a bond with the Yellow Vests. The problem is entirely in the domineering attitude of today's Trotskyists.

Trotsky would have likely said this: The Yellow Vests are a "pre-revolutionary movement" which will be routed, due to the lack of organised leadership. I don't agree, and it's possible that the presence of the 2019-2020 general strike would have changed Trotsky's mind.

They were definitely routed every Saturday, and they were a revolutionary movement in ideal, but they have not yet progressed to the actual waging of revolution, nor have they fully grasped that only a revolution away from Western Liberal Democracy can ever allow them to achieve their core demands. As we will see in the following chapters, their main problem was not understanding their political reality - the very different laws and constraints created by the 2009 Lisbon Treaty.

The Yellow Vests are thus at least a harbinger of coming revolution, I think we'd agree, at least.

What the Yellow Vests are doing is creating political enlightenment at every rural roundabout, urban march and Facebook page, and Western Trotskyists must either get on board or declare that they are not in favor of Socialist Democracy but of Western Liberal Democracy. If they continue to work more with Western Liberal Democrats than with the Yellow Vests then they are not Trotskyist, who wrote, and the emphasis is his: ***"There can be no greater crime than coalition with the bourgeoisie in a period of socialist revolution,"*** and this is what they have done so far during the Yellow Vest era.

Because they live in a leaderless times the Yellow Vests are the ones introducing clarity into the political consciousness of the struggling masses - I believe Trotsky would have called them the vanguard party of France today, and not France's Communist or Trotskyist parties.

If the Yellow Vests lack one thing it's in fully knowing that, as Trotsky wrote, *"Without a complete overturn in property relations - without concentration of the waning system, the basic branches of industry, and foreign trade in the hands of the state - there is no salvation for the petty bourgeoisie of the city and country."* There is no salvation because, again, the era of 1945-75 appears as a short anomaly compared alongside the eras of 1848-1944 and 1976-2022 - the short era of Social Democracy in Europe was easily overturned, aside from being always inadequate.

The USSR, China and Iran overturned property relations, but this overturning is actually not among the Vesters' demands, which were first made public in December 2018. Of course, many Yellow Vests knew that nationalisation is the only way, even if only instinctually.

> *Yellow Vest: "How Macron has handled these privatisations reveals exactly what we have been denouncing since the start. How can Macron sell off our national inheritance without even consulting the opinion of the people? This is exactly why we are demanding regular citizen referendums. Why are we selling something like the airport of Paris now, when it will certainly be worth much more in the years to come, and especially if we invest some money into it? Despite what the government is saying, we are losing money with this sale, and with other privatisations."*

In their bones and in their deeds the heroic Yellow Vests are revolutionary - it's the fault of other Western leftists to not have joined them, and to have feared joining them starting after the incredible police brutality and intimidation on May Day 2019.

The Yellow Vests suffer from a similar defect as Trotsky did: without a disciplined bureaucracy there is no way to institute the practical demands of the revolutionary masses. However, it's still early for the Yellow Vests. Trotskyism refused to support just such a bureaucracy in the USSR, and for that people like Du Bois admired Stalin, the USSR and *"real socialism instead of the sham Trotsky offered"* - the *"sham"* being revolution without a bureaucracy to install or preserve it.

Trotsky and his scourge of bureaucratism is similar to the Yellow

Vests insistence on being a leaderless movement which also makes a boogeyman of establishing a formal bureaucracy. The fault in both is that they think everyone is as politically advanced and committed as they are when they are not - they are vanguards.

Make no mistake, the Yellow Vest movement was ultimately not checked by poor leadership or a disdain for disciplined bureaucracy but by total war against it. Had this war been waged by a President Marine Le Pen it would have been called "Fascist", but because it was waged by a President Emmanuel Macron it was whitewashed. This absurdity can be easily recognised by seeing that Western Liberal Democracy has allied with Fascists for nearly a century, has subsumed key tenets of fascism into contemporary liberal democracy - is fascistic.

Trotsky really thought "*imperialist democracy*" and "*parliamentary democracy*" was totally discredited and smashed for good in 1939 - it was not.

It is ultimately most accurate to say that Trotsky may have correctly intuited, but did not correctly describe, that Western Liberal Democracy and Fascism were interchangeable and needed to be discredited and ousted for good - why don't you see this?

<—>

9

Growing up Yellow Vest: Seeing French elites, not French people, conquered by neoliberalism

World War II saw massive political gains by the lower classes and average person, but only via their own mass-murder. Many socio-economic demands which go back to 1789 and which animated the Revolutions of 1848 were put in place, finally.

The three biggest changes were that Socialism was now firmly implanted on the global scene, women got the right to vote in France in 1944 and that the Western Liberal Democratic elite were discredited worse than ever.

That forced Western elite, who were now allying with fascists to forestall further Socialist and anti-imperialist victories, to make political and economic concessions which they had resisted for a century. These subsequent 30 years - from 1945 to 1975 - are known as the "30 Glorious Years" in French history. During this period a broad economic stability was founded upon the stability, productivity, joy and long-sightedness which can only be provided by worker rights and influence, and by socialist-inspired levers and organisations.

However, the brief era of "Social Democracy" was officially terminated by the introduction of the euro (1999) and then the European

Union (2009). EU citizenship was introduced in 1992 but its official installation was not until 2009, with the elite-only ratification of the Lisbon Treaty, which amended the constitutional basis of the EU, the Maastricht Treaty (1992) and the Treaty of Rome (1957). The Yellow Vests would be the flaming leftist economic and political reaction to this political-economic regression away from Social Democracy. The introduction of this version the pan-European project was a major regression in the threat of modern political history: to reduce the autocratic rights of elite and to increase the empowerment of the average person.

Sadly, it was only 30 years - one generation - before the autocratic and oligarchical elite began to retake power. When they do this effort is called "neoliberalism", even though the first "neoliberalism" was with the start of 3rd Republic (1871-1940), which restored the immediately discredited and popularly rejected Liberalism of the 2nd Republic (1848-52). The goal of today's "3rd-liberalism" is to end the Social Democracy era and to redistribute its gains back to the Liberalist 1%.

This book ignores the upheaval of 1968 in France - when a General Strike attracted 8 million workers in a country of 50 million people - for this reason: This is a book is about political changes, and the rebellion of 1968 only produced cultural changes. It was indeed a cultural revolution, but because it was not state-sponsored, as in China, where cultural changes were embraced by leaders like Mao Zedong, the Western Liberal Democratic elite successfully broke any chance of fully democratising from Social Democracy to Socialist Democracy. There's no denying that this era's cultural revolution (note the lower case) won advances in everyday culture but that is not the same as formal political-economic changes.

The political failures/cultural gains of this era would eventually reveal the continued rightward shift within the elite of the French left, and this can be illustrated by the path of Daniel Cohn-Bendit, the most prominent of the student leaders in 1968. In his memoirs he wrote that he was not seeking Marxist-inspired equality but simply more control over his personal life. These freedom of expression types of changes can perhaps be encapsulated in the freedom of students to now question their teachers in class. Cohn-Bendit quit the Trotskyists, switched to the Green Party, became a devoted Europhile, rejected the Yellow Vests and is now a close advisor to Emmanuel Macron - it's an incredibly representative political trajectory of this era. Ecology is a subject completely neutered of class politics (even though the idea of a capitalist/competitive solution to ecological issues, and not Socialist/cooperative solution, is an obvious absurdity) and thus is the political outlet most encouraged by contemporary Western Liberal Democratic elite.

However, we should note that for many decades already French Socialism was primarily intellectual, and dominated by right-wing socialists: "*Before the war of 1914-1918 only 20% of socialist deputies were workers while they had been 80% of the German socialist party (SPD), and they represented the totality of the English Labor party. The socialism of Jaures and Blum is, when it comes to leaders, a socialism of intellectuals and liberal professions,*" wrote Pierre Rosanvallon in "*Accroître le 'pouvoir de vivre*" ("Increasing the 'Power to Live'". Jean Jaures and Leon Blum were the right-leaning socialist leaders of their respective generations. Jaures is notable in that both Francois Hollande and Nicolas Sarkozy both claimed to be continuing his legacy. Also notable is that whether worker or intellectual - 20th century West European socialists failed.

Between the USSR's fall (1991) and China's rise (starting in 2008) the French left's economic ideology was in disunity and disarray at best and total betrayal at worst. Many also went whole-hog over to neo-imperialist culture, espousing right-wing "universal values" and embracing neo-colonial wars in the former Yugoslavia and the Muslim world.

The change began in 1974 with the death in office of President George Pompidou, Charles de Gaulle's successor in the 5th Republic (1958-today), just a month before the presidential vote.

Neoliberalism starts to win over elites from Paris to Moscow, but the French keep protesting

Pompidou's death effectively ended Gaullism, which had helped win World War II, presided over the "30 Glorious Years" and insisted on French sovereignty. The closest election in French history saw the victory of the aristocrat Valerie Giscard d'Estaing, a politician who was thus extremely familiar but also a new breed: Giscard d'Estaing was liberal on social issues, rejected Gaullist Euroscepticism and was extremely close with high finance - he served as Minister of Finance twice. We see how the "Bankocracy" has gone from not existing in 1789 France to running the executive branch. He marks the start of the third restoration of extremist Liberalist thought.

Liberalists had been waiting decades to restore firm control, and they salivated at the prospect of dividing up the spoils created by the 30 Glorious Years. Using the excuse of inflation cased by a rise in oil prices in 1973, free competition was reimposed after decades of abandonment, austerity was imposed for the first time, salaries were frozen, compulsory salary taxes soared ten points to nearly 30% and the despised CDD work contract was created. (The *contrat à durée déterminée* is a temporary employment contract which renders life in France extremely difficult and unstable. It's usual length is one month and then it is renewed endlessly, without ever becoming a long-term contract. As the French do not have hourly wages, the CDD can perhaps be thought of as "part-time work".)

Seigniorial dues and tithes were not restored.

It would not be until 2016 that a team of economists at the International Monetary Fund would release a paper which admits that austerity doesn't work. The economic massacring of the lower and middle class which is austerity would be the reason for the upcoming years of recession, although the mainstream history is that it was entirely due to the rise in oil prices.

France was not alone in its first steps towards the restoration of Liberalism. The United States responded to energy inflation with the "Volcker Shock" in March 1980: a huge rise in interest rates which gutted the average person's primary asset class - the housing market. The UK and Germany turned to wage suppression. It's vital to note that the same elite capture was also occurring in the USSR. By Christmas 1991 it would be imploded from the top: their elite infamously ignored a high-turnout referendum in March in which 80% of the nation voted to preserve the USSR.

Unsurprisingly, the French voter rebelled: Giscard d'Estaing was voted out in 1981. A socialist-communist backing of Francois Mitterrand's economic platform - the most Socialist economic plan ever promoted in the non-Eastern Bloc Europe - was a repeat of 1936. However, by 1983 he infamously made his U-turn back to austerity (more on this shortly) - French elites had fully accepted the terms of Liberalism.

> *Yellow Vest: "I worked from the age of 14 until the age of 60, and in my entire life I accepted only 1 month of unemployment insurance. And yet, in the last 4 years I have seen my pension lowered from 1,150 euros to 1,050 euros. My rent is 800 euros a month, so I cannot afford to live, and I will never accept this injustice."*

By 1986 French neoliberalism was in full swing: the abolishment of price controls, the end of controls on exchange rates and the deregulation of financial markets in order to do what modern Western financial markets do - divert the wealth produced by people who actually work into the bank accounts of the 1%. Mass de-nationalisations began: General Electric Company, Suez, Paribas and Société Générale (banks), Saint-Gobain and Matra (industrial giants).

The average Frenchman would not accept the death of Social

Democracy as complacently as in the rest of the West, and that fact is certainly in keeping with the line of West European history since 1789 - the Yellow Vests only confirm this line further. The French responded to the restoration of Liberalism over Socialist-inspired ideas with massive, broadly-encompassing and successful social movements: protests against proposed university reforms in 1986 and rail reforms in 1987. The "*Touche pas à mon pote*" (Don't touch my buddy) movement marked the introduction of French Muslims into French political movements and truly into being represented in mainstream French cultural life.

> Romaric Godin, economics reporter of *Mediapart* and author of *La guerre sociale en France (The Social War in France* - 2019) wrote: *"The error of* (then prime minister) *Jacques Chirac in 1986 was to think that he could force through a new culture which could sweep away the past, as Margaret Thatcher did across the Channel. However, the French showed their capacity to resist the complete destruction of their social model."*

In France from 1986 until 1995 efforts at restoring Liberalism were stopped by massive social movements: against worse work contracts in 1994, retirement and social security cutbacks in 1995. The 1995 general strike was the largest since 1968, and the political introduction for a new generation. Starting in 1992, the excuse of the need to "qualify" for the euro currency - and thus right-wing fiscal rollbacks were needed to social programs - was unconvincing to the average Frenchman as well.

From 1995-2007 the attempts at major neoliberal reforms were less ambitious and, crucially, began to offer some monetary redistribution efforts as compensation for right-wing deforms. These redistribution are also partially explained by the inflation which immediately followed the introduction of the euro in 1999. The work contract reforms of 1994 would fail again in 2006, due to more protests.

But by 2002 the leftist and independent voter had partially revolted against the traitorous French left - the National Front made it to the 2nd round at the expense of the ever-more un-socialist Socialist Party. The far-right party - totally neoliberal in economics - was led by Jean-Marie Le Pen, a former intelligence officer in Algeria. Like with Cavaignac in 1848, once again Algerian colonisation has provided the entry point for the most extreme-right and anti-Socialist elements in French domestic politics.

The National Front's advancement to the runoff was precisely due to the left's now two decade-long embrace of neoliberalism despite the rejection of neoliberalism by its constituents. The French mainstream media like to blame Mitterrand's party-gerrymandering, but that's a distant secondary reality from the fact that voters opposed this third return of Liberalism. However, unlike in 1852 there was no Bonapartism to send Liberalists packing, and unlike in 1945 Liberalists had not yet had a long-running economic crisis deep enough and/or war to fully discredit them.

The 2005 French European Constitution referendum was essentially a referendum on neoliberalism, and it lost by a 55-45% margin. The majority of the French Socialist Party would vote yes, and that effort would be led by future president Francois Hollande. Three days later the Netherlands would also vote no, by a 62-38% margin. Aghast, Western Liberal Democrats decided that this would essentially be the end of putting the concept of the European Union to popular votes.

Yellow Vest: "The government doesn't listen to us at all. The economic situation keeps getting worse, the prices are rising, and the government's response is to attack the Yellow Vests to keep us from telling the truth."

In May of 2007 neoliberalism made a huge inroad in France with the election of Nicolas "*l'Américain*" Sarkozy, the son of a Hungarian nobleman. Sarkozy was the first French politician since World War II to break totally with even lip service to being an anti-monarchist in style and ideology. Giscard d'Estaing at least made regular and often poorly-received efforts to shed his aristocratic pretensions and appear close with the average person. The pernicious influence of monarchy was still grasped in France then, but the new millennium has seen Western culture re-cultivate the idea that greed is good and that the established neo-aristocracy are our betters.

Sarkozy would make France the first major European power to approve the new Lisbon Treaty, which put the installation of the European Union into the hands of the elite: the Maastricht Treaty was reformed to allow the installation of the EU via the approval of national parliaments and not popular referendums. French Socialist MPs overwhelmingly voted in favor of this coup in plain sight.

The method (oligarchical approval) and context (an economic collapse unseen since 1929) of the ratification of the Lisbon Treaty cannot be stressed enough, as it unmistakably reveals that in the history of Western Liberal Democracy the installation of EU was the latest in a never-ending line of autocratic decisions by their oligarchical elites. Again, by understanding modern political history (which began in 1789) as a move away from autocracy and towards democracy we see how the EU is a regression and not a progression.

Only Ireland was able to achieve a popular referendum on the Lisbon Treaty: when the first vote produced a rejection a re-vote was forced the following year, when it passed. Every other member approved the installation by a vote only in their national parliaments, as well as six royal assents.

This is a precise repeat of when the parliamentarians of the French 2nd Republic, the continent's first Western Liberal Democracy, committed coups against the people via voting to submit the 1848

Constitution to the majority approval of parliament, and then to gut the primary advance of the 1848 Revolution, universal male suffrage: government structure has been drastically changed changed solely via the elite and not by popular approval.

The vast majority of nations would ratify the Lisbon Treaty between February and July of 2008, a disastrous year. The collapse of Lehman Brothers investment firm that September is the official start of the Great Recession, but the US Federal Reserve held its first emergency weekend meeting in 30 years back in March, to negotiate the shocking collapse of the Bear Stearns investment group. Thus, it's not as if European elite weren't aware of major issues brewing. Four countries, including Germany, would not fully ratify the treaty until after the fall of Lehman Brothers. We can certainly call it an amazing coincidence: how the elite Liberalist politicians successfully forced through the European Union mere weeks before economic collapse struck?

The Treaty would be fully ratified in November 2009 amid mass bankruptcy, home foreclosures, unemployment and that slogan which is the essence of British conservatism: "Keep calm and carry on". The pan-European project was now complete and - as we'll see - largely unchangeable. The European Union thus joined only Saudi Arabia, Israel, San Marino and the UK Commonwealth as having citizenry but no constitution.

The European Union thus was born amid the Great Recession - it has never been willing or able to end it.

The next chapter will deal with three related events - the Great Recession, the European Sovereign Debt Crisis and the Age of Austerity - which left the French populace too skeptical, resentful and experienced to allow the extremist Liberalist policies and autocratic personality of Emmanuel Macron to go uncommented upon, as he apparently had assumed.

This chapter has thus far shown how the French people, but not the elites, successfully fought the 3rd restoration of Liberalism which so many other countries embraced even before the implosion of the Soviet Union. We should now turn to these new Liberalist structures.

I should note that in this era of Socialist Democratic collapse the last great progressive revolution of our contemporary times - the Iranian Islamic Revolution - victoriously emerged from the ashes of the Western-imposed War of Sacred Defense (Iran-Iraq War) in 1988. They found very few sympathisers to the Socialist-inspired country it had just forged, and then 9/11 would create not just skepticism but violent animosity towards seemingly all things Islamic.

The European Union - capitalist cartel or France's idea of a progressive & united continent?

Yes, it's pathetically easy to dismiss any discussion of the European Union as being merely an extension of aristocratic autocracy: since 1992 there have been eight national referendums which rejected key aspects of the European Union only to be either ignored or subverted by oligarchical elites. Nonetheless, if we insist (rightly) that another version of the pan-European project is possible then we need to see how France has repeatedly proposed an alternative vision of a united Europe, and one which wasn't embraced by the Liberalists of 1848 or 1871 either.

Just as Lenin saw that the principal feature of modern capitalism is monopoly, so the EU began in 1951 as an undemocratic cartel to fix prices for coal and steel. The European Coal and Steel Community also included a multinational bureaucracy which was empowered to ignore national parliaments and laws.

Was the EU always intended to be just a capitalist cartel? It's possible, but we cannot completely ignore France's historical trend since 1789, which is to be more often than not at the progressive forefront of the West.

In the WWII postwar reckoning France was excluded - de Gaulle was famously not invited to the Yalta Conference in February 1945. Thus, France immediately saw that the US and UK Liberalists were only dealing with the head of Western leftism since 1917, the USSR. After the Labor Party defeated Winston Churchill in July 1945, just two months after the defeat of the Germans, the rabidly anti-Socialist US called off the in-progress plan to de-industrialise Germany and instead tapped West Germany for their imperial collaborators in Europe. That is why Germany is the industrial powerhouse of Europe today even though they provoked and lost WWII: Western Liberal Democracy's alliance with postwar Fascists couldn't be more clear. This was a crucial historical decision which laid the foundation for German domination of the Eurozone and EU today. Many would correctly add that it is a US domination of the Eurozone and EU, and via their longtime dependant in Germany.

By the 1960s French elites were well aware that they could not compete industrially with America's creation of a German Frankenstein, so in their conception of a pan-European project they wanted to join with - not conquer - Germany. In some ways this is a continuation of the Franco-German elite alliance in 1871, but there is a very different factor this time: the imperialist United States.

Historically, no country's elite has pushed harder for European unification than France, and that's because the European Union was seen by many French elite as something which could serve as a Franco-German bulwark against imperial domination - that of the United States. The idea of total French enmity with Germany since 1871 is a short-term view - the two neighbors share a tremendous number of cultural similarities, values, multiple regions and several millions of Franco-German citizens in Alsace, Lorraine and in Alpine regions. France uniquely combines both the cultures of Latin/Mediterranean Europe and Northern Europe, after all. Some further add that France is a Latin country but run by a Northern elite. European unification was seen by many in Paris as an effort to preserve the sovereignty of both nations and to create a counterbalance to the obviously domineering US. In this way we can say that the European Union was the latest in two centuries of effort by France to unite Europe in a more progressive way - the problem is the awful, undemocratic structures which this version of a pan-European project would ultimately adopt.

The foundational Élysée Treaty of friendship between France and Germany, signed in 1963, was a clear attempt to separate West Germany from the Anglosphere. The US was livid at France's attempt at undermining the US-imposed postwar order: "*I can hardly overestimate the shock produced in Washington by this action or the speculation that followed, particularly in the intelligence community,*" said top US diplomat and banker George Ball.

The French understood that the 1944 Bretton Woods monetary system (when accounts began being regularly settled not in gold but in dollars) was not meant as a balanced system of international trade and financial flows but as an instrument of US domination via the dollar. Europe's participation meant it supported American living standards and subsidised American companies. That the US could print unlimited dollars for unlimited imports was famously deemed an "exorbitant privilege" by France, but postwar France could do nothing about it until 1965.

The US deficit exploded in the mid-1960s, mostly due to their imperialist wars in East Asia. France and de Gaulle openly demanded a reform of the Bretton Woods system, a return to the gold standard and began repatriating French gold from New York City banks. *"Perhaps never before had a chief of state launched such an open assault on the monetary power of a friendly nation,"* wrote *Time* magazine in February 1965. In 1967 France was the first to withdraw from the West's London Gold Pool, hastily constructed in 1961 to defend Bretton Woods. Unlike the UK and Germany, France was not always so subservient to the United States.

The truth which financial media never wants to tell is that France had a genuine commitment to a pan-Europeanism guided by a mixed Socialist/pro-growth/not-rabidly-capitalist economic plan. This mirrors France's own postwar "Mixed Economy" model, in which the state gives short- and long-term targets for industry to meet, and aids them to achieve it. There's planning and state ownership - not at the level of a communist state but enough to enrage Liberalists. There is also a commitment to a social safety net because endless austerity is simply not sustainable if French elite wish to avoid further revolutions. France's Mixed Economy is also not at the level of Japan, where the state's role was much larger (until the Plaza Accord of 1985, signed by Japan, the US, France, West Germany and the UK), and where economic success was spectacularly greater.

France's contemporary effort to fight far-right economics and austerity did not begin with Francois Hollande's 2012 election campaign campaign but began three decades earlier. So why did Mitterrand's anti-3rd Liberalist "Common Project" culminate in a U-turn in in 1983? Of course, just like in 1936, 1871 or 1848 the primary reason is that Western Liberal Democracy is an oligarchy which refuses to listen to the majority will of the people (as in a normal democracy). But in 1983 the power of a completely united globalist rich class - one undivided by royalist squabbles or support for the staunch national sovereignty proposed in Fascism - could be wielded as one. This same tool - the "Bankocracy" of international high finance - would also be used to provoke the 2012 European Sovereign Debt Crisis.

Despite a clear democratic mandate to end Giscard d'Estaing's austerity and restore growth polices, France was immediately foiled by high finance and currency speculators. Capital flight from France to Germany immediately took place and long-term borrowing rates (10-year bond) went from 9.6% in March 1979 all the way to 17.3% in May 1981, when Mitterrand was elected. Government bonds, as Marx foresaw, are the indispensable lifeblood of the biggest economic actor in any capitalist country: the government. After devaluing the franc three times Mitterrand was forced into submission. He made his U-turn and by March 1986 10-year bonds were at 9.3%.

> *Yellow Vest: "The British have shown us that it is possible to obtain a referendum on leaving the European Union. However, the French media refuses to ever discuss the issue at all, but many in France will not stop demanding a Frexit."*

What happened was that Germany and the Bundesbank, knowing that Western high-finance was philosophically in their corner and willing to destroy France's democratic will with every dollar they could borrow, joined with global high finance and professional currency speculators to strangle France into backtracking on Socialist-inspired policies. If high finance cared at all for democracy they would have supported France's anti-austerity plan. However such an idea is as absurd today as it was to Socialists, Fascists, political independents in the 1930s and revolutionaries of 1848.

France could not boldly defy high finance and keep devaluing their currency until growth took hold for another crucial reason: they would have had to abandon the 1979-inaugurated European Monetary System (EMS), the financial predecessor of the euro. This was an adjustable exchange rate agreement which linked 10 Western European currencies to prevent large fluctuations. It was France's brainchild for their long-term goal: wooing Germany away from the US and towards a genuinely European integration. Preferring to stay in the EMS meant violating the people's democratic will demanding an anti-austerity agenda - this process would obviously be repeated ad nauseam.

By 1993 the European Union would begin, which replaced the European Economic Community, which in 1957 had replaced the original European Coal and Steel Community. The euro currency would arrive six years later - the new structures would fully end the Social Democracy era.

In 2012 Hollande was the hope of an entire "Latin Bloc" against Germanic austerity, once again, but he would do the exact same U-turn. However, he showed far less resolve than Mitterrand and faced far less pressure: 10-year bonds stood at 2.75% when Hollande was elected and and they fell immediately - high finance seemed to know the long-time Europhile Hollande's anti-austerity promises were election nonsense. French 10-year bonds stood at 0.81% when he left office, in total disgrace and with the Socialist Party perhaps permanently smashed.

More important than the EU - the Eurogroup

Part of the problem of talking about the "pan-European project" is that you have multiple bodies which overlap. You also have some nations which are part of one, but not another. Or which pay into one body, but abstain from another.

The Eurozone is more important than the European Union because it controls the money in the world's second largest macro-economic bloc behind the US (in 2008 - now it is third: socialist China has soared since then). By comparison, the EU is mainly a regulatory body, and their modest annual budget – about the size of Denmark's – reflects that.

All serious studies of the eurozone - from Nobel Prize-winning economists, such as Joseph Stiglitz, to those with insider knowledge of how it operates, such as former Greek Finance Minster Yanis Varoufakis - stress that there is nothing in its structure which allows for the possibility for change. That's a pretty vital and damning conclusion to be consistently reached, especially when post-1991 Europe loves to stand on its hind legs and lecture the rest of the world about democracy. Objective studies reach another regular conclusion, and it's one which is shared by the lower- and middle-class: the euro has totally failed in its promise to bring about prosperity and economic security.

The Eurozone was a clear replication of the German *Zollverein*, led by Prussia during the 19th century, which was the world's first example of independent states creating a full economic union without also creating a political union. In 1834 much of Germanic Europe - excluding Austria - became united in a customs union which abolished tariff barriers and reduced the number of currencies from over 30 to two. It laid the groundwork for the eventual domination of Prussia within Germanic culture, the unification of Germany and the longstanding Germanic opposition to French economic conceptions of equality and fraternity. Germanifying an area of German-speaking peoples and cultures is one thing, but trying to replicate that for all of Europe has only led to dramatic inequalities because the distribution of money and resources is always inherently political.

The Eurozone thus embodies the victory of Germanic economic ideology in tandem with the victory of English oligarchic parliamentarianism in political ideology - this is perhaps the simplest essence of Western Liberal Democracy: England's Glorious Revolution of 1688 combined with the Germanic commitment to the economic autocracy of the elite. The French are often called the intellectuals of Europe, but it's far more accurate to call them the ignored intellectuals of Europe: the history of Europe since 1789 is the defeat of French intellectual egalitarianism and the victory of the aristocratic thought of Anglo-Germanic intellectuals.

To examine the Eurozone you have to bring up something which mainstream media is instructed to ignore – the Eurogroup.

The Eurogroup rules the Eurozone and its 19 member states, and it also governs the "bailouts" to member nations like Greece. The Eurogroup is, at face value, an informal monthly meeting of the finance ministers of the euro member countries.

However, it is no exaggeration to say that the Eurogroup is the banker cabal hidden in plain sight. It is truly the expression of the autocratic and oligarchical forces which go back to 1788. Gone are the Bourbons and Orleanists, though of course they remain on the boards of banks and hedge funds.

In his 2017 book *And The Weak Suffer What They Must?* former Greek Finance Minister Yanis Varoufakis provided a wealth of insider knowledge on how the Eurogroup operates.

> *"Moreover, the Eurogroup, where all the important economic decisions are taken, is a body that does not even exist in European law, that operates on the basis that the 'strong do as they please while the weak suffer what they must', that keeps no minutes of its proceedings, and whose only rule is that its deliberations are confidential – that is, not to be shared with Europe's citizenry. It is a set-up designed to preclude any sovereignty traceable back to the people of Europe."*

What can we say of Western Liberal Democracy when their most advanced economic achievement is governed by an entity with no rules, no records, no democratic process and no democratic accountability? It is truly a return to 1788 - the time when the average person had no say in politics or economics! Every French person should be able to recognise in 21st century Western Liberal Democracy the autocratic domination which even the many European kings of today recognise is no longer unacceptable.

Thanks to the whistle-blowing of Varoufakis we also know that there is also essentially no discussion at Eurogroup meetings: The Troika (the International Monetary Fund, European Central Bank and European Commission) initiates, dominates and outlines the terms and then the finance minister-members vote. The overwhelming majority of participants in this group which governs eurozone economic policy (and thus social policy) are bankers, former bankers or intimately tied to high finance.

When bankers run economic policy, one shouldn't be surprised if the resulting social policy is for the benefit of bankers and their biggest aristocratic clients. Yes, the EU is obviously a Bankocracy, but Bankocracy is simply the modern form of rule by an oligarchy of the rich and powerful. It is as if the new banker class in 1830's France didn't just put the House of Orleans on the throne and boot out the House of Bourbon, but as if the new banker class assassinated all Houses, restored serfdom and declared that they had a divine right to rule. Their obvious goal is the rollback of mere Social Democracy, and to reattempt a destruction of any Socialist Democracies.

The Eurogroup is not an EU institution and cannot declare any legally-binding decisions. It can never be blamed for a bad decision, nor held accountable, because it is not answerable to any parliament or body politic whatsoever. Many are increasingly asking in France and Europe: What's the point of voting for any national or EU politician if they have little to no chance of influencing policy? Many don't even realise that the highest level of policymaking is actually the Eurogroup.

Yellow Vest: "In France's 5th Republic when someone is elected president they can do whatever they want for five years because we truly have no way to influence them. This is why the Yellow Vests are insisting that Macron accept regular citizen referendums on his policies, because he is destroying French society."

(Of course, what will occur when citizen referendums oppose the decisions of the Eurogroup? The European Union will step in and either totally ignore the referendum, call it illegal or regulate around them.)

It is self-evident that that when politics does not rule – where there is no law or regulation – the rich are the rulers. It is also self-evident that in a climate of total deregulation the richest nations and persons will benefit the most, thus inequality will increase. It is also self-evident that when billionaires and hedge funds own the bulk of a deregulated and denationalised media there will be very little media discussion of the Eurogroup. This is what has happened throughout the history of the Eurogroup, which operated without formal recognition until the Lisbon Treaty.

Unsurprisingly, the US pioneered the concept of mass deregulation in the early 1980s, which they foisted on Europe as much as possible when their academics, think tanks and intellectuals helped oversee the writing of the new structures of the pan-European projects. It is thus no exaggeration to say that - coming after the so-called "end of history" and Liberalism's alleged total victory following the fall of the USSR - the Eurogroup has achieved the American dream of total deregulation even more than in America.

For the Eurogroup to become remotely democratic and not autocratic/oligarchic a Eurozone constitution would have to be created, an executive would seem useful, a legislative branch would be indispensable and approval power over national budgets would seem necessary. Only the last is already in existence, but why would they add any Liberal or Socialist Democracy to this Bankocracy? Answer: they never will create this in any sort of equitable format.

Such facts make it clear why the Eurogroup cannot be considered compatible with democracy, and thus cannot be supported. One might support *creating a new Eurozone or changes to the Eurozone structure, but supporting the current Eurozone is democratically indefensible.* The European corollary to the post-1991 dictum of TINA (There Is No Alternative (to imperialism and Liberalism)) is that there is no alternative permitted to this version of a pan-European project.

Because change is impossible the elites' goal is thus forced ignorance and silence, and when that fails, deflection: *"To believe that Europe's problem was debt. Not the architectural design of the Eurozone.*

Not its unenforceable rules. But debt. Debt was never Europe's problem. It was a symptom of an awful institutional design," wrote Varoufakis.

From 1999 until 2007 it's said that the Eurozone had a short period of success in redistributing wealth. This is based on the fact that rich Eurozone countries decided to loan to their Eurozone brethren in poorer countries. As is always the case in capitalist countries, and as was seen in previous recessions, and as is evidenced in the history of countless Third World client states of the West - once economic troubles hit these loans were called in and could no longer be repaid, creating even more crisis.

Liberalism fully restored for the third time - exact same result: immediate failure

The 2009 European Sovereign Debt Crisis will go down in history as the time when the EU both started working and then immediately started dying. The response to the crisis by Brussels and the newly rammed-through governmental structures made clear that the economic solidarity which would be required of richer nations to make "more Europe" work simply does not exist.

The parallel of its literally-immediate democratic discrediting with France's 2nd Republic should be striking to all readers of this book, and should remind that Western Liberal Democracy has only produced failure. This is especially true when the outlet of imperialist war is not an option for this structure - France's 3rd Republic (when Liberalism was re-imposed) took advantage of this option to the maximum, as the 3rd Republic's imperial empire was one of history's most expansive.

As the European Sovereign Debt Crisis turned into the Age of Austerity Europe's richer nations got what they wanted from weaker Eurozone countries - the ability to buy (often taking local, 1% compradors as junior partners, for show) ports, airports, water departments, laws favouring their own industries against local industries, etc. They did this all while claiming that Western Liberal Democracy was so much more just than any ideological competitors!

Pro-capitalist American media may be persuaded by the German accusation of profligate smaller countries, but most of Europe saw the democratic will of nation after nation get strangled until their national politicians surrendered. Around the continent (and in the brewing Leave movement in a still pre-Brexit UK) many realised that the EU and Eurozone was sucking the lifeblood of White locals the way White colonialists used to suck the lifeblood of Brown locals. Some understood that the forcing of the governments of Greece, Ireland, Portugal and other weak countries to assume the private debts of French and German banks was simply a repeat of what happened all over the 3rd World since the late 19th century - neo-imperialism was not just for Brown puppets anymore, but White puppets too.

2009 thus became the historical bookend to 1871's siege of Paris, when the elite of France and Germany colluded to destroy the first flowering of Social Democracy and Socialist Democracy in the Paris Commune. French and German banks were the most leveraged in Greece; are the two biggest funders of the European Central Bank; were the most insistent that promises of borrowers to their bankers are sacrosanct while the promises of national politicians to their voters are not. The victory of the neoliberal and neo-imperial EU empire was thus fully imposed, and - amid the heat - Bismarck and Thiers looked up and smiled.

None of this was missed by the as yet unformed Yellow Vests.

<—>

10

The pan-European project wanted a Great Recession, winds up with the Yellow Vests

Most damning to the claim that the pan-European project is benevolent is that there was no plan to relaunch the Eurozone economy after the 2007 economic crisis, unlike in China and the United States. The reason for that became clear: chaos was fostered in order force through "reforms" which would revert postwar European Social Democracy back to Western Liberal Democracy - that is what the word "reform" truly means in modern economic journalism.

The French truly had something to lose from these "deforms": France's model combined strong social protections on a Nordic scale but without their withdrawal of public ownership via de-nationalisations and certainly without their labor market "flexibility", i.e. poor unemployment insurance, reduced recourse to legal protections for fair conditions & pay and gutted worker protections via the proliferation of short-term work contracts.

The other critical aspect of the "French model" was its resilience to the cyclical busts in capitalism - buying low when there is blood on the streets is critical to keeping capitalism to the "200 families" with whom Socialist Prime Minister Leon Blum negotiated in 1936 because, as he said, *"Who else was there for me to negotiate with?"* After both the economic crisis and the coronavirus crisis top Western commentators were shocked that France's economy was a star Western performer, but avoiding prolonged crises is entirely the point of Socialist central planning, which influenced France's postwar "Mixed Economy" model. France's GNP grew 34% from 1998-2018, greater than the Eurozone average (33%) and alleged top performer Germany (32%). Combined with a worker productivity which is perennially leading or near the top of the Eurozone, it's clear: There is no stagnation of the French model no matter how often that is falsely cited as a reason for "reforms". The alleged "stagnation" is a euphemism to describe French resistance to reintroducing wholesale Liberalism for the third time since 1848.

The fall of the French model began in autumn 2010, when Nicolas Sarkozy backtracked on a promise to not raise the retirement age. The French responded with seven marches in eight weeks with at least 1.5 million marchers each time. One week saw three marches with perhaps 3 million people each, but Sarkozy didn't budge. Despite being even larger than the Yellow Vest protests, it was the first time since the re-reintroduction of Liberalism in the mid-1970s that major social protests failed to win any concessions. The reason for that was made crystal clear in the previous chapter: the Lisbon Treaty's firm establishment of the European Union in 2009 had created supranational masters to which the French president was now solely accountable. No longer was he or she accountable to the French people, and this vital misunderstanding still afflicts French politics in 2022.

If we want to look for a start of the Yellow Vest movement it would be with this failure in 2010; if we want to see what inspired Emmanuel Macron's autocratic style, it would be here as well.

As we wouldn't learn until 2015, in March 2011 European Central Bank president Jean-Claude Trichet threatened Ireland's newly elected government with a "bomb" should they follow through on promises to impose losses on the failed business decisions of the Anglo Irish

Nationwide Bank, despite this being a key plank of their election campaign. That "bomb" was assumed to be expulsion from the Eurozone. The Lisbon Treaty thus allowed Brussels to progress from negating referendums on installing the EU to negating national elections which disagreed with the policies of the EU. The most well-known example of this would be their strangulation of Greece after the anti-austerity Syriza party was elected in 2015.

In 2012 optimism in France was extremely high, probably like in 1981 and 1936: Socialist Party President Francois Hollande narrowly defeated Sarkozy, who had been the first mainstream French politician to absurdly suggest that France's economic problem was Muslim welfare and not banker welfare. The 2+ million Muslim vote got their revenge by playing kingmaker - they voted for Hollande to the tune of 93%, and the election was decided by just 1.1 million votes. People wanted to believe in the empathy of a famously formerly-fat guy from the countryside nicknamed "Mr. Normal". Out was the aristocratic Sarkozy, whose tenure was summarised by French media via a term from American rap music which describes the shining of jewellery: "bling bling". Hollande openly declared that high finance was his "enemy", the Socialists swept the legislative elections and they could undeniably boast of a genuine anti-austerity mandate. A united "Latin Front" was finally going to throw its weight around - Italy's call for a very necessary pan-Eurozone banking union broke the mainstream taboo against honest talk on this subject. The democracies of small Ireland or Greece might get pushed around, but surely not France?

Unlike in 1983, economic crisis was not set off simply because a Socialist took power in Paris - France's borrowing (bond) rates were always extremely low in this era of economic turmoil, as France was the world's 5th largest economic power and perceived as a low-risk haven. However, the bond borrowing rate for Spain hit an unsustainable 7%. This was the apex of the European Sovereign Debt Crisis, when many wondered if the euro would crumble, and like in 1983 it was provoked by high finance speculators - the Bankocracy strikes again.

Speculators had perceived that the 2007 economic crisis, the ragingly neoliberal structures of the pan-European project and the anti-solidarity nature of Western capitalism all combined to make what was then the world's second-largest macro-economy also the most unstable.

Speculators began attacking poorer countries, causing bond spreads between Eurozone countries to diverge sharply in what was supposed to be a unified currency bloc. If major economies like Spain or Italy had to borrow at high rates in order to keep the streetlights on then staying in the euro would be economic suicide. They no longer had a currency to devalue, and thus no way out. The solution as demanded by Liberalism - to devalue their workforce into competitiveness - would take many years. Until that dubious capitalist goal was achieved richer northern countries could borrow euros at low rates and even purchase the assets both big and small of poorer nations. The problem as presented by the mainstream media was debt taken on by poorer Eurozone countries, not the poor decisions of richer Eurozone countries to make those foolish loans, and certainly not faults built into the Liberalist structures of a pan-European project which was rammed through despite regular democratic disapproval and amid economic chaos unseen since 1929. Indeed, the crisis birth of the Lisbon Treaty can't be stressed enough, nor its autocratic installation by the elite Liberalist oligarchy, because both reveal how they clearly represent regression from the trend established in 1789: the move away from autocratic government and towards democratic empowerment.

In June 2012 France, Italy and Spain (the Latin bloc) forced a midnight meeting with Germany on the sidelines of a Eurozone summit - this gang of four would decide policy unilaterally for the entire Eurozone, and with major consequences.

They agreed that the European Central Bank would be the

supervisor of Eurozone banks - this made the ECB the most influential central bank in the world behind that of the United States. They decided to end the preferential status of governments over private investors in cases of default - the failed private banks in Spain were now as equal as the average Eurozone taxpayer, with the former having just a bit more lobbying clout. Bailouts would now bypass national governments and go directly to private banks. Finally, Spain gave up trying to rescue its ailing banks alone and accepted a €100 billion bailout from Europe.

This was the deal which allowed the president of the ECB, Mario Draghi, to famously "save the euro" in July by uttering just one sentence: *"Within our mandate, the ECB is ready to do whatever it takes to preserve the euro."* All high finance heard was *"whatever it takes"*, and that this came after a bailout of the shoddy banks of the bloc's fourth-largest economy. Draghi had implied that the ECB would violate the "no bailout" clause in the Maastricht Treaty, and bond interest rates fell bloc-wide, ending (or rather postponing) the European Sovereign Debt Crisis.

With the gang of four's new rules, in September the European Stability Mechanism (€500 billion in reserves to help eurozone economies) would be created to run alongside with and then replace the European Financial Stability Facility (created in 2010 with €440 billion in reserves). More no strings attached bailout money was poised to enter the system if needed.

Thus, that same month a third round of Quantitative Easing (QE3) began in the United States, and this is the unnecessary round which revealed to the world that Western Liberal Democratic financial systems were undergoing a radical transformation. QE1 bought the infamous subprime mortgage assets, what I term QE 1.5 bought debt securities in the credit market, QE2 bought longer-term US securities, but QE3 created much anger from developing countries because it became clear that Western QE was not a temporary measure designed to solve a few specific problems.

Instead, it revealed a plan to flood the entire globe with newly printed Western money to serve as an enormous debt trap; that the West could not admit that the recent three decades of failures by "neoliberalism" had crippled their "real" economies will falsely inflating their financial industries; that the West could not admit that no strings attached QE wasn't improving (via "trickling down") the quality of their real economies either; that Western central bankers had resorted to QE because Western private banks had lost faith in each other's integrity; that nobody knew what would happen when private banks then lost faith in central banks; that taking away this "cheap money" would produce economic chaos in the form of long-forestalled genuine valuations re-based on economic fundamentals; that the West was adding a "subprime central bank" crisis onto their "subprime loan" and "subprime bank" crisis.

The problems caused by the Great Financial Crisis - and by the failure of Western Liberal Democracy's implemented solutions - are obviously quite Great indeed. The collusion of governments with corporations and banks - which is one of the ideas of Fascism which Western Liberal Democracy subsumed, just as they had subsumed ideas of aristocratic monarchy earlier - makes it truly no exaggeration that Western Liberal Democracy suffers from a "subprime government" crisis.

The ECB would follow the Bank of Japan's original lead and start with no strings attached "Quantitative Easing" in March 2015. It was supposed to end in March 2017 but QE, after many prolongations, was not planned to end (allegedly) until the day this book was published (July 1, 2022). Because taking away this "cheap money" was certain to produce economic chaos QE would be passed like a baton around many of the G20 economies to keep the trick going. This was obviously a very real collusion between central bankers and corporate private bankers, and why I often refer to a "Bankocracy": this is who decides public policy in Western Liberal Democracy, especially when we consider the role of the Eurogroup.

In 2014 the ECB had pushed interest rates into negative territory, taking yet another cue from the Bank of Japan, truly the West's central banking innovator. The main reason they can be so innovative is that their debt is almost wholly owned by Japanese people - this is not at all the situation in the Eurozone, as the sale of Greek assets shows. ZIRP (Zero Interest-Rate Policy) was an effort to keep inflation down amid the banker bailout money printing, but also a way to encourage banks to finally loan some of this taxpayer bailout money downwards. However, with no strings attached here, either, banks never did. ZIRP proved to be another fiscal policy disastrous to public finances, as it was also manipulated by elite to fuel their lifestyle and to further inflate their preferred asset classes. ZIRP, like QE, would also be passed around the G20 to keep the money conjuring going.

> *Yellow Vest: "Of course the movement will continue because there is so much injustice in France today. Above all, there is economic injustice."*

But the European and Western elite wanted even more than just free money and no-risk loans - they also wanted an end to any Socialist-inspired drags on their profits caused by the advances of mere Social Democracy. On November 6, 2012, Francois Hollande made a U-Turn as bad as Francois Mitterrand did in 1983 when he also backtracked on his anti-austerity promise. His 2013 budget contained basically all the neoliberal, economically-regressive measures proposed by Sarkozy during the presidential campaign. It was a total shock to the average Frenchman, who had not grasped the power of the Lisbon Treaty. France's two-party system was officially a uni-party system: pro-Brussels.

On the very next day Hollande submitted to parliament a divisive, deflecting law to legalise gay marriage and gay adoption - it was a stunningly cynical move. November 7, 2012, is a perfect incarnation of what Western democracy has become: class-obscuring identity politics combined with far-right economics, which is then ludicrously passed off as progressive politics. Such preposterously false politics can be achieved only via forbidding Socialist-inspired analyses from regular public debate: Insisting that all political analysis promote Liberalism, combined with Fascism's obsession with tribe and identity politics, allows for "left" and "right" to lose solid definitions based on class, history and consensual agreements on reality, and to create nebulous definitions which are so grounded in personal whims and individualist nonsense that they are clearly reminiscent of the illogical rule of an autocrat.

The connection between the two events was rarely uttered, and the pro-gay news widely prevailed instead of the economic backtracking which would gut the lives of countless French people regardless of sexuality. If European citizens had assumed that France would continue its tradition of bravely being a primary torch bearer for progressive politics - they were now definitively mistaken. Hundreds of thousands of people would regularly protest against the extremely minority, pro-gay measures in the "*Manif pour tous*" (The Protest For All) marches, which ran regularly from November 2012 until May 2013, when the law passed. The diversion and safety valve worked perfectly.

In January 2013 the European Fiscal Compact came into effect: it was the official enshrining of austerity budgets across the Eurozone, and the official death of Keynesian government spending. The French left had gone from the radical equality of 1789, to majoritarian Marxism, to compromise Keynesianism and now to aristocratic Liberalism.

The stated goal was to appease international lenders and keep long-term interest rates down. The Compact's rule that a national budget deficit must not exceed 3% (a completely arbitrary number) of GDP would be wielded repeatedly in order to roll back Social Democracy into Liberal Democracy. Mass protests across France called for a referendum on the European Fiscal Compact - these were completely ignored, and the Compact was ratified merely by parliament, again. The anti-1789 regression back to autocratic oligarchy thus took another major step towards total normalisation.

The first budget of Hollande, elected on anti-austerity, was the strictest in 30 years. France was not alone - when other Eurozone nations budgets unveiled their austerity turn protests broke out in many counties, and lasted for months in places like Spain and Greece. By October 2013 Hollande was the most unpopular president in French history.

Thus from the forcing in of the EU in 2009 until 2013 the economic crisis caused by Western Liberal Democracy was used to strengthen their Bankocracy more than ever. Not just France but almost all of Europe was truly restored to its usual historical state - autocratic oligarchy.

In spring 2014 a headline first appeared which would be repeated over and over: stock dividends hit a quarterly European record. In 2012 France's CAC 30 stock index hit a low of 3000, but by 2022 it would reach 7,000 despite a lost decade of economic growth and then the coronavirus recession. This is not solely thanks to Western policies of Quantitative Easing and ZIRP: The economies of Western Liberal Democracies had clearly become totally untethered from economic fundamentals - as in Liberalist capitalism - and now clearly relied on Fascism's alliance of political power and corporate power.

The subsuming by Western Liberal Democracy of Fascism's economic policy, its obsession with identity politics and its authoritarian governance style simply cannot go unremarked upon by leftists. It's a conclusion which is as obvious as it is never mentioned, and fully fits in with the trend of Western political-economic history described in this book. The irony is that such conclusions are accused of being emotional and unscientific, and yet it's repeatedly stated that it's neoliberalism which is a "faith-based ideology" precisely because - even after a fourth decade - it lacks factual proofs of its broad success for the masses. This book shows that Liberalism also lacks such proofs for almost all of its two centuries of existence.

What is quantitative easing and how does it differ from another financial innovation of this era - Bitcoin?

Why is QE known as "free money" and what is the collateral backing QE?

The Eurozone did not discover any mines which yielded them trillions worth of gold. What they discovered was that the Bank of Japan was correct back in 2001: modern printing presses don't have to actually print in order to create real-life money. Digital zeroes simply need to be typed on a government computer and then copy-and-pasted into the computers of private banks. Thus, QE money was truly created out of thin air. Ironically, this was the common Liberalist accusation towards Bitcoin.

The simplest breakdown of what that means is: QE has taken printed money and given it to private banks so that private banks could give it back to central banks in the form of buying national bonds, which the government then uses to pay salaries and keep the streetlights on. No value is created for anyone except for the private banks - it is the ultimate victor of the *rentier*, he or she who adds no value but only parasitically extracts value. Western Liberal Democracy has evolved from constitutional monarchy to oligarchic Western Liberal Democracy to a fascist Bankocracy.

Here is a more detailed explanation of what that means in practice:

On their computers the ECB creates money out of "air", which they lend to national central banks in the Eurozone to bail out private bankers who made poor business decisions. (National central banker middlemen would be cut out via the European Stability Mechanism in 2012.) However, private banks would infamously refuse to loan this public money backed by the good name of the Eurozone's people out to the average person/small business. Instead of making these lower-yield but socially-productive investments, the elite spent the money to inflate the asset classes which only rich people can afford to invest in - stock buybacks are the most notorious example. Worse, this refusal to loan downwards actually has the real effect of creating even more "air" money: By actually investing the ECB's "air" in something high-yielding, such as in the stock market, this artificially boosts prices - the stock price has risen based merely on increased demand instead of due to hard-won improvements in its actual economic fundamentals. The same goes for something like real estate or jewellery or fancy art: increased demand is what raises those prices as well. This also allows stockholders and landlords, for example, to show private banks their "air"-inflated stocks or real estate as collateral to procure private bank loans (of quite real money) to further fuel their elite lifestyles. These loans of real money - despite being based on value increases based on "air" - also increases the balance sheets/assets of private banks and makes them look more stable, because they are powerful enough to loan out so very much money to elite individuals and institutions. That gives them even more borrowing power. Most importantly about the ECB's "air" money" is that it empowers private banks to loan real money to national governments - in the form of buying their bonds - in order to keep the streetlights on, and we are back to the start: the money has been fully washed. Thus it is not the ECB but the private bank which allows the Eurozone's national governments to fund their national budgets, and thus the ECB has truly given money to private banks in order to make national governments even more indebted to private banks, even though private banks have just been bailed out by both taxpayer money and "air". The national governments of the Eurozone thus remain solvent/avert bankruptcy/don't disappoint investors, but they do keep on paying usurious interest fees and effectively hand control of public policy to these creditors. Marx realised that bond buying was the corrupt, phony game upon which Western Liberal Democracy is entirely based, and properly condemned Louis-Napoleon Bonaparte for perpetuating it.

This dance happened every month to the tune of €60 billion per month and is supposed to stop on July 1, 2022. Forgive my skepticism: they have been saying that since autumn 2017.

> *Yellow Vest: "The government is deaf! For three months we have been in the streets to call for social and fiscal justice, but they have done nothing. The past 10 years have seen more taxes on the average person, while the rich, corporations and shareholders get tax cuts."*

All this "air" did not produce broad economic growth precisely because there were no strings attached forcing them to do so - the rabid capitalists merely shared the money among their elite friends. The failure to loan downward kept the "real" economy profoundly depressed in a self-defeating cycle: the failure to loan bailout money downward created a lack of confidence in the economic situation, which deterred economic activity, which created poor economic results, which then created more lack of confidence in the economic situation, which created more poor results, etc.

The everyday purchases of the people is always the main economic driver, just as the government always has the most measures to influence the economy. However, Western Liberal Democracy has always been constructed to benefit an autocratic aristocracy, and the war against Socialist Democracy - which demands strings be attached and which demands efforts at just redistribution - has always been total. The idea that Europe post-2009 did not follow this long-time trend of history is obviously a total fiction. Another fiction held dear by many in France is that the French government has more influence over the French economy than the government in Brussels, post-Lisbon Treaty.

How was the "air" in which central banks created unbacked trillions different from the "air" which private bankers accused Bitcoin of being based on? Bitcoin offers many advantages over the 19th century-based banking system: transactions without the usurious fees of private banks, plus the transparency and security provided by blockchain technology. Perhaps most important is that Bitcoin's "air" has the credibility granted by being impossible to inflate via over-printing - this is precisely the credibility which Western fiat (paper) money had lost via no-strings attached bailouts and QE. The amount of Bitcoin which can ultimately be created and used is limited to 21 million - it's a finite, public, international, 24/7, secure system.

Crucially, Bitcoin was created precisely as a populist reaction against the obvious economic disaster which was created as result of the West's reckless and inflationary over-printing (and then the irresponsible use of this money). The first ever block of Bitcoin, known as the Genesis block, was mined in January 2009. It contained a message which referenced an article by British newspaper *The Times*. The message read: "*The Times 03/Jan/2009 Chancellor on brink of second bailout for banks.*" Bitcoin is thus a response to the fact that Western Liberal Democracy is autocratic and oligarchic, and that it's fascist-influenced economy suffers from a "subprime government" crisis.

Bitcoin is thus the biggest financial weapon against capitalism with Western Liberal Democratic characteristics since the cooperative. Unfortunately, Bitcoin is rather infested with an anti-government, rabidly individualist libertarianism - they fail to see that the blockchain technology upon which Bitcoin rests contains the same virtues of Socialist Democracy: communal, consensus, decentralised, transparent, egalitarian. Another issue which must be remedied is the fact that an estimated 1,000 individuals, known as "whales", own 40% of the market and thus leave Bitcoin open to the same valuation manipulation, collusion and monopoly upon which modern capitalism is based.

A Socialist-inspired usage of cryptocurrency will undoubtedly reshape global economics. It is now drastically destabilising the Western Bankocracy, but capitalism repeatedly demonstrates it needs no help in cyclically destabilising itself.

If a 'Lost Decade' falls but nobody reports on it, does that make it 'Found'?

The term "Great Recession" is commonly defined as running from December 2007 through 2009, but this is a historical analysis which comments only upon the fortunes of the rich - they got bailed out, so the recession for the 1% is alleged to have ended by the start of 2010. However, for the average Frenchman the "Great Recession" has never ended but was continued all through the "Age of Austerity".

"Economic austerity" contains four essential ideas:

Firstly, it's the cutting of governmental social services - Liberalism hates "big government" precisely as a monarch hated the idea of even a small parliament. In practice, this means passing the costs onto households for what used to be provided by the government. Second, it's refusing to invest taxes in or sell bonds for public infrastructure programs which would benefit the nation regardless of economic class - government policy must focus on favouring the needs, success and confidence of the rich class. Thirdly, it is reducing worker stability and conditions in order to reduce profit drags for owners, bosses and stockholders. Lastly, it's increasing the tax burdens on households and individuals in order to finance cutting taxes for the rich and corporations in the hope that the latter pair will good-shepherd the economy back to strong growth. Crucially, there can be no strings attached to such tax cuts, in the form of promises to hire, invest sensibly, etc., as that would make it not capitalism but Socialist central planning.

By following these policies the economic growth which will eventually be produced is promised to be vastly superior to Socialist central planning, *and will also even render* the governmental social safety nets inspired by Socialism to become so cheap that they will become unnecessary for governments to provide. This is the precise central claim of modern Western Liberal Democracy, though never openly formulated as such because it is so obviously absent, distant and preposterous.

This set of policies is on the far-right of the spectrum of economic thought because it implicitly relies on the individual, autocratic, unaccountable decisions of a member of the rich elite class. It posits that by placating/encouraging/protecting/promoting the biggest owners of capital they will then willingly engage in economic practices which benefit the nation/bloc. This anti-statist (and thus anti-people/pro-person) "voluntarism" is also espoused by many libertarian/anarchist misleaders in the nascent Bitcoin community.

Cutting social services, refusing to invest and increasing taxes are obvious to all, but what exactly is "reducing worker stability and conditions"?

In brief, Eurozone capitalists want every member nation to go through the reactionary "Hartz Reforms" of pre-crisis Germany, which promoted part-time work and subsequently, of course, shot poverty and inequality through the roof. The German model is: part-time work + old age poverty + low wages + lower productivity + increasing inequality + finding neo-imperial advantages (Germany has found this in the former East Germany and the ex-Eastern Bloc - this is covered up in Western media, just as any profit from neo-imperialism is covered up) + less public investment + just enough of a social safety net to prevent embarrassing mass homelessness = "being fiscally responsible". Clearly, this is not the German model but the "American model"; it is the "precarious" model which has nearly always guided Western Liberal Democracy; it is Western imperialism turned inward - gutting the resources of their nation's own people for the benefit of an international 1%.

So how did the Age of Austerity actually perform for the Eurozone?

In January 2018 the Eurozone officially achieved a "Lost Decade": From 2008-2017 the average annual growth rate was 0.6%, which was a worse score than either of Japan's two Lost Decades (1991-2010).

The news went completely unnoticed, although of course PressTV and I reported on it immediately. Because the Eurozone's annual growth rate in 2017 was 2.5% the mainstream media were amazing in their apparent conspiratorial collusion to produce headlines like that of the *Financial Times*, who optimistically penned, "*Eurozone growth hits highest figure in a decade*".

For comparison, from 1975-1987 the US, UK, Germany and France all had between 1.8-2.5% annual average growth, and this era is universally considered a recession era. From 1945-1975 France's growth rate dipped below 4% in less than a handful of years.

China's growth rate from 2008-17 was 7.4%, but Western financial media ran countless propaganda variations such as this headline from *Fortune*: "*Why China's GDP Growth Rate Tells Us Nothing About Its Economy*". Iranian growth over this decade was five times better than the Eurozone's, at 3%, despite an ever-strengthening blockade. Cuba, which has far less resources than either China or Iran to combat an even longer international blockade, produced 2.8% growth over this time frame. We see clearly that presenting 2.5% growth as some sort of great achievement is clearly capitalist propaganda which hides its inferiority to Socialist Democratic economics. Western Liberal Democracy is good at preserving inequality, not at producing economic growth - the Social Democracy era (1945-75), contrarily, was ok at producing solid growth.

During this era France was on the brink of a headline-blaring "triple-dip recession" several times, only to be saved by the official reporting of a quarterly growth rate of 0.2% or less. Such repeated close-call accounting was never questioned by mainstream media journalists - who are usually even worse at economics than they are at basic math

- or even in the financial media, which one assumes would be more rigorous for their investor-readers.

All other capitalist metrics revealed the depth of the economic distress: Eurozone GDP per capita averaged €29,400 in 2008, and achieved only 0.1% annual growth by 2016 to reach €29,700. Considering that austerity also passes the buck for social services, €33 more per year was undoubtedly not enough of an increase for the average person. Nominal GDP, dropped from €14.1 trillion in 2008 down to €11.9 trillion in 2016. The bloc's debt-to-GDP ratio, so often used as further justification for austerity measures, went from 69% to 89% over this time period - the price tag of austerity cuts to national budgets (usually a median of roughly €12 billion annually in France) were obviously dwarfed by the huge taxpayer-funded banker bailouts. It was not a "Lost Decade" for bankers, but for the Eurozone's citizens.

Just as "national finances" referred to the king's purse in 1788, the Western Liberal Democratic "Bankocracy" cemented by the Lisbon Treaty stopped caring about these low rates of economic growth because their preferred sectors - finance, insurance and real estate (the FIRE sector), dominated by unproductive and parasitical "*rentier*" usury - became completely untethered from economic fundamentals. During this decade their favourite asset classes - bonds, stocks, real estate, luxury goods, Leonardo da Vinci paintings, cases of rare wine, etc. - all hit record highs despite the undeniable tanking of the real economy.

Thus everyone living under Eurozone austerity felt and knew the reality that all of the ECB's "free money" had gone for nothing which benefited the average citizen nor society overall. It was unproductive "bad debt" because it did not strengthen the "real" economy by building any infrastructure, which would have improved the ease of doing business and thus increased state revenue; nor funded any pension, health or education programs, which would have reduced fiscal drags and produced productive tax streams; nor gone into wage increases which would have increased consumer demand and resulted in economic growth. Any of these would have qualified as "good debt", which would have produced multiple euros for every euro invested. This is something which Socialist-inspired countries comprehend, and which explains their economic resilience during this decade of global recession.

Unsurprisingly, the net effect of QE on employment in the Eurozone was negligible, as economists say that job growth does not even begin until growth rates hit 1.5%. Unemployment in France thus steadily climbed to nearly 11%, a level unseen since the mid-1990s. It should be remembered that official unemployment rates should usually be tripled, as they generally avoid including the underemployed, those whose unemployment insurance has expired and those who have given up looking for work. In this era of the West, however, part-time work became the goal of austerity "reforms". Indeed, "underemployment" is perhaps the dominant theme in the life of the average Westerner during this era. The unemployment rate in France would only decrease in the Macron era thanks to shameless number-rigging and ignoring entire official classes of unemployed persons - the mainstream media, ever-illiterate in basic economics, played along.

The official inflation rate from 2000-19 revealed an increase of over 30% in France, though trusting official figures on inflation is certainly to accept a drastic and wilful undercounting also based on shameless number-rigging and mainstream media sycophancy.

> *Yellow Vest: "We pay our taxes to support public media, and we pay to help privately-owned media as well, but they both relay the exact same opinions and exclude or slander any dissenting voices. All we are asking is that the diversity of opinions be respected, and we are telling these journalists to stop their censorship and propaganda."*

Frankly, there is no limit to the number of statistics which can be used to describe the economic failures of Western Liberal Democracy during this era.

Combined with economic repression was the actual repression of the Hollande era

The autocratic demand from Brussels for austerity required the restoration of police states unseen since the era of Hapsburg domination and Metternich.

This is epitomised by the fact that from 2015 through 2021 France was in a state of emergency for 4.5 years. The final two years of Hollande's reign a state of emergency held, and when Macron took power one of the first things he did was to legalise, and thus normalise permanently, the excessive powers granted during the state of emergency.

Given the brutality against the Yellow Vests it's entirely too easy to forget that the Hollande era was also an era of absolutely constant protests. I estimate that at least 10,000 citizens were arrested at anti-government protests during the Hollande era, with truly countless hurt, tear-gassed and harassed by cops. Four thousand protesters were not just arrested but actually prosecuted during the 2016 labor code rollback protests alone, so how many more were arrested but never charged? How many more would have been arrested and tried had not over 600 demonstrations been banned during the terrorist-related two-year state of emergency, with countless other protests strangled in the cradle?

(For comparison, when maimed Yellow Vests marched a week before the first round of presidential elections in 2022, here are the widely cited statistics: 11,000 arrests, 1,000 imprisonments, 5,000 protesters seriously injured, 1,000 critically injured, dozens maimed for life and 12 deaths).

The banning did not really work - France averaged about 10

protests per day prior to the coronavirus - because the undemocratic installation of the EU, Hollande's backtracking on austerity and the economic failure of austerity provoked an absolutely massive backlash.

After his backtracking on austerity anti-government sentiment immediately ballooned: a 2013 poll showed that 70% of France viewed their politicians as corrupt, marking a 30 % increase in just three years. A tone of trying to criminalise social movements and intimidate politically-active citizens was set on March 2013, when one labor union activist in a crowd of 1,000 was shockingly fined €40,000 for participating in a non-violent rail protest in 2006. The fine was upheld.

Rail workers were targeted because they are the most combative protesters in France: they led both the 1995 and the 2019/20 general strikes, and also because they were about to take to the streets over the EU's forced breakup of national control over France's railways. The 2014 rail strike was the biggest labor movement since 2010, inspiring other movements - such as major protests in favor of Palestine - and brutal police tactics. Personally, I remember them as being more brutal than in 2016, albeit on a smaller scale. However, Brussels could not be stopped here nor in 2019, when similar EU orders to privatise the air industry forcibly opened French skies.

In January 2015 the Charlie Hebdo attacks saw workers at the xenophobic journal killed over needless cartoons of Prophet Mohammad. Omitted in Western media coverage was that one cartoon showed Prophet Mohammad filming a pornographic movie and another showed him bent over with a star where his anus would be. Disgusting, childish and not at all intellectual, but that's what they drew. The "*Je suis Charlie*" (I am Charlie Hebdo) marches would bring several millions to the streets of Paris in the name of tolerance, and then introduce essentially perpetual Islamophobia. Gay rights could only deflect for so long - France's Liberalists needed Islamophobia to implement Fascism's creation of fractional identity politics, which deflects from majoritarian class politics.

Many wondered how the attackers could have fought in Syria, returned, be under police surveillance (one had already been jailed on terror-related crimes) and yet were still successfully able to carry out a terror attack? Adding to these questions was why terrorists would feel the need to take their state ID on a terror attack, much less be daft enough to leave it in their getaway car?

Regardless of how: the attack occurred, and Islamophobia has ruled the media-politico waves ever since. It was one attack of many in this violent era: At that time France had 20 foreign military operations in place. In 2014 Hollande had admitted that starting in 2012 he violated the EU arms embargo to militants in Syria by sending them cannons, machine guns, rocket launchers and anti-tank missiles. This was preceded in 2011 with France's illegal airlift of 40 tons of weapons to Al-Qaeda-linked militants in order to overthrow Ghadaffi. As widely predicted, these arms would be used to destabilise the African continent. In 2013 Hollande would send troops to Mali, and without prior UN permission. In every attack from 2012 onwards these foreign interventions would be cited by seemingly every terrorist who was not deemed mentally unfit.

In May a "French Patriot Act" had been rushed into law to put everyone under mass surveillance, legalise computer hacking by the government and end the need for a court warrant. Like the United States in the wake of 9/11, France's judicial branch effectively stopped deciding on anything if the word "terrorism" was attached. France's judicial branch no longer acted as a check and balance - they were simply secretaries: they branch merely had to be informed of decisions taken by the the executive branch, its ministers and its police.

Many said the new powers weren't even necessary because France's executive branch was already the most powerful in the West, but executive branch power grabs were indispensable during these first formal years of the pan-European project: Because the pan-European project cannot win approval via democratic votes they must increase the power of their executive branches, who then implement the policies ordered by Brussels.

Only a week after Charlie Hebdo Hollande brought back the "49-3" - an undemocratic legislative loophole (called a "bazooka" in France) which allows for the executive to force through laws without consulting parliament. The obviously autocratic tool had been used rarely since 1993, as voters had proven their opposition to it. When it was used it was only for more limited issues, whereas here Hollande used it for the economic centrepiece of his term: the Macron Law, named after the young Minister of the Economy. Ominously foreshadowing his own autocracy, Macron brushed aside accusations of 49-3 as being anti-democratic by saying, "*Is it democratic to keep procrastinating? There is a moment when you have to act.*" A few days before the Charlie Hebdo attacks, Hollande had declared that he would not use the 49-3, which he had previously strongly criticized.

The autocratic 49-3 was used three times to pass the legislation of the Macron Law, and it drastically shook up France: at a time when the global "*Je suis Charlie*" protests had convinced France they were the world's leading light of liberty, Frenchmen knew there was an autocratic rot in their own government.

Culturally, while Sarkozy introduced xenophobia, Hollande made it mainstream (Macron would then legalise it). Hollande persecuted the Roma worse than Sarkozy and totally ignored the 2015 European Refugee Crisis which he was a major factor in perpetrating, thanks to France's efforts to destroy Libya, Syria and elsewhere. 2015 saw refugees flood the streets of the working-class areas of Paris, adding to this era's massive economic, cultural and governmental malaise.

When the El Khomri Law, aimed to be a Hartz reform for the French labor code, was announced for 2016 many in France were well aware that major protests lay ahead.

However, in November 2015 a state of emergency had been declared - for the first time since it was used to forestall Algerian independence

- in response to an atrocious massacre at a rock concert in Paris and two other coordinated attacks, causing 137 deaths. Once again fighters in Syria had returned to attack Frenchmen. This was not the deadliest day in France since World War II, as is often reported - in October 1961 some 300 peacefully protesting Algerians were killed, many thrown into the Seine River. However much the Hollande administration might have hoped the bloody flag of the Bataclan concert hall would smooth the passage of the labor code rollback, they were mistaken.

All of spring 2016 was near-daily strikes: oil refinery, electricity, air traffic controllers, railroads, garbagemen, pilots and dockworkers all held multi-week strikes in the biggest labor action since 1995. Riot police inflicted violence seemingly as often as there was a protest. Furthermore, every night in Paris for months were the unprecedented "*Nuit Debout*" (Up All Night) protests, which were hailed as an effort to create a new form of democratic politics. Hundreds, sometimes thousands, of protesters gathered at *Place de la Republique* to sit and discuss the disastrous political and social situation. Every single night police forced them to dismantle their camp, and every day activists rebuilt it.

In this context of a terribly hard social spring Brexit occurred (June 2016), and the link is as obvious as it is ignored by the Mainstream Media : The disastrous and despised leadership of Brussels was on display every night just across the Channel. "Remainers" chose to blame racist rural citizens while "Leavers" exhaled at escaping a continent which had been mired in chaos since 2009. It's appalling that the context of a disastrous 2016 is pushed aside as a reason for Brexit thanks to the privileging of an absurd xenophobic narrative. Given the decade's political, economic and social disaster it's amazing that there was only one "-exit". However, the coronavirus would put a 1.5-year stop to all political protests.

After almost four months of near-daily protests, France's prime minister finally agreed to sit down with labor unions for the first time

- Macron clearly neither invented rubber-bullet Liberalism nor the refusal of Western Liberal Democratic politicians to autocratically rule without discussion.

Hollande did eventually make some minor concessions to the labor code rollback, which were then used by Macron as a reason for quitting his cabinet. Despite public disapproval, Hollande rammed the final version through by 49-3.

Defying the mainstream media pundits, Hollande never made an about-face on austerity even if only to win-election. Instead, he threw in the towel before the ringing of the 2017 first-round bell: he shockingly refused to stand for re-election. It was a first in French history, and one with few parallels in Western Liberal Democracy. His final approval rating was just 4%. Hollande thus was never held directly accountable by voters - he ruled like an autocrat and left on his own autocratic terms.

> *Yellow Vest: "This is an admission of weakness. The government is using the last advantage it has to increase the repression of protesters. The military already has a job to do when they are deployed inside France – to protect us from terrorism."*

Hollande was surely thinking something like, "One day they will look back and thank me". Mikhail Gorbachev is probably thinking the same thing, too, as will Macron. The only persons thanking these elite imploders are their fellow elite.

The fault is in not repeatedly not predicting totally predictable consequences

The Lost Decade could have been limited to just 10 years - Europe's Quantitative Easing was originally scheduled to end September 2017.

Of course, realism about how capitalism works prevailed - rather than opening the door to European Sovereign Debt Crisis II it was accepted that Quantitative Easing could not end.

What added to the alarm is that a once-risky Eurozone situation has grown even more unstable, because the Eurogroup's policies did not correct whatsoever - economically or politically - any differences in risk among the different nations of the Eurozone.

Further adding to the alarm is that the Eurogroup did not strengthen the resilience of the "real economies" in their member nations – austerity policies and labor code rollbacks have worsened the fundamentals of the "real economy". Should something like a pandemic hit and strain finances, the results will be… well, we will soon find out.

There's a life-or-death question for which Western Liberal Democracy is only starting to answer, at the time of publication, and which they hoped to avoid asking: When the era of free money ends, and knowing that the 1% can never be satiated, how long do the devilish speculators wait to strike the poorer members of the Eurozone?

The other existential question facing the Eurozone is: How can any sort of redistributive, equalising era of "free money" for the 99% ever start when the solidarity required for a pan-continental project clearly does not exist? For Europe there must first be a *political* agreement on this question, which is the only way to finally create economic growth, equality and equal growth across its regions.

In May 2016 a team of economists from the International Monetary Fund admitted that austerity doesn't work, that rising inequality was bad for growth and that governments should use controls to cope with destabilising capital flows. It fell on deaf ears among policy makers, who - as always in Western Liberal Democracy - refuse to employ Socialist-inspired ideas to prevent the next looming inevitable bust in capitalism.

In August 2016 Nobel Prize-winning economist Joseph Stiglitz released perhaps the most popular American critique of Europe's economic choices with, *The Euro: How a Common Currency Threatens the Future of Europe*. Stiglitz is perhaps the most prominent left-leaning economist in the United States, and I should note that he grew up in a small city in which I lived for several years: Gary, Indiana. Gary is the home of once-mighty US Steel, but which has been reduced into a regular contender for the per-capita murder capital of the world via globalisation, offshoring, White flight and total Western Liberal Democratic neglect.

> *"Austerity has always and everywhere had the contractionary effects observed in Europe: the greater the austerity, the greater the economic contraction. Why the Troika would have thought that this time in Europe it would be different is mystifying,"* Stiglitz wrote.

It is not "*mystifying*", but "left-leaning" economists and figures continually make this claim of, essentially, "but surely they had good intentions" even though we know that the capitalist opponents of Socialist Democracy routinely aim for and perpetuate catastrophic scenarios for the average person. What happened in the Eurozone has happened all over the 3rd World during the two-plus centuries of European-led imperialism: countries were flooded with loans from Europe which they could never repay, resulting in Westerners taking over government policy with an aim of picking apart the newly-indebted economies. This is what capitalism does over and over and over, from the Bey of Tunisia in the 1860s to Greece today. Stiglitz is guilty of viewing the Eurozone as some sort of isolated case in capitalism - it is his wilful insistence on remaining "*mystified*" which allows his merely left-leaning ideas to maintain mainstream dissemination.

> *"A cynic might say that this was the intent of the law: to preserve power relations. But I am convinced that the rule in Europe was*

driven more by ideology and misguided economic beliefs than narrow self-interest," wrote Stiglitz.

It is not at all cynical to say that capitalists in the Eurozone have not yet rectified a long-standing criticism by the left: that capitalism needlessly and inefficiently promotes international competition and imperialistic rivalries. To say that the bankers, the Troika and top national politicians didn't know what they were doing is pathetically collaborative. Worse, it shows that a Nobel Prize-winning economist doesn't even understand how the Eurozone works post-Lisbon Treaty? It also lacks sufficient contempt for a negligence which undoubtedly produces mass suffering. But lacking contempt and rigour for Western capitalism while still making obvious criticisms is how a person such as Stiglitz becomes reportedly the fifth-most most frequently cited author on college syllabi for economics courses in the US.

Yet the fundamental misconception that high finance *actually wants* a "high-growth" model – but just can't figure the darn thing out – is likely to persist. The true reality is that regular forced recessions are a tool of social war against the 99% to restore 19th century living standards and rights. From 2018-2021 the Eurozone produced a growth rate of just 0.5% - it seems inevitable that the Eurozone will achieve a "Lost Score", just as Japan did.

Five months after Brexit Donald Trump would be elected on a platform of "draining the swamp" in Washington of its corrupt, essentially uni-party political hacks, and also of ending "this American carnage", a reference to the social destruction caused by the Great Recession. Trump would become one of the least warmongering US presidents in history, so some carnage was indeed reduced.

Would France follow the Anglosphere's lead of rejecting mainstream political-economic ideology in favor of populism in their 2017 elections? The mainstream parties would lose, but not mainstream ideology. Since 1789 France has often rejected the ultimately right-wing politics of the Anglosphere, as mainland France has often followed the lead of other, rather unexpected, sources.

France's overseas colonies are repeatedly at the crest of the wave of French politics, providing innovations which later spread to the mainland. We will see this with the Yellow Vests, but in spring 2017 French Guiana burst into the news with a general strike, demanding an end to their colonial status and far more autonomy.

It was amusing to see how France's mainstream media printed promises that "the strikes are over" almost daily - an effort to strangle them in the cradle - but they would last three weeks. Just as historically notable was the arrival of a people's militia called the "500 Brothers Against Delinquency". The first rule of any government is to provide security for its citizens, but Guiana had been allowed to become the most violent "overseas *département*" of France. The citizens' brigade wore masks, were called absolutely necessary by locals I interviewed in Paris and were expectedly denounced by Liberalists as extralegal vigilante justice.

All 11 of France's neo-colonies are rife with atrocious inequality and French-led hypocrisy, but none more so than French Guiana. Just as colonial England prohibited colonies like Barbados, Jamaica or Monserrat to manufacture even a needle or a horseshoe, so does France and the EU treat French Guiana as an economic hostage. More than 60% of their imports are from France, but by prioritising France instead of trading with their neighbors the growth of French Guiana has been incredibly retarded. The advent of the EU made this situation one of the worst neo-imperial situations on record: Goods from nearby South American nations are blocked out by EU tariffs, thus the Guyanese have to favor goods from the Netherlands and Germany instead of from Venezuela and Brazil despite the obviously higher shipping costs. This arrangement is regularly called a "paradox" in the mainstream media, who is mystified as to how capitalism works, of course.

French Guiana is thus emblematic of how the Eurozone is a system which is rigged to increase inequality in favor of the rich as long as there is such an obvious absence of political solidarity among member nations. Such solidarity is anathema in Western Liberal Democracy, of course.

As Varoufakis underlined, because deficits and surpluses are inevitable between two nations which trade, there must be a multi-national mechanism/parliament/executive which redistributes wealth from surplus nations in the Eurozone to deficit nations in order to ensure economic balance and social/regional harmony. In the absence of such a mechanism a multi-national project like the Eurozone will never be able to create growth or equality for perpetually poorer members like Greece or French Guiana. Such areas are doomed to permanent debtor/deficit nation status, with all the loss of real political influence to 2012's "gang of four" that obviously entails.

What the Age of Austerity proved is that European elite are not only opposed to a redistribution of wealth among classes, but also to any redistribution of wealth among nations sharing the euro. This is not an economic question but a political one, because only a government intervention – a *political* agreement/decision – can create equality, growth, and equal growth across Eurozone regions. However, many in the Eurozone still believe that their national governments are in charge, despite all of this era's evidence to the contrary.

The future of the Eurozone is so hopeless because the Bankocracy which controls it will never promote or allow political agreements which redistribute wealth and political power. The spirit of 1789 has been supplanted by a Western Liberal Democracy which takes many cues from Fascism, and this would soon be encapsulated in France by Emmanuel Macron and then bravely opposed by the Yellow Vests.

<—>

11

To Yellow Vests he's the radical: Macron imposes 'radical centrism' for Brussels

During the only debate featuring the five principal 2017 presidential candidates the National Front's Marine Le Pen zinged Macron with the night's best line:

> *"Do you know what, Mr. Macron? You have a crazy talent: You just managed to speak for seven minutes, and I am incapable of summarising your thoughts – you've said nothing. It's completely empty,"* she said, and then turned around to the audience and admired, *"It's an art, huh?"*

Macron and Le Pen would barely emerge from a four-way dead-heat in the first round. Twenty percent of France gave their vote to a candidate whose main plank was to start over by founding a 6th Republic - Jean-Luc Melenchon, who had previously broken with the Socialist Party over its Europhile stance. Clearly, many in France realised that still using a governmental structure which was created before the elite-forced installations of the European Union and the euro has produced inadequacies, conflicts and redundancies - total social disaster.

As in 2012, enormous geopolitical issues were at play. Le Pen had refused to ignore the public's perception of economic, democratic and pan-European regression since 2009. She promised to hold a "Frexit" vote within six months of victory, the repudiation of banker debt and somewhat seriously discussed leaving the euro. She savaged Macron's past as a Rothschild banker and acted every bit the outsider politician intent on overturning the status quo. However, when the moment of truth came - the lone presidential debate between them - Le Pen clowned and mugged for the camera, looking every bit the joker and not the concerned patriot.

In the two weeks between the first and second round of voting terrorism-related news found surprising ways to make the headlines nearly every day. Anti-terrorism raids and arrests fell on April 24, 25, 26, 27 and May 2. One day featured a national homage to a slain cop. High-profile court judgements for being an "apologist for terrorism", a sensationalist charge created after the Charlie Hebdo attack, were released. The day after the debate the media was consumed by a national homage for all the slain policemen across France.

Fear and hysteria was in the air, not serious political debate. There was not one major media in France which was pro-Le Pen, which contrasted sharply with a pre-Brexit United Kingdom that saw daily discussions of the pro-Brexit rationale prior to the June 2016 referendum. Fake-leftist newspaper *Libération* would even break the law requiring total impartiality on the day before the presidential vote with a cover that read, "*Do what you want but vote Macron*".

Macron had saved his big public relations gun for the final week of campaigning: "The National Front is the anti-France party". It resonated, even though the National Front is the most hyper-patriotic party: but by including pathetic xenophobia (a form of identity politics which

Western Liberal Democracy adopted from fascism) Le Pen obscured her patriotic aspects and became easy to caricaturise and demonise.

Macron won what appeared be a resounding 66-34% victory, and both Brussels and high finance exhaled. The National Front continued to be a mere safety valve and the ultimate paper tiger: in 2016 they held just 0.4% of all French elected offices.

Contemporary elite had every right to exhale because they knew that they couldn't be bothered about France for five more years. In post-Lisbon Treaty Europe it had become clear that - once elected - politicians were unconstrained by popular opinion. Nicolas Sarkozy's undemocratic end run to install the Lisbon Treaty and Francois Hollande's backtracking on austerity had shown anyone with a political or even legal mind that France truly had become no different than tiny Greece or Ireland. The Macron era would repeatedly remind that this is not hyperbole but 21st century reality.

Macron never had anything close to a broad mandate for his policies but would dangerously govern as though he did: When we subtract abstention, blank or purposely spoiled ballots (the best protest vote allowed in France) and those voters who said they voted for Macron simply to block Le Pen (43%), then Macron's 66% final tally translated into only 24% of the total electorate having actually selected Macron for his policies or personality.

Like Brexit and the United States, which had elected Donald Trump in November 2016, mainstream Liberalist ideology was also harshly reprimanded, but the least so in France. In the June legislative vote the two deeply discredited mainstream parties were swept out of national dominance, which had been the second-most popular motivation voters had for choosing Macron over Le Pen. This legislative victory had now been guaranteed for all three presidents since 2007, when France aligned the timing of their presidential and legislative elections. Still, if we assume Macron's campaign promises of a new anti-corruption regime to be sincere, then it appeared to some like a clean break with the two mainstream parties which had united to establish the current pan-European project on a basis of "neoliberalism": the Socialists, who falsely claimed to be leftist, and the conservatives, who falsely claimed to carry the legacy of Charles de Gaulle and *La Résistance* (sovereignty and anti-fascism).

Again, the lack of a mandate was obvious: Abstention was the lowest not just in the history of the 5th Republic, but in the 4th and 3rd Republics as well. A final round turnout of 43% represented an absolute democratic catastrophe, as French legislative turnout had averaged roughly 75% for almost 150 years, until the alignment. Even though Macron's parliamentary alliance won 49% of the second round vote this translated to just 21% of the total electorate, but 61% of the National Assembly's 577 total seats. Macron would constantly join his alliance with the mainstream conservatives - which is what Macron always was, despite his campaign claim of "centrism" - to combine for an unstoppable 486 seats. The almost always-agreeable Socialists would hand him another 45 seats for a uni-party-sized 92% of the National Assembly. Furthermore, the National Front and Melenchon accumulated 24% of the first-round vote yet would walk away in the second round with just 4% of total seats combined.

Western Liberal Democracy was already infamous in 21st century Europe for its lack of democratic representation, elite capture and electioneering - the last thing they needed was someone who would pointedly remind angry and embittered French voters of this reality. What France needed was time to heal the anger caused by Francois Hollande's appalling backtracking on austerity and to calmly discuss the perceived failures of a pan-European project which hadn't been fully implemented for even a decade.

That did not happen.

Macron's 'centrism" was quite openly a 'Revolution'

Macron's November 2016 book which delineated his program was titled *Revolution*, and it was not ironic. Macron clearly saw himself as a Liberalist revolutionary, and his war was to roll back the gains which Social Democracy had made from 1945-75 in order to fully re-impose Liberalism. This is clearly in keeping with the pattern of French and Western history since 1848 as aimed for by its oligarchical elite, and Macron's ability to understand this explains how he rose from a political neophyte to the chief executive so quickly and with such universal elite support.

Macron's primary "revolution" was this: he no longer cared about preserving the social peace whatsoever. Sarkozy autocratically ignored protests for his centrepiece economic legislation - raising the retirement age -, and Hollande did the same for his economic centrepiece - the Macron Law -, but neither dared to make autocracy their governance style in all matters like Macron did. Macron quitting Hollande's cabinet over indignation that minor concessions were made on the 2016 labor code rollback showed how absolutist his conception of governance always truly was.

Macron was the first French leader to have no memory of the 1968 protests and that means - crucially and without a shred of irony - he missed a cultural revolution which was dominated by a peacefulness and utopianism the likes of which a rabidly imperialistic West hadn't seen in centuries. Neither did Macron have any experience with war, and what that instability, deprivation and hardship means. Thus he was very much a throwback to the sheltered, protected aristocracy of the Bourbon royalist era. He was the child of an elite which had told him to be convinced by the neoliberal and neo-imperial pan-European project for his entire life, an idea pushed by the elite-dominated French media. Macron infamously married his high school drama teacher (and a chocolate heiress), and it is widely assumed that their sexual relationship illegally began while he was still in high school (as his wife refuses to give the exact date - chocolate heiresses are apparently extended this right), which would make Macron a victim of statutory rape. The man clearly embraces standard authority figures, and he is clearly no revolutionary against the conservative status quo. His *Revolution* must be understood for what it truly was: a reversion to elite autocracy.

Macron's lack of contact with and empathy for the French masses explains his constant public relations gaffes (too long to list here), which would force his handlers to keep him away from the French public as much as possible. Unlike the also aristocratic Valery Giscard d'Estaing, Macron could not even attempt normal public relations efforts and nor did he appear to desire to do so. Stunningly, in a France pushed by the Charlie Hebdo attack to think of itself as a nation which demanded a strong press, Macron did not hold his first press conference until two years into his term and five months into the Yellow Vest crisis. An oft-publicised rationale was that he wished to restore kingly grandeur and respect to the French presidency by acting as a remote god - "Jupiter" was constantly cited, pathetically - but his aloofness was actually forced by his arrogant, out-of-touch manner that galled the average voter struggling to make it through Austerity Era France. The "Jupiter" canard was deployed to hide what this mere mortal was: a major victory for royalist conceptions of government, economics and culture. Only a Western culture so blind to the modern scourge of royalism could miss this, but this book aims to remind that ending royalism (and its cultural legacy) is the first necessary step in progressive, leftist politics.

Macron is not completely exceptional - he does have a base of electoral support, and it is the bloc which has been the most firmly united throughout Western Liberal Democracy, starting with the "Party of Order" in 1848: the bourgeois. The term "bourgeois bloc" gained currency after Macron's election, but it hails from an actual coalition of conservative and elitist parties during Weimar Germany.

In the 21st century the bourgeois bloc can be most easily described as the "winners" in Western Liberal Democracy, and they are joined by those who aspire to also "win" via unquestioningly accepting the values of the bloc. The actual math in Western Liberal Democracies appears broadly like this: the 1%, who own a third of the country (we could call them the "neo-royalists"), their so called "talented tenth" of professionals, managers and technocrats (the "Liberalists"), who also own a third of the country, and then a "toadying tenth", class traitors who adopt the values of the top 10% in order to join them one day. This computation corresponds almost exactly to Macron's actual base of electoral support (24%). The opponents of the bourgeois bloc are no longer labelled Socialist but instead are labelled "Fascist" - i.e. racist, misogynist, homophobic, extremists, etc.

The idea remains the same as it did with the 1848 Party of Order: Allow the bourgeois bloc to rule, with their wisdom which is superior to both king/queen or their mass of subjects, until their riches trickle down and a *democratic majority in favor of Liberalism will eventually be created.* This majority was not evident in 1852, 1871, 1914, 1936 and other points besides, notably in national referendums which rejected the Liberalist pan-European project. As this *democratic majority in favor of Liberalism will eventually be created*, then the anti-democratic and inegalitarian methods of Western Liberal Democracy are only a temporary, even necessary, evil for the bourgeois bloc. This explains why there was a bloc of 25% which ardently supported the repression of the Yellow Vests. The Yellow Vests immediately and durably had about 75% popular support - thus we see the two blocs which modern France is truly divided into: one convinced of Western Liberal Democracy and one skeptical.

The political vision of the bourgeois bloc is best described as "radical centrism". What is radical here is that this so-called centrism insists that it knows the only way to see reality, and grants itself the right to reject any contrary view as an outright lie, and thus subject to Metternich's censorship. Godin described the situation appropriately: *"In a 'neoliberal democracy,' the checks and balances are those of the 'experts,' in other words, those who validate neoliberal thinking in 'independent' institutions charged with ensuring a political path that escapes the 'popular passions'."* Those who affirm the bourgeois bloc are "*experts*" and "*independent*", and those do not become classified (increasingly officially) as misinformation.

Want to discuss the democratic and economic failures of the European Union and Eurozone? Then you are either just ignorant, supporting Fascism, or dangerously pushing misinformation because Liberalism is (or, as most prefer "neoliberalism"), quite simply, the eternal, constant, unchangeable truth. Of course There Is No Alternative - encapsulated by the famous acronym "TINA" -, as is waiting to install "neoliberalism". This explains Macron's comment referring to the deeply unpopular use by Hollande of the 49-3 executive decree: "*Is it democratic to keep procrastinating?*" To the bourgeois bloc any procrastination from a full restoration of 1848-style Liberalism is not just normal dissent but evident of being anti-democratic. Preposterous, but this was all the unstated basis of Macron's *Revolution*.

The main point here is not that cutting off political debate violates a core tenet of Western Liberal Democracy which they insist makes it superior to Socialist Democracy, but that: this is not centrism, because centrism - by definition - seeks a consensus interpretation of reality. Radical centrism is thus an elitist snobbery as old as Western Liberal Democracy itself. Godin noted: "*The 'hateful mob' (foul haineuse) of Emmanuel Macron responds quite exactly to the 'vile multitude' of Adolphe Thiers.*" Indeed, there is no politician whom Macron resembles as much as Thiers, who colluded with occupying royalist Germans in 1871 to turn the Paris Commune into a bloodbath and into another failed French revolution which aimed to move away from autocratic oligarchy. The American version of this is Hillary Clinton's infamous assessment of Trump supporters as a "basket of deplorables". Western culture has gone from insisting that royalists/elitists are the "deplorables" to it is the working poor which is "deplorable" - the obvious cause of this change is the suppression of Socialist Democratic culture, and the obvious solution is Socialist Democratic-inspired policies.

Macron's *Revolution* is precisely that of an elite talking to another elite about fully restoring elitism, i.e. Liberalism, by any means necessary and immediately. His backers should have modified the pro-sovereignty slogan of the Iranian Revolution - "Neither East nor West but the Islamic Republic" - into "Neither left nor right but the Bourgeois Bloc Republic". In a West which can no longer see the pernicious culture, economic and political influence *still being pushed* by shahs, kings and aristocrats, and which views Islam as an existential threat to "the truth" of Western radical centrism, this recent historical parallel cannot be perceived much less rebroadcast.

A primary Western problem is that the bourgeois bloc is actually the most politically united. Contrarily, those who reject neoliberalism are clearly in the Western majority but they have no political organisation or expression of their will - an "anti-bourgeois bloc" clearly doesn't exist in an any politically effective, organised way. How could it, when anti-bourgeois bloc ideas are classified as misinformation and extremism; when a handful of billionaires control France's privatised media in total unity? Who could get a stable, much less influential, job as a journalist in the West by discussing the need for such a bloc on a regular basis? The arrival of the bourgeois bloc's now-ceaseless censorship campaign of social media - after having initially and falsely assumed that social media would easily and successfully broadcast "the truth" of radical centrism to the unenlightened masses - is thus easily explained: social media could be a force for the anti-bourgeois bloc.

The Yellow Vests, which effectively began as a movement on social media, are so important because they prove that the Liberalist model is - after almost two centuries, still! - a minority model which can only be imposed by anti-democratic force. In Macron-era France to demonstrate against government policies progressed to making one an enemy of the state and of society, which gutted Western Liberal Democracy's claims of superior political tolerance and openness. The Yellow Vests also buried the world's "*Je suis Charlie*" sympathy because the freedom of assembly is far more critical to the average person than is the freedom of the press, because rich people own nearly all the printing presses and airwaves in the West. However, the internet (which gave everyone their own printing press) cannot be put back in the box in the West - the bourgeois bloc's biggest fight will be to control the moderators of social media, and they will eventually lose their battle to perpetually hide the discrediting facts of Western Liberal Democracy.

The Yellow Vests showed to all what French leftist revolutionaries like Napoleon Bonaparte noticed in 1789: that oligarchical English parliamentarianism does not prioritise representativeness but mere governability. This explains why the Yellow Vest crisis could go on, brutally, Saturday after Saturday after Saturday for six straight months in a Western Liberal Democracy without resolution, in a rarely asked question). The will of a majority-supported grassroots group like the Yellow Vests could not be (and will not ever be) translated into Liberalist politics because this impasse is baked into the very structure of Liberalism. No understanding is permitted.

> *Yellow Vests: "If the country is blocked for a few days, that would certainly provide a good tool to pressure the government. I hope Macron will understand by the night of December 5th, but we will do whatever we must to force him to drop this reform."*

What the bourgeois bloc had gained from the undemocratic installation of the pan-European project was not shared tangibly or in perception with the 75% "grassroots bloc". The 1%, talented tenth and toadying tenth salivated over the prospects of perpetual and astronomical gains - they cannot admit or realise their profits come at the expense of the grassroots bloc located in France, the Eurozone and the Third World. Shorn of its Social Democratic concessions and tethered to a new supranational government Western Liberal Democracy in France appeared for what it was: neither rule by the people nor even rule by the majority, but simply periodic elections with ever-worsening outcomes, ever-decreasing voter interest and ever-decreasing actual influence. This did not meet the definition of "democracy" to many in France.

Given these current realities, which are the product of historical legacies, a showdown between the bourgeois bloc and some grassroots group appears in hindsight as an eventual certainty.

The record of Macron: exterminating Social Democracy to restore the Liberalism of 1848

The term "liberal strongman" was first used in reference to Emmanuel Macron by the mainstream media as soon as July 2017 because everybody saw what was coming: Macron had normalised the state of emergency, had an executive branch supercharged by the repeated use of the 49-3 executive decree, control over a brand new party (titled "La République en marche!" (Republic On the Move/Advancing) - the last two words corresponding to Macron's initials, and also being the term Canadian dogsled drivers use while whipping their dogs onwards (corrupted into "Mush!")) half-filled with totally dependent, first-time politicians who had absolutely no political power bases of their own, an absolute majority in parliament with an "opposition party" (the mainstream conservatives) which was happy to move in lockstep with rolling back Social Democracy. Macron was gong to rule as he himself saw fit, and that's exactly what he told people immediately after taking office.

Macron had campaigned on the idea that France has bad finances because France's model is wrong - and it's me or Fascism -, which was a very far cry from Hollande's platform in 2012 that France has bad finances because finance is our enemy. Furthermore, Macron insisted that he was the one opposing the rent-seekers in French society: those who can't be easily fired, allegedly-cushy union jobs, old people daring not to die sooner and thus collecting pensions, etc. It's an inverse of reality, of course, but nothing can ever be said about the true *rentiers*, such as bankers, landlords, financial services, etc., in Western Liberal Democracy, who had fully overthrown France's monarchy by 1848. Prior to 1789 all rentiers in France were confined to the royals and the Catholic Church, of course.

Thus Macron's open goal was to destroy France's model as fast as possible - with its "Mixed Economy" concessions and Social Democratic safety net - and this is why many viscerally hated him immediately and viewed him as an anti-patriotic traitor. He said he needed 10 years to effectuate his revolution - paradise arrives for all after he leaves office, apparently.

Many expected Macron would naturally incline towards 57-year old Laurence Parisot for prime minster. She became majority owner of the nation's top polling institute, IFOP, in 1990. In 2005 she then became the youngest chief of the MEDEF bosses' union, the union with the most positive media coverage in France. Parisot incarnates the revolving door between politics and polling agencies which had come to exist in France, which is alarming given the reliance of modern journalism on polls to shape the news and public perceptions.

Here is what his first prime minister, the unknown mainstream conservative Edouard Philippe, thought of Macron in a January 18, 2017, interview with *Libération*: "*Who is Macron? For some, impressed by his ability to seduce and his reformist rhetoric, he will be the natural son of Kennedy and Mendès France. We can doubt this: the first had more charisma and the second had more principles. For others, he will be Brutus, the adoptive son of Caesar. ... Macron, who takes no responsibility but promises everything, with the ardor of a youthful conqueror and the cynicism of an old truck-driver. If I dare to say it, he acts like a used-car salesman."* This was the opinion of the #2 public servant in France of the #1 public servant - Philippe accepted the job offer, and it's expected he'll essentially continue Macronism - House of Philippe version - in 2027.

Macron's first major move let France know where the alleged "centrist" truly stood: He ended the ISL (*impot du solidarity sur la fortune*/ solidarity tax on fortunes). The ISL was created in 1981 and helped Mitterrand get elected. In 2018 it only represented €5 billion a year but it was highly symbolic as a longtime anti-neoliberal effort in favor of wealth redistribution. This is when Macron earned the enduring moniker "president of the rich". The approval rating of the man hailed as the new leader of the free world dropped faster in his first three months than any other president, except Jacques Chirac.

With the unveiling of the 2018 budget the fig leaf of the "3% fiscal deficit rule" was simply discarded for the arbitrary lie it always was: even though in March it was announced that a decade of austerity had shrunk the public deficit to 2.6 percent GDP austerity continued anyway, and worse than under Hollande. Macron's popularity would plummet - never to return - when these cuts to social security incomes alienated his core elderly voters. Many of these elderly voters had grown up resisting Vichy France and then the National Front - they would have voted for Satan himself rather than vote for a Le Pen, but many regretted that now.

In 2018 calculations showed that all of the average Frenchman's wages from January 1 until July 27 went to the tax man - seigniorial dues, tithes and harvest taxes were never so bad. Frenchwomen had it even worse in 2018: due to the gender pay gap they essentially worked for free from November 8 until the end of the year. It doesn't have to be this way, but Western Liberal Democracy has always regressively relied on heavily taxing the populace instead of business profits and the elite

- contrarily, in Iran half the population pays no taxes, including every farmer. The French also could not live off fantasies about hoped-for windfalls from Quantitative Easing: in 2016 just 7% of France owned stock, compared to 50% in the US.

In September 2017 Macron rectified what he claimed was Hollande's failure of a labor code rollback (making it "easier to fire") by signing his own version into law by executive decree. Not only was it not approved by the legislative branch, it was not even debated there. Furthermore, it was written, autocratically, entirely by his team - unions, grassroots groups and "social partners" were given just two hours to read the final 159-page version of 36 changes to French labor law. Protests against this laughable "democratic" legislation were widespread and just as spirited as in 2016, but they not only produced no concessions but not even any involvement. Macron had not yet given a press conference but he did sign the autocratic legislation live on television. This is modern royalism in action, and Western Liberal Democracy swooned over the start of boyish Macron (most especially old ladies).

The following year saw a whirlwind of far-right reforms similarly written autocratically, which would often passed into the law via executive decree. The ELAN law: a rollback in social housing despite 1 in 4 Frenchman suffering from a housing problem. Reforms of teaching and university - to align them with the needs of employers. The *Pacte* law - privatisation of the national lottery and airports, and further deregulation of the economy. Cap 2022 - reduced state expenditures. Fiscal advantages were created to attract financiers from the City of London post-Brexit. (Economy Minister, Bruno Le Maire incessantly repeated: "*Finance is our friend.*") Ending efforts at a financial transaction tax. De facto raising of the retirement age to 64. *Revenu universal d'activité* - called France's Hartz IV, was constantly pushed but never made it through. Mobility Law - to allow major internet, transport and distribution platforms to replace the salaried worker with a fictitious "entrepreneur", i.e. the "Uberisation" of the workforce.

It's an incomplete list, but all these changes thrilled the bourgeois bloc and were a counter-revolution of France's Mixed Economy model with its Social Democracy half-measures.

The 2019 budget contained €19 billion in no-strings attached tax cuts to businesses, caps to senior pensions, regressive tax increases on consumer goods, and cuts to thousands of government jobs. Austerity was continuing even while it continued to fail: the Eurozone's GDP was down 12% since 2008, whereas China's was up 266%. There was essentially zero mainstream media usage of the description of "*austerité*" (or even Mitterrandian "*politique de rigueur*") for this annual budget - the French voter had lost any allies in all four estates, and all this simply must be accepted patiently if one is not to be accused of being "anti-democratic".

And then the Yellow Vests appeared on November 17, 2018. They are still marching every Saturday at the time of publication of this book, July 1, 2022.

> *Yellow Vest: "We will continue no matter what the results of the vote are. There are too many people who have been hurt, blinded, and killed, and we must think of them. All we have ever asked for is not to keep starving at the end of every month, and to protect our children's future."*

The reminder of the book is dedicated to analysing the Yellow Vests in detail, so only the broad historical points of the unfurling of the movement are necessary here.

The Yellow Vests: The unanswerable rejoinder to proponents of Western Liberal Democracy

The initial protest was over a diesel gas tax hike, and it was unknowingly symbolic of what "leftist" politics have become in the West: a regressive tax (one which costs the poor more) was claimed to be an pro-ecology gesture, but of course it was designed to cover the gaps created by tax cuts for the wealthy, banker bailouts and Eurozone economic failure. French leftists almost uniformly responded to the initial protest by implying that the fate of the world's health depended on making sure dirty diesel was taxed even higher. In a literal sense, France's auto industry had made what was now acknowledged as a failed bet to become the global leader in diesel passenger cars: The state had gone from pushing the average Frenchman to buy diesel cars to not just onerously taxing them for doing exactly that, but to also accusing them of being backwards, selfish, anti-ecologists just for resisting yet another tax hike.

Stunningly and electrifyingly to a France which seemingly assumed that Macron and the bourgeois bloc would never be confronted, the protests continued. Nothing captivated the world or France as much as protest graffiti on the famed Arc de Triomphe on December 1 which read, "The Yellow Vests will triumph". But Macron was not Thiers - no troops from Germanic areas were coming to help, and he could not limit the protests to just the capital. France's most famous roundabout had been occupied but so were they in the rest of the country. The state-sponsored repression shocked the entire world - global perceptions of French democracy changed permanently.

Yellow Vest: "We have a president who is trying to give lessons on democracy to places like Venezuela, and yet Macron is firing on his own people for expressing their discontent with his polices."

All of a sudden things had changed, even though France had already been wracked by intense protests for a decade. The past decade was entirely the cause of the Yellow Vests' discontent - and yet the past decade did not matter anything compared to the revolutionary moment. Did the reflective safety vest which French car owners are required to own contain a magic power?

Immediately the radical centrists went into overdrive: the Yellow Vests were stupid hillbillies, fascists, racists, anti-Semites, anti-ecology, luddites, losers, berserkers ruining the economy (the economic impact of the Yellow Vest protests was ultimately decided to be 0.1% of GNP), minions of the Kremlin and fuelled by the misinformation that Liberalism is somehow not the eternal, constant, unchangeable truth.

Why did the protests continue despite the immediate and total establishment war against them?

The determination of the Yellow Vests is not explained by any negative accusation of the bourgeois bloc but by the Yellow Vests' knowledge that a "neoliberal" minority has unfair and unpopular control over France's government - they knew, correctly, in their marrow *that they were in the democratic majority and in the democratic right.*

Previously explained is the reason why the Western Liberal Democratic establishment was not just unable but unwilling to appease the protesters. In covering France I had already reported that Macron curiously seemed to be safely out of France on any major day of protest - there was no chance he would engage with the Yellow Vest protesters directly. Thus the executive branch would not intervene to pacify the protesters, the legislative branch knew that they should not pacify the protesters lest they incur the wrath of the executive, and the judicial branch (pathetically citing the same bogus need: to remain "independent") could not get involved in politics no matter how many laws protecting the political rights of citizens were being broken like so many Yellow Vest bones.

> *Yellow Vest: "It's all a masquerade. The government wants to give police total impunity to hurt Yellow Vests. Doctors reported that what they were treating were similar to injuries during war. This is*

all easily verifiable by countless online videos, but the government doesn't want justice."

There was a widespread belief that Macron would be forced to resign: "Macron resign!" was the primary chant. The spectacular and unprecedented demonstrations hadn't been seen a century, and France had swiftly become totally discredited at home and abroad. After four Saturdays Macron finally had to actually respond to mass social protests - the first setback to his pathetically self-unaware, gaslighting *Revolution*.

Macron's initial concessions were the abandonment of the diesel tax, a slight rise to the SMIC salary (the minimum salary level) and a slight rise for pensioners. These €11 billion in total concessions were mere crumbs compared to bailouts and concessions to the rich, of course, and not nearly enough to remotely achieve the promises of Western Liberal Democracy.

The protests continued into 2019 with unthinkably high approval ratings for the Yellow Vests, unprecedented and ubiquitous evidences of everyday support for a French social movement, stunning police violence and an executive who seemed personally insulted that his subjects wanted more popular opinion in the shaping of government affairs more than just once every five years.

Instead of concessions to stop the bloodshed Macron announced a three-month national consultation known as the Great National Debate. It was a series of town hall meetings in which a president who somehow felt justified to be totally aloof now got twice as much daily television speaking time as Fidel Castro ever did. "Debate" was false because it implies that Yellow Vests had an equal (or even non-negligible) amount of speaking time. When we recall that radical centrism simply does not allow for true debate, then we understand why it was derided by the Yellow Vests as the "Great Instruction" - from Macron down to the ignorant masses; from the bourgeois bloc down to their lessers.

What's worse, Macron put the idea of immigration at the heart of his Great National Debate even though it figured nowhere in the demands of the Yellow Vests. Immigration and identity politics was first an obsession of fascism and now of Western Liberal Democracy.

> *Yellow Vest: "Macron just said 'blah blah blah' and offered us nothing. He was just trying to put us to sleep with his long-winded answers. He should be listening to the huge part of France which is awake, which is fighting and which is suffering."*

The Great National Debate began as a stalling tactic: hopefully the protests would die out. When the protests continued to rage perhaps some in the bourgeois bloc sincerely thought that the Debate would explain to the stupid French masses the eternal truth and beauty of "neoliberalism", thus ending 45 years of mass rejection. When neither happened the Debate allowed the bourgeois bloc and their sycophants to rationalise that a democratic solution "had been tried", and thus overwhelming, coordinated, state-sponsored repression to crush the movement was now justified.

How was the Yellow Vest movement stopped, in just one sentence? The average person simply became too intimidated to protest in a yellow reflective vest anymore.

This process of intimidating a French public habituated to not only regularly protesting but to enduring police violence required many brutal machinations.

Any state's first responsibility is to provide security, but French riot police were not deployed to allow peaceful demonstrations - they were deployed to prevent them. Only those who never attended a major Yellow Vest demonstration could insist otherwise.

> *Yellow Vest: "The police did everything they could last week to orchestrate violence in Paris. They did not lift a finger to stop Black*

Bloc rioters, and the poor Yellow Vests were trapped in the middle. The government wants radical and violent anarchists to infiltrate social movements in order to discredit us with the average person and journalists."

In February 2019 what was known as the "Anti-Yellow Vest law" was announced: The law allowed police chiefs to pre-emptively ban citizens from attending protests, something never resorted to in 1968, and a power previously reserved for judges. The law gave police the power to search citizens without warrants, and imposed fines and prison terms for any protester covering their face even to avoid tear gas. Yellow Vests had already been sped through the justice system with great fanfare, and their trials had received countless criticisms: overly harsh sentences, often despite a lack of evidence, and for people with spotless records; arrest procedures which were not followed correctly; arrests of people who were only trying to leave the demonstration; arrests of people trying to help medics treat injured protesters; and many others. The certainty of not just permanent physical difficulty but long-running legal difficulty should one put on a yellow vest and go protest was thus constantly increasing.

Yellow Vests: "Now, the Yellow Vests must demand not only economic and social justice, but legal justice as well! The government is targeting people from the lower classes with heavy and unfair punishments. Any simple citizen can not only get hurt, but then fined and imprisoned."

It wasn't until late February 2019 that top Western-led NGOs like Amnesty International finally condemned the ongoing weekly violence. It took three months for the Council of Europe to ask France to stop using rubber bullets - golf-ball sized and fired by what French media pathetically rebranded "defense ball launchers" - against protesters.

It wasn't until April that the United Nations called for an investigation into the widespread allegations of police brutality, while also recognising the economic and democratic demands of the movement. The entire Western system was being permanently discredited by the Yellow Vests: the refusal of Western-led structures to condemn a Western leader like France was laying bare Western hypocrisy.

> *Yellow Vest: "I don't know why the United Nations hasn't reacted until now? But we are glad the UN finally denounced the government, because they are using weapons against their own people, and causing people to be permanently handicapped and mutilated."*

The Anti-Yellow Vest Law was yet another example of a Western executive branch making a permanent power grab amid chaos, like after terror attacks and later the coronavirus. Similarly, in February Macron used the false slander of the Yellow Vests as racists to announce that public opposition to Zionism (opposition to the colonialist political project which seeks to establish the state of Israel) would now be classified as anti-Semitism (opposition to Jews and Judaism) even though the two are obviously quite distinct.

> *Yellow Vest: "This is a political operation on the part of Macron and those around him. They are manipulating anti-Semitism in order to smear the image of the Yellow Vests, and it's amazing what a huge effort they are making to achieve this goal."*

The Debate ended March 15 and the mainstream media loudly broadcast that democracy was satisfied and that public opinion would now be incorporated into public policy - few actually believed it. The March 16 protest saw the worst police brutality in months. The Paris police chief was fired, but precisely because there wasn't enough brutality: one of the reasons given by the prime minister was that he had given orders which had reduced the usage of rubber bullets. At 6:15 in the morning on March 16th Macron called for a parliamentary vote regarding the biggest wave of privatisation in 15 years: only 45 parliamentarians were present. The bill was approved, and the mainstream media spared no effort to explain why such a vote was still legally-binding.

For the March 23 protest the army was deployed for the first time since the War to Prevent Algerian Independence. Approval ratings for the Yellow Vests were still between 60-70%. Protests were banned in many major cities for the first time - the mayor of Bordeaux orders the metropolis to become a "ghost town".

> *Yellow Vest: "This is turning into a civil war, and that is exactly what will happen if President Emmanuel Macron doesn't back down! We Yellow Vests have solidarity with all the workers of the world, including the victims of France's imperialism, and we will not stop until our demands for greater economic equality are fulfilled."*

Macron continued with autocratic reforms to the unemployment system and thus the spring protests against austerity returned - it's now an annual event in post-Lisbon Treaty Europe. Nearly 10,000 police continue to lock down swathes of Paris every Saturday. Much of Paris assumes a pose of ignorance and nonchalance - much of Paris is now bourgeois bloc and not proletarian, of course - and tries to make people believe that all this repression is normal and boring.

> *Yellow Vest: "The government has chosen to repress us from the very beginning. Not only has this destroyed people and their lives, but it has destroyed the quality of France's democracy. The job of the French president is to find a consensus and not to act as a tyrant, and certainly not to hurt French citizens."*

An hour before Macron was scheduled to appear live on national television to give his results of the Great National Debate the nation instead watches Europe's most-visited spiritual centre - Notre Dame Cathedral - gutted by a devastating fire. French malaise has reached incredible spiritual proportions. Europe's primary church would remain closed for years. Four months into 2019 nearly as many French cops have committed suicide as in all of 2018. Macron's approval rating reaches just 27% - it was the bourgeois bloc versus everyone else and the result is total catastrophe.

On April 25 Macron deigned to hold his first press conference ever, to finally give his conclusions of the Great National Debate, and he says the words "Yellow Vests" for the first time ever in public. The mainstream journalists permitted to attend dare to ask just one direct question about the Yellow Vests. Polling agencies now cease publishing findings on the Yellow Vests - the last poll gives them a 50% approval rating, and despite the total establishment war to discredit them.

Macron's concessions after the Great National Debate were considered inadequate to nearly all: polls show just 6% of the country called it a success, while 80% (the anti-bourgeois bloc) correctly predict it will not resolve the current political crisis. Macron says he will drop the plan to de-index pensions to inflation (a nod to his pensioner, anti-National Front base) and a lowering of the income tax, which was the only real concession to the working middle class after all these protests. Macron's austerity-inspired "deform" programs, as listed earlier, never ceased - autocratically organising and autocratically implementing them continued until the coronavirus struck in March 2020, and then sometimes even after normal governmental functioning, transparency and accountability totally broke down in that era.

The faux-democratic sideshow thus had been concluded; it was sanctioned by the participation of a fourth estate trusted by almost as few people as who own it; the judiciary had been sidestepped and was preoccupied with sentencing uppity protesters; the legislative branch approved the formal democratic changes to empower the executive branch, lest the executive branch come after them; the less brutal of the police force had been replaced with the arrival of the army; five months of protests - 24 "acts", as the Saturdays were termed - had culminated by merely making clear that there was going to be no solution offered except violence. The French state, Macron and the bourgeois bloc had no interest in democracy, much less redemption.

May Day - International Workers Day - was intended to be so brutal that nobody except a hard-core Yellow Vest would think of protesting for years, and it worked.

From a radius of 150 kilometres around Paris rural *gendarmes* made warrantless searches at highway checkpoints and toll booths. In Paris a squadron of riot police were posted every 50 meters along the approved parade route - an unprecedented deployment designed to allow police to forcibly divide the marchers into smaller groups, whom they then attacked with rubber bullets, tear gas, water cannons and batons. The parade route was turned into total shambles. Protesters fleeing tear gas and rubber bullets entered into the Pitié Salpêtrière Hospital for shelter - this enrages the mainstream media for about 36 hours, who falsely accuse the Yellow Vests of attacking the hospital, and this misinformation prevails as the dominant story of the brutal day. The real story finally comes out, and the event provides the basis for the first French big-budget cinematic portrayal of the Yellow Vests, *La Fracture* (2021). I reported live directly from outside the hospital during that episode. It was obvious what had truly transpired, but I only saw one other television journalist reporting live from the street that day - a woman from Italy's state-owned RAI - so it's perhaps no wonder the French media got it so wrong. In a decade of covering almost every major protest (and from the front lines, as good television journalism requires) I can report I saw no state-sponsored violence as brutal as May Day 2019. May Day was not aimed at suppressing the protesting Yellow Vests (though they were there, of course) but a day to send a message of violence to anyone else (unions, leftist groups, pensioners, students, etc.) who was thinking about protesting anytime soon, and perhaps with the Yellow Vests.

> *Yellow Vest: "Just like at the beginning of the movement, it was the same old tactic from our government. They want the protest to degenerate as quickly as possible in order to discredit the movement. They launch round after round of tear gas, to the point where people are stepping on protesters who have fallen down! They want to scare us into staying at home, but we will never stop protesting!"*

Protests immediately began to lessen - the average person was simply not willing to attend another May 1 on May 4 (Act 25) or anytime soon. Protesting - such a vital part of French culture, and which for decades had been the key to keeping neoliberalism from sweeping the country as easily as in Anglo-Saxon and Anglophone countries - had become denormalised: only a Yellow Vest could handle it.

On May 11 rural Yellow Vest protests were now officially banned in countless areas. Police claimed the right to "control the pace" of protests: this meant that the fronts of Yellow Vest marches were now never-ending scrums between people trying to walk forward and cops determined to prevent them from doing that anytime they felt like provoking a slowdown. A Yellow Vest march was now easily portrayed on television as simply constant, almost oafish violence.

On May 25 Yellow Vest demos went "wildcat" - they stopped requesting permits, in an effort to avoid the now-perpetual provocation of the brutally armed and brutally-tempered riot police. Hundreds were arrested nationwide - the main difference here being that the arrests were immediate.

On May 26 the far-right won June's elections to European Parliament - the only place they had ever been given any actual power by French voters. Turnout soared to 50%, compared with just 35%

in 2014. Three Yellow Vest lists combined for less than 1%, while the Animal Rights Party scored 2.2% - the intelligence of Western Liberal Democracy had partially devolved into a literally subhuman level in places. At the continental level the so-called "Grand Coalition" of Socialists and conservative Christian Democrats lost their majority for the first time ever. Eurosceptic parties won 23% of the vote. An era of unprecedented dissent seemed certain for the pan-European project - the coronavirus era would provide unity, simplicity and an end to political talk.

Ignoring the widespread banning of protests, the fear, the certainty of undeserved violence, the indignity of personal intrusions, the arrests, the fines, the court cases, the injuries, etc., the French media gleefully claimed the protests are finally "over". French media stops covering the protests completely. By the start of June only Russian and Iranian state media are covering the Yellow Vests in Paris any more. The banning of Russian media in the wake of their military operation in Ukraine means that by spring 2022 only Iranian media is there.

In July a "cyber hate" bill passes, targeting Yellow Vests trying to organise and discuss on social media, and Palestinians

> *Yellow Vest: "The paradox is that Macron is acting just like King Louis XVI: people rebelled against him and his prisoners at the Bastille prison, and today Macron has political prisoners and denies democracy. Macron also wants the rich class to dominate, but this time it's the bankers who gave him millions for his campaign and media barons who gave him free media coverage."*

At six months into the protests the government issues new data, which was accused of being drastically undercounted: 50,000 demonstrations, 12,000 arrests, and the use of 13,000 rubber bullets. Media groups counted 12 deaths, 800 serious injuries and scores of mutilations/blindings. What was easier to verify is that 4,000 activists had been rushed to trial, with nearly 1,000 receiving prison sentences, usually of one year.

By Bastille Day in July there was still routine police violence at Yellow Vest demonstrations but the difference is that only committed Yellow Vests were now showing up, not the average Frenchman. When the Yellow Vests broke through to march on the Champs-Elysées for the first time since mid-March hundreds were arrested amid mass brutality.

> *Yellow Vests: "Tourists are getting tear gassed and witnessing major violence, when they are only here out of curiosity. Some people are led to believe that only bad people get tear gassed, but these tourists now know better. If the tourists had stayed a bit longer they would have been beaten, as well."*

However, the spirited protest was something of a last gasp - protests immediately returned to being ignored by the media, repressed by police and watched from afar by the average Frenchman. Eight months of protests and the crisis was not resolved, but it certainly was repressed.

The Yellow Vests were initially thought to be merely Macron's "Thatcher moment", or the air traffic controller strike which Ronald Reagan subdued with the army - the most basic analysis, facts and statistics prove that's false. Once the 2009 Lisbon Treaty affirmed that the pan-European project would be implemented on anti-democratic lines there simply cannot be (nor has there been) structural concessions which oppose neoliberal "deforms", and no matter how sincerely desperate and democratically supported the protests are. Democratic opposition to the restoration of Liberalism is not allowed in France, Greece, the Eurozone, the European Union, the West and probably even Earth.

Many will dismiss the above paragraph as opinion, speculation, ideology and even propaganda but what the repression of Yellow Vests proves is this:

The burden of proof is now squarely on the supporters of the pan-European project, specifically, and Western Liberal Democracy (Liberalism), in general. The Yellow Vests are an immediate, unanswerable rejoinder to the ardent proponents of Western Liberal Democracy.

That's a massive, massive, massive achievement because the Yellow Vests end an era which started in 1991: complete certainty in the worth - in every sense - of Liberalism.

How very far France had fallen from its longtime position as the Western and even global leader of progressive political thought - 1789! Napoleon Bonaparte! the only revolution to succeed in 1848! the Paris Commune of 1871! - and how very much the Yellow Vests suffered to restore France.

The failure is to see Macron as something new, which would make 'neoliberalism' something actually new as well

The Yellow Vests are not the singular result of Macron but the historical result of the failure of Western Liberal Democracy to deliver on nearly two centuries of post-feudalism promises to the middle and lower class of employment, stability, security, liberty and dignity. The failure is to not see the same autocracy and elitism in Macron as French revolutionaries perceived in Louis XVI, and not to see that political progress means to move away from autocracy and elitism towards greater citizen empowerment, involvement and equality.

The entire first part of this book proves that the historical expansion of power and wealth from the coterie around an absolute monarch, and then to a slightly expanded oligarchy in a constitutional monarchy, and then to the embrace of lawyers and some professionals in Western Liberal Democracy may be enough to satisfy the bourgeois bloc but that it has never received majority satisfaction or approval. Nor will it. Nor should it.

An obsession with Macron occurred among some Yellow Vests because of Macron's unprecedentedly arrogant and autocratic style, but the previous chapter proved how in even France's most recent history (Hollande, Sarkozy, Brussels) such autocracy was not at all new.

We should not even go so far as to say that Macron achieved what Louis-Napoleon Bonaparte allegedly achieved 150 years ago according to Marx: a "*maturation of the executive power*" only in order to prove how Western Liberal Democratic executive branches inevitably so discredit themselves that they become "*the sole subject of reprobation in order to concentrate against it all the revolutionary forces of destruction.*" To believe this of Macron would be to not only uselessly repeat history but to uselessly ignore it. Historical progress is linear and not cyclical - or else there is no progress but mere progression of repeated cycles.

Concepts and terminology matters: It is not result of the failure of "neoliberalism", because Liberalism has always been opposed to even the ameliorations offered by mere Social Democracy. The Macron era and the pan-European project give French and European history a stunning new clarity - the 1945-75 period is clearly a 30-year exception in the 1848-2022 history of Western Liberal Democracy. The Yellow Vests remind that the bourgeois bloc will never allow Socialist Democracy, Social Democracy or even a genuine Liberal Democracy. Marx was correct at its very start: Liberal Democracy denounces even the most basic rights of Liberalism as "Socialism!"

In two centuries there has only been way to combat the bourgeois bloc - zero tolerance for their autocratic, oligarchic privilege and appropriation of their wealth and political influence. Until that is done France (and any other nation) will continue to be ruled by them, with all the repression that inevitably implies.

<—>

12

The Yellow Vests: At worst, the most important French movement for 100 years

At the very worst they will be as forgotten as the sit-ins, factory occupations, strikes and marches of 1936 have been: 1936 was, however, the most important political movement in a century - between 1871 (The Paris Commune) and 1968.

This is no small achievement.

If nothing comes of the Yellow Vests and France sleeps for several decades they will be looked to by that next generation of Frenchmen who have recovered their spirit. If for another 50 years France's elite avoids provoking another uprising, and Western Liberal Democracy successfully deflects away from its endless recurrence of discrediting failures, then in 2072 that powerful new French movement fighting for equality, freedom and sovereignty will say, "The Yellow Vests were the most important movement between us and 1968."

So the Yellow Vests are definitely worthy of your attention and analysis.

At the very best the Yellow Vests - their recovery of a class-based and inspirational *esprit de corps*, methods and demands - have redefined and revitalised Western progressive politics, which will hopefully lead to the permanent discrediting of ever-oligarchic Western Liberal Democracy.

What Iraq, Vietnam, Algeria and all the other unjust wars proved is: no matter how many imperialist wars the West fights the final discrediting will only ever come from within. The Yellow Vests did not set out to do this, but in the failure of their earnest desire to interject some public opinion into public policy our living generation must inevitably conclude what their ancestors did: that Western Liberal Democracy will never accede to this point - democracy.

It is facile to say - and I have heard many international leftists I respect say it - that France's Yellow Vests are spoiled; that they are just fighting for a 6th week of paid vacation; that other countries, especially ones subjected to French neo-imperial rule, are more genuine leftists and have more necessary struggles. I don't agree, and I will relate my personal experience to explain why:

Very few Westerners have ever understood the Iranian Revolution, and most did not even want to. This caused me to realise that Iran is actually not that important to most people, despite its importance to me. If I removed my egotism I realised: It is a very big world, and Iran is just one of almost 200 countries. Most people are not interested in politics, anyway, and remain disinterested even no matter how exciting a country's successful revolution is. Most people are mainly interested in their own country, region, community, etc., and my epiphany fully arrived when I realised they actually have plenty of good reasons to consider such things more worthy of their time and attention than Iran. My point is: We cannot blame French people for being in France and for being preoccupied with the unique problems of their own unique country.

The fundamental achievement of the internationally vital Yellow Vest movement is that they have put a contemporary human face - and a politically revolutionary one - on the Western working poor and their issues. They have also put a face, crucially, on the long-faceless White Western working poor.

The Yellow Vests demand the respectability and influence which the working poor should have. The Yellow Vests are not people in social housing and on the dole - they are the people who make just enough so that the French system can exclude them from social services which they deserve and need. The Age of Austerity swelled these ranks to bursting. Thanks to the Yellow Vests the working poor could no longer be falsely portrayed as only recent immigrants, criminals and the lazy. This was a major, much-needed and long-awaited reformulation of the social question in France, but also with obvious parallels to other Western nations.

I have constantly written that all popular revolutions are - to the elite and their enablers - essentially "trash revolutions". The Iranian revolution was derided, by the autocratic monarchists and their bourgeois sycophants, as a "revolution of the barefooted" because it was primarily staffed not by the nation's relatively few college communists but by poor "Iranian trash" who couldn't even afford shoes. This idea was actually embraced in Iran, not rejected, because it showed the egalitarianism, morality and progressive change at the heart of the Iranian Islamic Revolutionary project. The French, Russian, Chinese and all other leftist, progressive revolutions were also lower-class revolutions, and how long they endured seems directly proportional to how many righteous lower class cadres were allowed to endurably rise to positions of policy influence.

"Trash" refers to the American phrase "White trash", and this is the most common description - behind closed doors - which Americans use to describe people like the supporters of Donald Trump, but it's a centuries-old epithet. "White trash" is as potent a term to a White American as "nigger" is towards an African-American - using either can start an immediate fight.

The bourgeois bloc in France undoubtedly views the Yellow Vests as "French Trash", and they have attacked them with all the same insults contemporary White Americans use for their White working poor: racist, stupid, lazy, incorrigible, untrustworthy, unfit for office, impossible to work with, easily manipulated and even traitorous. In a Western society which has been "politically-correct" for three decades such epithets can only be publicly used to describe only one bloc: the White working and lower classes. African-Americans have embraced "nigger" (with the extremely minor change to "nigga", quite often) so effectively that only they can use it publicly, but there has been no such proud reclaiming of "White trash".

The reason why the war on "White trash" is so enduring is history and simple math: In White countries the biggest and longest historical enemy of White elite culture is the White working class, and not non-White slaves/colonial subjects. That simple fact is easily forgotten in a Western culture whose view of history is incredibly short: the class war has been national *and not international* for most of human history. Horrendous Iranian monarchs have been the Iranian working poor's antagonist for 2,500 years - the British were annoying but far more easily removed, and this is an almost an absurd comparison.

White Western elite may have waged imperialist wars since 1492 but they have oppressed the White working poor for millennia longer than that. Their hated of this class is total and embedded far deeper than their hatred for their relatively recent non-White acquaintances. This is why places like the USSR, China and Iran have had Cultural Revolutions. This is also why Western Liberal Democratic elite are so in favor of identity politics and so against the anti-elite focus of Cultural Revolutions.

The West has few who are willing to say this but its truth remains: Removing the hatred and contempt for the White lower classes in White countries is only possible if one progresses to championing Socialist Democracy. When the 21st century arrived the West suffered from a lack of people willing to stand up for both Socialist Democracy and the White lower classes, and thus their domestic politics are now as catastrophic as their foreign politics.

France, the US and the UK: the three biggest contemporary colonialist empires were until recently essentially inseparable in the Third World mind, like New York and California. But are these three Western Liberal Democracies now separable?

The difference between the French and the American struggle can be easily pinpointed: race, and all the useless baggage that implies. Only an simple-minded person would interject with "but French Muslims": Muslim immigration is recent, was politically exploited only since Nicolas Sarkozy and the Yellow Vests upended this phony attempt to say that Muslim welfare and not banker welfare is France's problem. An important reality that proves this point is that, while in the Anglosphere the Yellow Vests were most often misrepresented as xenophobic, in France such an accusation held less sway - so they were mostly misrepresented as mere violent hooligans or "*casseurs*.

The difference between the French and the British struggle, however, sharply diverged after Brexit in 2016: France separated into a different continental struggle - against the pan-European project of which the UK was no longer a part. The UK, having kept their pound currency, was always only a partial part anyway.

Thus the Yellow Vests are a group in which race plays a tiny part but which the failure of the pan-European project is by far the most important factor in their rise. The economic, democratic and cultural disasters wrought by the rise of the pan-European project: this is the ultimate *contemporary* cause of the rise of the Yellow Vests, even if many of them choose to blame Emmanuel Macron. The British are not going to revolt over being a junior partner in an alliance with the Americans, but the French are indeed revolting at being a colonial subject of the pan-European project. There has been a major historical divergence recently, and the Yellow Vests mark this - few seem to understand that.

This is a book about France, and the Yellow Vests are a French phenomenon, so we need to also understand the *historical* causes of their rise, thus the first part of this book. The elite Western class wanted to portray Trumpers, Brexit Leavers and Yellow Vests as all the same but that is a spectacularly inadequate analysis. Where they coincide with their Anglophone Western counterparts is in how they reveal the oppression of the working poor class, which is one dominated by Whites in these countries. This class-based parallel is hugely important, but the solutions offered by these three groups are entirely different.

By July 2019 the average Frenchman had become too fearful to attend the Yellow Vests, even though the last polls permitted showed massive support by French standards. The hard-core Yellow Vests were all that was left - what were they like?

They often had faded tattoos, poor teeth, weathered faces - at first glance some might call them French White trash. That's a term people often don't like - "Barefooted" is much less abrasive. Upon talking to them it became clear: they had big smiles, large laughs, open eyes and infinitely more courage and fortitude than the preening riot cops covered in armour who surrounded them. The core of the movement was revealed - the working poor and the poor. I also discovered that they had just as much political intelligence as I had (even though I am paid to learn), and certainly far more intelligence about the subject of France. They were older, around 50, and at that age in life where one does not fear consequences or disapproval but only to have lived a life of indignity. They are the rightful and righteous vanguard of French politics - though they would never presume any such authority - and they wait every Saturday for new comrades.

Indignity for the working poor is what the pan-European project seeks to permanently install - it is a resolutely Liberalist project ("neoliberal" to some) which is hell-bent on rolling back the modest advances of a merely three-decade era of Social Democracy. Slight changes to the pan-European project, if they ever even arrive, will be no panacea; changing the president from Macron will not be one either.

Forcing indignity on the working poor is the very hallmark of Western Liberal Democracy since the first of the Seven European Wars Against the French Revolution, and indignity is what the Yellow Vests refuse to accept.

And so they marched, and still keep marching.

A structural look - a totally different mass movement

The book *Dans la tête des gilets jaunes* (*In The Head of the Yellow Vests*) begins with an impressive list of all the things the Yellow Vests are "outside of" in order to illustrate how radically different the movement is to France.

"It was an 'out' movement:

- *Out of institutions, mediations, and usual representations of the protesting categories (out of unions for example); therefore out of the radar.*
- *Out of the traditionally supervised zones (the suburbs), a movement born of a geographical alliance (the 'peripherals'* (i.e. the outer suburbs/exurbs), *the housebound of the countryside and small towns) and social alliance (from the workers to the small bosses).*
- *Out of political categories, since it expresses claims of right and left according to our usual grids.*
- *Out of class, or more exactly by an unprecedented alliance of classes that share the feeling of declassification.*
- *Out of norms. by its capacity of mobilisation (especially after the relative failure of the traditional union movements of 2018) and by the speed of polarisation of the struggles.*
- *Out of reach of the usual media discourses. Thus it seems impossible to make this social movement feel guilty by saying that it has*

brought up the Champs-Élysées to the brown plague (Nazi brownshirts), that it threatens democracy and that there will be deaths or that the planet will perish because of its silly need to drive SUVs. The guilt-tripping discourse - that one is playing into the hands of the National Front, extremism and company - does not stick with them.

- *Out of code: the demonstrators do not march as usual, they do not speak like the well-known representatives of the masses, they do not express themselves through well-formatted strategic and political speeches; they do not have the same relationship with violence, they do not play the same part, they do not present themselves as the traditional actors (they call themselves at the same time the people, the small, the middle class, the despised, those from below, the invisible, but also those who will hold and give back the power to the citizens).*
- *Out of the law, or at least out of the law of the type with a moderate respect for the rules of traditional demonstrations: authorisations to march, negotiations with the authorities, mediation by delegates, etc.*
- *Out of the attempt of recovery or rather beyond.*
- *Out of the traditional logic and political rhetoric: these people do not speak like politicians, enarques* (a reference to the National School of Administration *(ENA)*, where so very many elite French politicians went to school) *or commentators. So much so that on certain television sets we see the dismayed faces of the regulars who obviously lack simultaneous translation* (i.e. the ability to understand their idioms, experiences, demands and political point of view).
- *Outside the hierarchy (imperative mandate* (for a leader), *revocable delegates...): they have been reproached enough for not having leaders or representatives.*
- *Outside Paris. It is enough to have spent a few hours in the*

> *demonstrations almost exclusively composed of provincials to understand that, for many, Parisian, 'bobo'* (hipster, literally "bourgeois bohemian") *and exploiter are three very close concepts."*

This excellent list isn't even exhaustive. Taken from the book *La victoire des vaincus* (The Victory of the Defeated) by Edwy Plenel, the publisher of Mediapart, which since 2008 has become the best written journalism media in France:

> *"The egalitarian use of social media, the refusal to be exploited/joined by politicians, the willingness to film meetings with the authorities, the spontaneous invention of new modes of action, the holding of citizens' assemblies: these are all symbols of a new democratic demand, whatever the tensions or contradictions that run through it. Suddenly, the people took hold of the institutional question which, from then on, took life and body beyond the political programs and the learned colloquiums. By evoking referendums, the demand for consultation, the request for deliberation, the yellow vests say that democracy is not reduced to the right to vote. And that a democracy where the sovereign people lose all power once they have voted, are dismissed from the political debate and invited to pray in silence, is no longer a democracy."*

The Yellow Vests implemented all these radical changes in the country *which was already the most politically active* in the West, and which had long-established codes of vigorous political involvement.

They were routinely supported by 75% of the country, which is to say everyone but the 25% of France which supported Macron, i.e the "bourgeois bloc". The Yellow Vests achieved such massive support precisely because they are a completely different type of movement.

What is the fundamental basis of this different movement?

When we condense the two above lists we see that the Yellow Vests are not "normal". What needs to be understood is that since World War II "normal" in the West has been synonymous with total support for Western Liberal Democracy. However, the Yellow Vests are a revolution against Western Liberal Democracy; they are so supported because they are a revolution against Western Liberal Democracy. This conclusion is not widely understood, and certainly not allowed to be discussed in the mainstream media, but it is a correct conclusion.

institutions

A broad word indeed. I tried to encompass everything that word means in a November 2021 column which reshuffled my papers into order for the coming election, titled, *Catastrophe since 2017: How to cover France's presidential election?* I listed how every major French institution had been discredited in recent years:

> *"Emmanuel Macron: Marketed as Prince Charming but who quickly became Evil King Manu I of the neoliberal empire of the European Union.*

- *The Yellow Vests: It's as if France has spectacularly grown a fifth limb, no? Yet there it is – muscled and grasping. By now the followers of France should know what it is and what it wants, but what we can't say for certain is what it can do to a presidential election because this is its very first.*
- *Eric Zemmour: And you thought Marine Le Pen was repugnant? If the 1% can fabricate a Macron out of nothing and in mere weeks, of course they can create a Zemmour to divert attention/split the right-wing vote/divert attention again.*
- *Marine Le Pen: Joan of Arc was not just another ineffectual leader (hereditary, even) of a discredited system – Marine has been totally unmasked by the Yellow Vests. After all the authoritarian beat-downs,*

mosque closures and states of emergency since 2017 – do you still believe Macron was the better choice?

- *Traditional political parties: Routed. They're down to their last party-machine fiefdoms, such as the mayorship of Paris.*
- *France's left: Routed. Always a paper tiger – now barely there on paper.*
- *Unions: Routed by the Yellow Vests. Only the media cares what they have to say anymore, and also the tiny percent of France (8%) which is still unionised.*
- *Mainstream media: Routed by the Yellow Vests. If in Western Liberal Democracies politicians are the new aristocracy then media are the new clerical class. The miracle of transubstantiation which they insist on, and which few outside of their class actually believe, is that the universal value of Western relativism means that impiety can be the same thing as piety.*
- *Catholic Church: France, long-known as the 'daughter of the Roman Catholic Church', has just been embroiled (seemingly rather tardily) in a massive pedophile cover-up scandal.*
- *Notre Dame Cathedral: Europe's most famous house of worship is still closed and will be until 2024. Recall that the fire began just an hour before Macron was due to give an exceptionally rare speech – to finally discuss the then 5-month long Yellow Vest crisis.*
- *France's polling agencies: They are so discredited that the most popular newspaper,* Ouest-France, *has already refused to run any polls ahead of the election. They are perceived as being tremendously biased in large part because they are now staffed at the top by the mainstream politicians who recently lost their public posts.*
- *The French were as dismayed by their country's involvement in Afghanistan* (and their internationally embarrassing retreat in the summer of 2021) *as any other member of the Western colonial coalition.*
- *The war in Mali - launched by François Hollande, and before the*

initial consent of the United Nations - has been declared an abject failure and the withdrawal has begun.

- *France has been in a state of emergency for most of Macron's tenure.*
- *The longest labor movement in French history – the general strike of late 2019/early 2020 – failed, and for too many reasons to list here.*
- *In short, it's a total catastrophe.*
- *I don't mean to be negative, nihilistic or to sow despair, but who can look back at France since 2017 and see otherwise?*
- *Did you notice that I haven't even mentioned the coronavirus? Now do you see how bad it is?"*

any hierarchy, including one for themselves

Simply look at how the hierarchies of every major French institution have been discredited. The Yellow Vests always steadfastly insisted that if they had created a hierarchy or joined another one, then they could have never mushroomed in popularity - France simply doesn't know who or what can be trusted anymore. The success of the Yellow Vests is based on the fact that they actually trust each other, and their mass approval is an expression that the average Frenchmen sees them as worthy of trust.

Paris

In the chapter on the Paris Commune I discussed how the Anglo-Irishman Edmund Burke, the father of modern Western conservatism and his generation's leading reactionary voice against the French Revolution, correctly foresaw that Western Liberal Democracy would be eternally centred around the city. The urban-rural divide is something which cannot be solved by Western Liberal Democracy - only socialism has reconciled the two. It has become the most pernicious divide in Western society, and the Yellow Vests are the French illustration of this vital fact.

the normal capacities of political mobilisation

The simplest way to describe this is: The Yellow Vests were the first French political movement which refused to take Christmas or summer vacation off: No matter how much momentum union-led political movements had during the Age of Austerity there was this guaranteed semiannual pause, apparently under the assumption that urgent political mobilisations are not more urgent than vacation from them. The Yellow Vests also marched as though they never had done it before and as if their lives depended on it - both were true. A Yellow Vest demonstration in the first six months of the movement was to speed into tear gas for 15 kilometres around Paris while being chased by cops. They had no personal security to rope them off from the public and police, like the unions do, and they apparently didn't think giant balloons were absolutely necessary.

the normal capacity of the mainstream media comprehension (thus their vilification)

As a media member (though not mainstream) all I can say is: One cannot comprehend a movement without actually talking to the members of that movement, and from a point which begins with the journalistic ideal of objectivity.

the normal codes of demonstrations: from how they demonstrate to the fact that they don't presume an air of speaking for the masses, as most in politics do

The Yellow Vest killed the idea of the French protest as the height of "militancy". Protests, if they are to be taken seriously, cannot be seen merely as the city-centre middle class out for a stroll. Compared to what the Yellow Vests faced such protests seem like mere virtue-signalling by tribesmen to others in their tribe.

the norm of a specific demand, trying to salvage/reclaim/prevent something

In revolutionary periods political demands explode, as Trotsky pointed out. Their primary demands will be listed in the next chapter.

the normal intellectual and political rhetoric

Such rhetoric is one which approves of, works within and insists There Is No Alternative to Western Liberal Democracy and neo-imperialism. This is the "radical centrism" of the post-1991 West, which leaves no room for dissenters to the pan-European project, permanent economic austerity and for any accusations regarding the possible failures of the West's elite-led democracy.

the law: they are not easily intimidated nor cowed by threats, paperwork, etc.

One has to be familiar with France to understand how one can be "cowed" by mere paperwork. I have always found France's complaints about excessive paperwork to be uninteresting and mundane - merely a way to break the conversational ice by finding common ground, like complaining about the weather. Of far more importance is the way the Yellow Vests defied the law.

The forces of the law were actually the ones in violation of the law, namely they violated the Yellow Vests' Liberalist rights to freedom of speech, press, assembly, petition, illegal search and seizure, self-defence, cruel punishment, resistance to oppression, being innocent until proven guilty and especially the right to hold accountable every public agent of the administration. These are all the Franco-Anglo-American rights which Western Liberal Democracy is based upon - such rights have always only been for the elite, as the Yellow Vests remind us.

politics, or rather, politics as currently allowed to be grouped in "proper" French society

"'Proper' French society" is a euphemism of course: it means "bourgeois", "royalist", "upper-class", "elite", and evincing the aspiration for approval from these classes - i.e. the modern bourgeois bloc. The Yellow Vests show that Western Liberal Democracy is a tool of this "proper" class to perpetuate keep the working poor poor but working.

usually monitored areas (as the most hard-core are from small town petit-bourgeois/their workers)

The idea - and significant misperception - of the Yellow Vests as all hav-

ing country mud on their boots will be dispersed in the next chapter. Simply ask: How can a country which is more than 80% urbanised support at levels close to 80% a movement which is supposedly based around rural life? The truth is simpler: the *"usually monitored areas"* in Western Liberal Democracy means the centre of the capital.

political classes, though this is acceptable to those with the most inflexible and rudimental ideas of what class struggle is

The concept of class struggle is indeed inflexible and rudimentary - at least the concept of the upper, dominating, appropriating class is. Thus the Yellow Vests are not really "*outside*" of the class struggle at all - to assert so is either to have ignorance about the movement or is fake-leftist nonsense. The concepts of the "lower class", "middle class", "proletariat" - I agree that the Yellow Vests have forced the politician from every part of the spectrum and the ivory-tower academic to reassess what "class struggle" in the 21st century means in France, mainly because such groups rarely care about the working poor, or the White working poor in the contemporary West.

outside of any specific roots and yet they are deeply rooted in France

They are a truly grassroots movement, with the vital democratic imprimatur that implies. They are new, but after three and a half years of marching their roots are still growing.

The upcoming chapters will describe some of the components of these lists, in order to delineate the biggest achievements of the Yellow Vests.

What the Yellow Vests did is something very common in cliquish French culture but not in grandstanding French political/media culture: the Yellow Vests talked only among themselves. They were joyously thrilled to the marrow to find that - in an increasingly atomised and lonely Western society - there are other people like themselves, socioeconomically and politically. This charge produced the explosion of demonstrations which soldered them together permanently in a life-changing political experience that may culminate in something greater, but which has already been a once-in-a-century occurrence.

What they have done was to succeed in changing the media and political agenda from that of the rich to the agenda of the people - of Yellow Vest agenda.

What they have done is not just rejuvenate the proletariat but to finally redefine it in modern terms: the office drone working on an unstable month-to-month contract, the 50-year old who never had a job with great earnings potential but with two kids, the most ignored class in society - the middle aged woman -, the worthy pensioner who still can't get by, the student too broke for anything, the shopkeeper being crushed by big box stores - all of these can be the vanguard of a revolution.

What they have done is to replace the agenda of the ecologists, which is totally devoid of class struggle, with a human-centred agenda. The ecologists apocalyptic cry of *"fin du monde"* (end of the world) was replaced in France with the Yellow Vests' cry of *"fin du mois"* (end of the month), certainly one of the primary slogans of the movement. What ecologists fail to realise is that unless the end of the world happens before the end of the month bills still have to be paid, or the repo men arrive to inflict a personal apocalypse.

What they have done is rout the Western obsession with identity politics - which is the diametric opposite of broadly-inclusive class struggle and which was first fashioned by Fascism - by making identity economic, social and intellectual and not one chosen by your parents (religion) or birth (ethnicity or sex). The Yellow Vests are also the incredibly rare modern political movement which is completely devoid of what has been referred to as divisive "gonadal politics" - there is no role for sexuality, but plenty for feminist equality. Simply put on a Yellow Vest and your identity is that of one who supports the people. This is perhaps the most important "*outside*" of the Yellow Vests.

What they have done is to end the insults of the Western working poor - they insist that you simply cannot ignore them in the same way anymore.

> Trotsky wrote: *"When historical development poses before society an unpostponable revolutionary task as a question of life or death, when there exists a progressive class whose victory is linked to the salvation of society - then the development itself of the political*

> *struggle opens up before the revolutionary class the most varied possibilities....*"

That is what the Yellow Vests have done: Their bravery in the face of guaranteed state repression proved to France that there is an unpostponable revolutionary task which is a question of life or death. The Yellow Vests are that progressive class who willingly linked their victory to the salvation of French society.

Once-in-a-century....

<—>

13

Who are they really? Ask a reporter who's seen a million Yellow Vest faces

If I am permitted only one word to describe the Yellow Vests it is this: civic-minded.

They are always referring to the common good and not the individual - in Western Liberal Democracy, with its emphasis on individual rights, competition and elitism, that is a revolutionary idea.

What are the Yellow Vests? It's not easy to define because they are a social revolt instead of a social movement, which is focused on only a single area. Given all the Western propaganda against them it's best to start by refuting what they are wrongly accused of being.

They are "**rural-based**":

The near-total urbanisation of France is a completed fact: According to Aurelien Delpirou in *"La teint de gilets"* (The Complexion of Vests) 92% of France lives - "*according to modes and styles*" - an urban, and not rural, life. This is a complete inversion from 1822.

And while we can argue about the details of "*modes and styles*" the undeniable point is that mass *jacqueries* (peasant rebellions) simply cannot be rural-based in the 21st century. Rural life isn't what it used to be, and while that doesn't make rural life "urbanised" it does means we need new and more accurate conceptions.

The rarely understood reality is that the Yellow Vests are a result of suburbanite turmoil even more than rural dissatisfaction. The cause of this misunderstanding is poor translation and poor understanding of modern French urban development. The best translation for "suburban" in the French context is actually "*periurbaine*". *Periurbaine* is best translated as "exurbs" or "outer suburbs". The far more common usage of "*banlieue*" as being the less-populated barrier between city and country misleads because that refers to something quite different in France - namely, the settlements just outside the city limits but often as dense as the city itself. In the US, for example, the slums are inside the city limits - not so in France anymore.

Modern France has developed thusly: a historical city centre, followed by a ring of ugly suburbs for workers, and then recently a larger, well-built and thriving *periurbaine*/exurbs area.

The *periurbaine* area developed far later in France than the "suburban" areas of the United States, where they first sprouted on its un(war) scarred landscape immediately after World War II. In France the urbanisation of this exurb area didn't happen until the 1980s and 1990s.

To many of France's isolated city elites these outer suburbs are still thought of as being essentially rural even though they are not cow towns any longer - this is the most common home of a Yellow Vest.

These historically new *periurbaine* areas have infinitely more political and social representation than the impoverished *banlieues*, and they even have higher average incomes (€20,975) than the average city centre inhabitant (€19,887). The *periurbaine* is neither urban hellhole nor rural wasteland - they are vibrant places, but what the Yellow Vests have proven is just how little political influence they have in policymaking compared to the city centre. The economic quality of life of those who live there - petty-bourgeois shop keepers, minor professionals, intermediary positions, government workers, working-class employees - have been absolutely gutted by the Age of Austerity's successful imposition of Liberalist rollbacks to Social Democracy.

It's not for nothing that the Yellow Vests began over a petrol price tax increase - 85% of French households own a car. A car is is indispensable for living in the *periurbaine* exurbs but not for living in the city centre, which benefits from well-funded public transportation. It's also not for nothing that the most repeated violent assaults on property were the smashing of the toll booths on the outrageously priced tollways on France's denationalised highways. (Current price of tolls to drive from Paris to Marseille, on the Mediterranean: €61.90 - wow.) Speed-ticket cameras also bore a major brunt of the Yellow Vest's wrath.

This geographic/demographic recalibration should instantly make the Yellow Vest movement more clear: a primarily exurb population, and then secondarily rural and *banlieue* dwellers, who are disempowered by the rich elite and disrespected by the snobbish city centre hipster.

They are "**populist**":

In an elite-forced pan-European project which has exacerbated and manipulated the Great Recession worse than any other area of the world, we can see why the call for "populist" solutions is such a personal affront to the elite - they think things are going great with how they are running things.

The term "populist" is mainly used to describe lower- and middle-class people who disagree with the prevailing Liberalist orthodoxy.

However, "populist" also asserts that it has found the material to bridge the unbridgeable chasm between leftism and Fascism, when no such material exists. A "red-brown" (Leftist-Fascist) alliance is fundamentally impossible - the irony is that it is usually talked of without an open denigration of Liberalism, which is the only thing they agree on.

A far more interesting concept is that the Yellow Vests are "counter-populist", a term defined in *Le sens du face-à-face* (The Meaning of Confrontation) by Etienne Balibar as being equidistant from both the political oligarchy (i.e. Liberalism) and the ideological populisms of the left (the struggle of the working class) or of the right (the struggle of the ethnic nation). The adding of a key adjective makes it "transnational counter-populist", which acknowledges that the ideological problem is international capital, and that the practical solution for a multi-national Europe now run by Brussels cannot be limited to one nation.

> *"It was (and remains) just a **name** to indicate that we need a concentration of forces and an assemblage of ideas to recreate a politics made **by the people and for the people**. With populism 'counter-populism' shares a formal characteristic: criticising the dispossession or disempowerment of the masses in the oligarch regime. Against populism, it doesn't confer the task of ending dispossession to the dispossessors themselves, but seeks and requires the empowerment of the citizenry, therefore pushing its capacity beyond the limits and across the borders that in the past defined the political."* (emphasis his)

Balibar isn't going to openly write that Liberalism and *"the oligarchic regime"* are synonymous, and nor does he openly write that the fundamental motivation of Socialist Democracy is the *"empowerment of the citizenry"*. But terming the Yellow Vests as a "counter-populist" movement has more than just newness going for it: it takes the best of "populism" - resistance to the Liberalist oligarchy - and leavens the right-wing connotations it carries. Certainly, conflating Brexiteers, Trumpers and Yellow Vests as all "populists" - as all the same - is a way to avoid and prevent any serious political analyses.

A major criticism I make of the Yellow Vests is that they don't understand how they need to be more "transnational" - a point I'll clarify later in this chapter.

They are "**anti-migrant**" and "**anti-immigrant**":

What the Yellow Vests oppose is *travail détaché*, which can be translated as "temporary workers" or "posted workers". This is a problem which is specific to the pan-European project.

Travail détaché was created in 1996 to allow European Union members to work across national lines, and on an industrial scale.

Travail détaché has been a way to gut the power of the local artisan/craftsman/small businessman by flooding the market with cheaper labor, greatly damaging the economic prospects of both the French artisan/craftsman and the French petty bourgeoisie, who cannot organise the influx of such workers as easily as corporations. *Travail détaché* is an obviously neo-imperialist device which allows a rich international class to reap enormous profits while eliminating competition and reducing costs.

Being against this, in pro-capitalist Western media, is falsely conflated as being equivalent to wanting to deny asylum to refugees from war!

The Yellow Vests are completely right to insist that every foreign person who works on French territory must have the same rights and salary as a Frenchman, and that their employer must pay the same taxes as a French employer would.

Travail détaché is a subject which strikes at the core of the neo-imperial and neoliberal pan-European project, but many leftists are so woefully misinformed that they do not see how it proves the vital need for an alliance between the proletariat and the petit bourgeois shopkeeper, which the Yellow Vests exhibit. Such persons falsely see these two groups as having opposite interests, when they are in fact united against big capital.

They are "**a tool of Russian disinformation**":

In the book *Dans la tête des gilets jaunes* (In the Head of the Yellow Vests) the authors provided a quantitative study of supposed Russian influence, which the French government and mainstream media repeated endlessly.

In 2018 from November 10th through December 4th there were 200 Twitter accounts presumed to be linked to Russia, which provided 1,600 tweets and retweets on the Yellow Vests. Wow, hundreds of accounts - seems like a problem, right? Well, over that same timeframe in English and French Twitter there were 360,000 accounts which emitted 1.6 million tweets and retweets about the Yellow Vests.

Obviously, Twitter was abuzz about the Yellow Vests because an unpopular government was sponsoring unprecedented attacks on protesters, and not because malign Russian influence had duped 75% of France into supporting the Yellow Vest anti-government movement.

The authors of the book concluded with what should be obvious to all:

> *"Well, even before getting into quantitative analysis, it seems at least surprising to us that the activity of 200 Twitter accounts could spark an important impact and, worse, lead certain observers to see in them the mark of foreign interference. Making this one of the causes of mobilisation of the movement seems a tenuous argument, to say the least. ... This approach doesn't say anything about the profound causes of the movement, and closes the door to all sociological and political analyses."*

They are "**outside agitators**":

Well, they could never expect the rich areas of Paris to march against Emmanuel Macron and the failed leadership of the "bourgeois bloc", so they had to bring the march to them every weekend.

This accusation was constantly levelled by mayors of France's major cities but it held little currency in the small cities and towns, where some locus of activity was necessary.

If there's one thing the Yellow Vests have reminded everyone here it's that France is the world's number one user of roundabouts, a fact repeated ad nauseam in coverage of them. They were a smarter modern choice than the small-town centre: far more people pass through the roundabouts than small-town downtowns. What has been delocalised is not the protests, but French economic success and vitality.

They are "**half-revolutionary**":

An idea among the French left is they have proletarian incomes but hopes for bourgeois lifestyles. Such an idea can only stem from total non-contact with the Yellow Vests, and it obviously contradicts the primary description of them: civic-minded. The Yellow Vests are concerned with the lack of economic equality in France - they are not grasping capitalists.

Nor is it "bourgeois" for the working-poor Yellow Vests to want a stable middle-class lifestyle in modern France - to believe that is to completely neuter "bourgeois" of its indispensable historical context.

So who are the Yellow Vests, really?

At the beginning the Yellow Vests included every class and type of Frenchman, with one exception: the "bourgeois bloc", a bloc which has historically been against democracy and in favor of oligarchical elitism. This was clear from the very beginning.

In December 2018 researchers in Bordeaux published the pioneer analysis of the Yellow Vests in *Le Monde*, which immediately revealed the unique composition of the group.

Nearly half (45%) of all active Yellow Vests were office workers/clerks, and that's even though such workers only make up a quarter (27%) of the overall workforce. Also overrepresented by double (14%) were craftsmen, shopkeepers and lower-level bosses, who make up only 7% of the workforce. At almost the same rate of Yellow Vest involvement as in the national workforce were laborers/workers (20%), farmers (2%) and the inactive (retirees, housewives, unemployed, students). Drastically underrepresented were management, intermediary- and upper-level professions and intellectuals.

The median income of a declared Yellow Vests household is €1,700 per month, which is 30% less than the national average. The poorest

10% of Yellow Vest households earn less than €800 per month, compared with just €519 for the poorest 10% of French households. Thus they are the working poor: not enough to get stability, too much to get social assistance.

This allows us to make a point which is rarely touched upon: the Yellow Vests are certainly not anti-youth, but this is clearly a "grown person's" movement. It's a movement of the people who pay the bills.

In the West the political leadership is so often handed to their totally inexperienced youth class, something I have always found bewildering. Over and over again the youth are told to inspire new political movements even though they have the least experience, usually the least emotional fortitude and the fewest resources with which to sustain their combat - it's a recipe for failure. However, that seems to be precisely why Western Liberal Democratic societies pick them to lead movements which demand political change.

The average Yellow Vests was found to be 45, which is to say several years older than Macron. Here is another rarely touched upon point: This is a middle-aged person's revolt, and a revolt against a youth made heartless by four decades of the restoration of Liberalism. However, a less dramatic - and more far-reaching - reality is that Yellow Vests are people who have grown up with but become disenchanted by Western Liberal Democracy.

The political spectrum analysis revealed the biggest difference was that 33% of Yellow Vests declared themselves to be "neither right nor left", compared with just 22% of the overall population. For those who did pick a side you had three times as many far-left (15%) as far-right (5%) with 43% being on the centre-left. Of course, the mainstream media constantly accused the Yellow Vests of being fa-right, in a lie which was disproven almost at the very start. We see that the far-right is the least represented spectrum among the Yellow Vests and that the Yellow Vests are movement in which the majority is leftist and centre-left. There are a lot of independents, but that's merely due to modern Liberalism's scrambling of what left and right means, mainly due to the alliance between Liberalism and Fascism. As we'll soon see below, their list of demands left no doubt as to the leftist nature of the group.

A whopping 47% of Yellow Vests said this was their first time demonstrating, which does buttress the importance of political independents in the movement. Nearly 9 out of 10 said they rejected violence to property as a way to make their political message or demands known - a civic-minded group is not trying to tear down the community, even though this was precisely the primary claim of the mainstream media and government. Educationally the level of the Yellow Vests is mostly close to the national averages, with an overrepresentation of vocational degrees, as reflected by the abundance of craftsmen, and a bit fewer college degrees.

Their reasons for protesting were dominated by calls for increasing purchasing power, reducing taxes and a better distribution of wealth. Down at the very bottom of the list were ecology and immigration, two subjects obsessed over by the bourgeois bloc.

There were also major numbers of working-class women, a group historically not known for political activism. It's certainly in keeping with French history: it was a women's march which first apprehended Louis XVI and his family in Versailles, on October 6, 1789. (In an infinitely less significant event 188 years later: the author would be born.)

The reasons why working-class women would be spurred to action is obvious: Austerity's biggest victim has been women - this has been justly reported countless times. In general, women are paid less, they are more often underemployed via part-time work, that leads to reduced pensions thus they are poorer in old age - so add in Austerity's cuts to much-needed social services and it's clear why this is a feminist movement as well. In a Catholic France less and less inclined to accept the sacrament of marriage, single parenthood is widespread, too.

Thus it's no surprise that Martiniquaise Priscillia Ludosky provided the first major petrol price petition, which garnered over 1 million signatures, and that she was also a co-organiser of the premiere protest on November 17, 2018. It's notable not only that yet another leading French activist is a female, but also one with roots in France's overseas neo-colonies - they have consistently been the political canary in the coal mine, or rather are at the crest of political consciousness, for mainland France.

So what do the Yellow Vests want, really?

As Trotsky witnessed, during a pre-revolutionary time economic demands for social legislation does not cease but *"on the contrary, expands to an unheard-of extent."* This was proven during the Paris Commune as well.

Here is the list of the Yellow Vests' demands, based on online surveys of over 30,000 people and first delivered to the government in December 2018:

1. *Zero homeless people - urgent*
2. *A more progressive tax system*
3. *Minimum wage of 1,300€/month, net*
4. *Measures to protect small businesses in villages and city centres (stop building malls, no more "big box" stores), more parking spaces in downtowns*
5. *Government program for insulating homes & other buildings*
6. *Big businesses (McDonald's, Google, Amazon, Carrefour,...) should pay big taxes & small businesses pay small ones*
7. *Same health insurance system for all (including self-employed). End of RSI* (social security scheme for freelance and independent workers).

8. *Keep retirement system the way it is now, based on solidarity and thus socialised (no new system based on points)*
9. *No more increases on fuel taxes*
10. *No old age pensions below 1,200€/month*
11. *All elected officials should earn French median income + reimbursement of travel costs if justified + meal tickets*
12. *All salaries & all government benefits must be indexed on inflation*
13. *Protect French industry, outlaw de-localisations* (moving overseas). *Protecting our industry is protecting our know-how and our jobs*
14. *End the European system whereby workers from other European countries are paid lower salaries and benefits of their respective countries rather than French wages and benefits*
15. *Job security. Larger businesses should be obliged to give more employees permanent contracts (CDI)*
16. *Create a French industry of hydrogen powered automobiles*
17. *End the politics of austerity. An end to the interest payments on debt which is declared illegitimate, and start to repay the debt without taking that money from the poor and the lesser-poor and instead going after the €80 billion lost to tax fraud*
18. *Treat the causes that are forcing people to migrate*
19. *Those requesting asylum must be well-treated. We must give them lodging, security, food, and educate any minors. Work with the UN for camps to be opened around the world, while asylum-seekers wait for France's decision.*
20. *Accompany those who are not granted asylum back to the countries they came from*
21. *Create a program for integrating immigrants. Living in France entails becoming French (certificate program in French language, history, civics)*
22. *Maximum salary fixed at 15,000€/month*
23. *Jobs for the unemployed*
24. *Increased assistance for those with disabilities*

25. *Rent control. More social housing and in particular housing for college students, contractors, gig economy workers, people without steady jobs*
26. *Outlaw the sale of French public property (dams, airports…)*
27. *Allocate much more money to the justice system, the police and the armed forces. Pay police officers overtime or allow them to take the corresponding hours off*
28. *The totality of sums collected at toll booths should go to maintaining the country's highways & roads and road security*
29. *As the prices of natural gas & electricity have risen since these sectors were privatised, we demand the re-nationalisation of these industries and the lowering of prices*
30. *An immediate end to the closing of smaller train lines, post offices, schools and maternity wards*
31. *Well-being for our elderly. Outlaw for-profit elderly care. The time of "grey gold" has come to an end, and the time of "grey well-being"*
32. *A maximum of 25 students per class from nursery school through high school*
33. *More public financing of psychiatry*
34. *Write a popular referendum system into the Constitution. Create an on-line referendum site where citizens can propose new laws, overseen by an independent body. If a proposition receives over 700,000 votes it should be introduced into Congress, accordingly completed, amended and discussed before all citizens are allowed to vote on it (within exactly one year of obtaining the 700,000 signatures)*
35. *Return to a presidential mandate of 7 years. The election of parliamentarians to be held 2 years after the presidential election, which permits to send a positive or negative signal to the president regarding his or her policies. This will allow the voice of the people to be heard*
36. *Retirement for all at 60 years old and at 55 for people in professions that are hard on the body (construction work...)*

37. *A child cannot be alone at 6 years old: Extension of public aid to parents paying for day care for children up until 10 years of age*
38. *Incentivise transportation of merchandise by rail*
39. *No withholding of income tax*
40. *Presidents should no longer receive a salary for life*
41. *Outlaw the tax paid by shopkeepers each time a client pays by credit or debit card*
42. *Tax kerosene, air and maritime fuels*

What the list reveals is a primarily economic movement - half the demands are related to economics. This obvious rejection of "Liberal economics" has often been summarised in France as "moral economics", which is an obvious euphemism - based on either fear or ignorance - of using the term "Socialist economics".

The relative dearth of political demands reveals that the Yellow Vests do not realise the incapacity of Western Liberal Democracy to care about how economic policies affect the average person - not caring is entirely the point of "Liberal economics".

Their demands and group composition was summarised in *Dans la tête des gilets jaunes (*In the Head of the Yellow Vests) thusly:

"Among the versions of their demands which have circulated they singularly resemble those of France Insoumise (a left-wing party headed by Jean-Luc Melenchon, who came 3rd in the 2022 election and 4th in the 2017 election)*: anti-capitalism, super-Keynesian in economics, welfare state, 6th Republic. ... Nothing at all like the February 1934 complacently evoked by members of the government."*

(In February 1934 a royalist and Fascist demonstration led to the deaths of 15 people in Paris. It spurred strikes, sit-ins, the formation of the Popular Front leftist coalition and was a political movement unrivalled in modern French history - until the Yellow Vests.)

After clarifying the aims and composition of the Yellow Vests we see that the slandering of them as royalists and Fascists is particularly odious, but that is precisely what Liberalists and the bourgeois bloc did.

What a great list! What a disappointing list!

The list makes it clear the ambiguous nature of the Yellow Vests as regards to revolution.

The list shows there is no overt call for an overturning of property relations in the form of mass nationalisations, but there is a call for nationalising the industries of natural gas and electricity, a call to end future privatisations and a call to refuse to pay illegitimate debt. It's instructive to return to a quote from the chapter on Trotsky in order to delineate the basic definition of a progressive revolutionary country:

> *"Meanwhile the hypothetical government* (Trotsky is referring to a Western Liberal Democratic government which actually stood up to fascism) *would give nothing either to the workers or to the petty-bourgeois masses because it would be unable to attack the foundations of private property; and without expropriation of the banks, the great commercial enterprises, the key branches of industry and transport, without a foreign trade monopoly, and without a series of other profound measures, there is no possible way of coming of the aid of the peasant, the artisan, the petty merchant."*

Jean-Luc Melenchon and his movement also have an ambiguous relationship with revolution: their call to found a 6th Republic is revolutionary, but many of its guiding principles are half-measures rooted in Social Democracy and Liberal Democracy. So it's not surprising that on an ideological level the Yellow Vests - so fundamentally patriotic in their civic-mindedness and so inculcated to believe There Is No Alternative (to Liberalism) - also fail to realise that seemingly all of their 42 demands can only be realised in a situation where a Socialist-inspired revolution has taken place to progress onwards from Liberal Democracy.

It's a great list, sure - but because it's so surely impossible to implement in the pan-European project there will not even be serious discussion about them. There is one lone demand which has been seriously discussed: #35. The alignment of the presidential and legislative elections in 2002 is widely regarded as a disaster in France: it has caused abstention levels in the latter to soar to levels which threaten France's democratic credibility.

Extremely, extremely revealing is that the words "Europe" and "European" do not figure in any of these demands. It shows that there is a widespread lack of understanding of the rules governing post-Lisbon Treaty France.

The total lack of transparency regarding the activities of the Eurogroup and the lack of discussion permitted on the undemocratic passage of the Lisbon Treaty means that many in France assume that the French president has far more power to control French policies than he or she really does. It's a fatal political misunderstanding - some people are playing chess while other people are playing checkers.

This would be evidenced during the 2022 presidential debate between Macron and Le Pen: Macron easily portrayed Le Pen as being anti-Europe because he pointed out that many changes she is naively espousing - no matter how sensible - are violations of pan-European treaties, and thus impossible without leaving the pan-European project. She had no retort for that because there simply is none. Thus, Macron called Le Pen a "vote against Europe" over and over, which she was even though she didn't seem to know it, just like so many Yellow Vests.

There is simply a dearth of honest reporting since 2009 which has engendered a lack of comprehension that *France does not control its own* currency, public services, budget, trade treaties, laws, skies, rails, prices, the ability to end austerity and much, much else. Western Liberal Democracy decides these things in an autocratic fashion, but Macron is actually not an all-powerful autocrat who can implement these 42 demands even if he ever wanted to.

The above paragraph represents a huge problem because it shows how far away from contemporary political reality truly is the most enlightened and popular political group in recent French history. Western Liberal Democracy clearly has two different political realities which exist simultaneously: there is that of the bourgeois bloc (formerly limited only to the royal aristocracy) and then that of masses - the former rules the laws and policies, as they always have.

The Yellow Vests do not realise that not only are their demands impossible in Western Liberal Democracy in general, but that their demands are specifically impossible in this version of the pan-European project. This obvious impossibility means that the bourgeois bloc views such demands to change - from Le Pen to the Yellow Vests - as nonsensical, uninformed and exasperatingly infantile. That is precisely the affectation Macron repeatedly took towards Le Pen during the 2022 debate: a repeatedly disrespectful posture of a professor dealing with a student who has wild ideas engendered by having only a partial understanding of fundamental precepts.

Any "counter-populist" movement should be "transnational", but *especially* any such movement within Europe. The Yellow Vest movement spread to 30 countries and yet within France it was, paradoxically, insufficiently transnational in its outlook and demands.

Trotsky pointed out that communists contradict themselves when they say that society is based purely around economics: *"The truth is just the opposite: the masses make hardly any response to appeals for strikes on a purely economic plan. In politics, how can anyone avoid facing the facts."* It takes more than just economic demands.

The list revealed the lack of an ideological demand - which is to say a demand for a new *political* system, not merely just a new economic system - which is the only sustaining spark that can keep combusting a pre-revolutionary situation into a revolutionary situation, and this ideological demand was missing *precisely because so many do not understand the reality of the post-2009 political system in Europe.*

*I*t is a new Europe.

Now that the British have (sensibly) left, Hungary is proving over and over who has sovereignty and who does not in the pan-European project: they kept their own currency (the forint) thus they do have the ability to push against the dictates of the autocratic oligarchy running the European Union. Countries who accepted both the euro and the European Union - like France - have handed away their national sovereignty completely, but even the Yellow Vests haven't fully grasped that yet.

The French masses did respond for six months on primarily economic demands, but it wasn't enough. The conclusion is clear: it was a revolutionary situation, but the fault was in thinking that a revolution against the French president was needed *instead of a revolution against the pan-European project.*

The group with truly revolutionary potential is pursuing reforms which are impossible without a Frexit or without major reforms to this version of the pan-European project. It may take some years but a revolution is certain because the failure of the pan-European project - for the average person - is baked into the Liberalist project itself, and certainly into the "neoliberal" and neo-imperial pan-European project.

Even if the next step - promoting the inadequacy of Liberalism - is not taken for years, the Yellow Vests still represent a major step in understanding of what revolution means within the contemporary Western context. It may not be expressly written in their demands yet, but it certainly is already engraved in their spirit.

<—>

14

Yellow Vest victory: Ending the West's slandering of all popular movements as right-wing xenophobes

"The Radicals (Western Liberal Democratic reformists) *are the democratic party of French imperialism - any other definition is a lie."*

— Trotsky

It is too facile to refute the Western Mainstream media's "manufactured consent", to use Noam Chomsky's famous phrase, which gave overwhelming support to the police brutality and legal repression of the Yellow Vests. They did this by a tactic which has become common in the post-Lisbon Treaty West: calling them a "basket of deplorables", racists, xenophobes, fascists, homophobes, etc., despite all the abundant evidence to the contrary.

On October 16, 2022, the Yellow Vests were finally allowed to start what they termed "Season 2": normal political activity, which had been banned by the coronavirus lockdowns starting in March 2020, was allowed to be resumed. The pause was welcomed by no global leader more heartily than Emmanuel Macron. Given pride of place to lead the Paris demonstration was a banner of a Muslim woman wearing a hijab and a medical mask.

There had been no conversion during the lockdowns - the Yellow Vests have always been anti-racist.

In July 2020 they had marched to remember the 3rd anniversary of Adama Traore, a young Muslim Black man infamously killed while in police custody.

In February 2020 they had marched against anti-Semitism. At a previous Yellow Vest march far-right thinker Alain Finkielkraut was called a "dirty Zionist" and was told he was not welcome at Yellow Vest demonstrations. This allowed for an immediate media slander campaign which, shamefully, culminated in Emmanuel Macron's criminalisation of anti-Zionism (opposition to the colonialist political project to create Israel) by falsely conflating it with anti-Semitism (opposition to Jews and Judaism). The irony was that just three months earlier Macron had caused international shock by publicly praising the anti-Semitic leader of Nazi-collaborating Vichy France, Philippe Petain. In 2014 France had became the first country ever to ban pro-Palestinian marches. France has the world's third-largest Jewish population, and even though French Muslims outnumber them around 10 to 1 there is no comparison between the political and cultural influence of the two groups.

> *Yellow Vest: "The French media wants to make people believe that Yellow Vests are anti-Semitic because they insulted Alain Finkielkraut, but the vast majority of Yellow Vests are in favor of solidarity and against any form of racism. Yellow Vests are here tonight to say we are against anti-Semitism."*

Not that the French mainstream media cares about French Muslims, but many French commentators accused the Yellow Vests of being Islamophobic because they didn't have enough Muslims marching with them, they insisted. It was a false claim. The problem is that these commentators were looking for Muslim caricatures, not French Muslims. They wanted to see burqas, beards, African clothing and signs in Arabic - but these types of Muslims are not representative of the average Muslim in France. The same accusation against Muslims during the "Je suis Charlie" march was also made, but many Muslims protested then as well. Also, Muslims are a small minority in France, relatively equal to the number of those with red hair. I can't immediately recall seeing a single redheaded Yellow Vest, and yet I would not accuse proudly-Celtic Brittany and Normandy of not joining the overwhelming majority of France and supporting the Yellow Vests.

The most important reason why Muslims may have hesitated from marching with the Yellow Vests is because they would have certainly been the first victims of police brutality. A group of dark-skinned people with Yellow Vests standing together would be like waving a red flag at the idiotic bulls and bullies who are French CRS riot cops (*Compagnies républicaines de sécurité* - Republican Security Companies). Thus, an absolutely vital concept which the Yellow Vests proved to France is that police brutality is not just against the Adama Traores of France, but that police brutality is rooted in class oppression above all. The Yellow Vests proved - emphatically - what non-Whites (and the United Nations, and countless NGOs, and countless protesters) had said for years: French police brutality is among the worst in the world.

> *Yellow Vest: "I didn't suffer from police or state repression because I am White and because I don't live in a poor area, but because I joined the Yellow Vests demonstrations I have now suffered from police violence. This issue* (of police violence) *concerns everyone."*

When Emmanuel Macron put the idea of immigration at the centre of his Great National Debate - even though it figured nowhere among the demands of the Vesters - the goal was twofold: the classic

Liberalist/Fascist obsession with identity politics, and also to maintain the false link between xenophobia and the Yellow Vests, i.e. guilt by association. Liberalist elite now insist that they are supreme not because of royal blood, but because of their incredibly decent blood - thus, the poor must portrayed as embittered people with closed minds who want to close off their communities.

> *Yellow Vest: "From the beginning of the movement they have tried to slander us as racists, xenophobes and crazy people, and now they are trying to accuse of being anti-Semitic. All around the country there were marches this week against anti-Semitism, but the media only covered Paris and ignored the anti-racism marches in small towns."*

I could go on and on with actual proofs and quotes of the anti-xenophobia efforts of the Yellow Vests, because I was there so often, but this discussion is entirely false to begin with.

At the beginning the Yellow Vests were as heterogenous as France itself, so of course it went across the entire spectrum, from the far-left to the far-right. The only class which refused to join were the bourgeois bloc, Macronistas and blinkered Europhiles. The two previous chapters fully described the characteristics and composition of the Yellow Vests, revealing no allegiance, ideological ties or even Facebook chatter which inclines to the far-right. Academics found that the Yellow Vest demands resembled the political party *France Insoumise* (Unsubmissive France Party). This is a political party which is invariably labelled as "far-left" and "extreme left" in the mainstream media (although I rank them as simply "left"), and which is led by Jean-Luc Melenchon, who to the mainstream media is invariably a "far-left firebrand". How can this be true and yet the Yellow Vests are also right-wing xenophobes? They are leftist in economic and political ideology yet far-right racists in cultural matters? What an absurdity and falsehood!

It is an outright lie, but the dearth of reporting on the Yellow Vests means that most people are operating on total ignorance regarding the Yellow Vests, and on the realities of Western Liberal Democracy in general.

What's more necessary to ask is: why are the slander campaigns necessary? Above all, it was to manufacture support for Western Liberal Democracy's inequality-guaranteeing 1%-centred political agenda, and for its false electoral tactics, which serve as a safety valve for actual political progress.

The Yellow Vests sought to put the issues of the working poor and the working class back at the front of the media and political agenda, and this is something which the 1% who run Western Liberal Democracy cannot allow.

Their "xenophobic" crime was this: fact-based bias against the elite minority.

To use nonsensical Western terms: it is 'xenophobia' to question the rule of the 1%

Thus a primary conclusion we must draw from the Yellow Vest experience is that Western Liberal Democracy will portray anyone who tries to put economic issues on the agenda as being fascists.

Just as crucially, they will emphasise only the xenophobia of 1930s fascism while totally omitting the anti-Liberalist, anti-Bankocracy and social redistribution aspects of 1930s Fascism.

The point of chapters 7 and 8, discussing the 1930s, was to make it clear that Western politics has never reconciled (has never wanted to reconcile) with the arrival, meaning and legacy of Fascism. Those groups came to power because they publicly and correctly condemned the oligarchic and autocratic nature of Western Liberal Democracy, which was gleaned from their acceptance of Marxist-inspired analyses of

19th century politics and economics. However, they irrevocably broke with Marxism by replacing the international brotherhood of the class struggle with a self-worshipping and competitive xenophobia. Precisely because fascists (like so many socialists) assumed that Western Liberal Democracy had been irrevocably discredited by the modern industrial horrors of imperialism (such as during the French Third Republic), by World War I, by the Great Depression etc., they concentrated their efforts on crushing Socialism in the USSR - Western Liberal Democracy was already smashed, they assumed. When they failed the fascists were eagerly subsumed by Western Liberal Democracies because they always, of course, sought to smash Socialism, anti-imperialism and the working class worldwide. A major reason why Westerners cannot comprehend their own contemporary and 20th century politics is because they fail to remember that Western Liberal Democracy was broadly considered the most "evil" prior to World War II, and they are now kept in the historical and ideological dark regarding Western Liberal Democracy's subsuming of Fascism via the most false propaganda regarding the benevolence of their 1%-focused ideology.

This brief but accurate retelling of 20th century Western historical development helps us understand why Western politics in the 2020s is so very similar to the 1930s - we are constantly being warned of a "Fascist" threat.

The enormous difference is that - thanks to the Socialist-led anti-segregation, anti-apartheid and anti-racism movements, as well as the much maligned lens of "political correctness" - racism and xenophobia has been decreased to the point where pogroms are no longer possible in the West (and in a West now often reconstituted thanks to unprecedented immigration). There will be no mass murder of Muslims in France, to give one example - too many non-Muslims would come to their aid. Morality has changed, just as morality changed in the 19th century to ban slavery. Xenophobia as a political ideology has lost in the heart of the average Western person - it is only the Western Liberal Democratic 1% which keeps xenophobia going.

It is kept going by the bourgeois bloc-elite because a hysterical fear-mongering against a "Fascism" which is not even Fascism - which carries no threat of Germanic genocides but all the corporate-government alliance which Fascism promoted economically (as opposed to the worker empowerment and egalitarianism of Socialist Democracy) - has proven to be an effective electoral and capitalistic culture tactic to prevent the century-long delayed revolution against Western Liberal Democracy.

The Yellow Vests implicitly call for just such a revolution - thus they had to be deemed "Fascist": they pointed out the failures of Western Liberal Democracy.

The electoral tactic is a repeat of the failed safety valve in 1936 France - the "People's Front", an alliance of all parties centre and left (and green) in order to keep the scourge of Fascism at bay. In the 21st century this new coalition is twice as retarding of social progress than the one in the 1930s because it is not even half as leftist.

I call this new ideology "PFAXIsm", and it is what Western fake-leftists have incessantly called for since 2016 (which is when the travesty of the 2008 Financial Crisis and the Great Recession began to be registered in the political ideologies and votes of many Westerners, such as with Brexit and the election of Donald Trump): a "People's Front for Anti-Xenophobic Imperialism". It is pronounced very similar to "fascism" for an obvious reason.

This acronym describes the paradox of someone marching against xenophobia, but doing so upon the corpses perpetually caused by capitalism-imperialism. By not only rejecting Socialist Democracy but even much of mere Social Democracy modern Western politics sees their "righteous" elite marching against xenophobia while also marching their lower classes off to distant capitalist-imperialist war. The proofs of this are too legion to mention. PFAXIsm is the result of neutering leftism of any demand for redistributing political power and wealth while insisting that non-Whites and non-heterosexuals get an (allegedly) equal chance to climb up to the Liberalist 1% elite.

This is not progressive politics.

The fact that one can be the most rabid "neoliberal" while being also anti-xenophobic shows that anti-xenophobia cannot provide the foundation of a leftist, progressive political doctrine.

The most false claim by PFAXIsts is that they are "tolerant and inclusive" of minorities, but the are only tolerant of minorities who share their Liberalist views. Thus, they are not tolerant at all - they are actually fighting class warfare, and their class is that of the elite.

Above all, PFAXIsm is being pushed precisely because of Western Liberal Democracy's struggle *to keep from being completely Fascistic*: The only legacy Western Liberal Democracy wants to keep from Socialism is anti-xenophobia, but they cannot because xenophobia is an inescapable component of imperialist capitalism, while elitism is an inescapable component of Western Liberal Democracy

The undemocratic installation of the pan-European project, the brutality against the Yellow Vests and the rollback of Social Democracy prove the accuracy of these conclusions.

Thus a good definition of Western "fake-leftism" during the Yellow Vest era was to being flailing wildly, ignorantly and falsely about fake Fascism (and Russian interference for any anti-"neoliberal" development) in order to distract from the obvious errors, inequalities and autocracies of Western Liberal Democracy.

A "progressive politics" which must rely on wilfully ignoring the crimes of Western Liberal Democracy is by definition not progressive, and any other definition is a lie.

The Yellow Vests smashed PFAXIsm just as they re-discredited Western Liberal Democracy

Just as modern Western Liberal Democracy cannot or will not define Fascism properly, they also cannot identify what true Western leftism is even while watching it getting beat up by cops every Saturday. Just as Edmund Burke and the Whigs falsely insisted that they were still the true progressives in 1789 - despite being Rights of Man-denying sycophants to pro-monarchy oligarchs - so modern Western fake-leftists falsely insist the same, totally behind the times.

This why what Trotsky wrote about France in the 1930s remains a valid electoral analysis today, and even across the West.

> *"The whole meaning of the present political situation resides in the fact that the despairing petty bourgeoisie* (the small businessman class) *is beginning to break from the yoke of parliamentary discipline and from the tutelage of the conservative 'Radical'* (i.e. Liberal Reformist) *clique, which has always fooled the people and which has now definitely betrayed it. To join in this situation with the Radicals* (Reformists) *means to condemn oneself to the scorn of the masses and to push the petty bourgeoisie into the embrace of fascism as its sole saviour. The working class party* ***must occupy itself not with a hopeless effort to save the party of the bankrupts****. It must, on the contrary with all its strength, accelerate the process of liberation of the masses from Radical* (Reformist) *influence."* (emphasis mine)

The entire problem of contemporary Western politics - with its schizophrenic inability to delineate "left", "right", "fascism", "Nazi", "socialism", etc. - has just been summarised: Not understanding that *any Western Liberal Democratic party is a party of the bankrupts.*

Trotsky, Socialists, Fascists and even the average European knew this in the 1930s but the message has been obscured and forgotten. This concept also provides the best explanation for the domestic popularity of the Yellow Vests in France: they refused to associate with any of the "*party of the bankrupts*" of the re-discredited French political establishment.

Western Liberal Democracy has waged propaganda wars that it was redeemed by winning World War II. Even though the Socialist USSR and China paid the overwhelming costs for victory, somehow the war provided redemption for the Western Liberal Democratic horrors of industrial imperialism, World War I and the Great Depression. It's preposterous propaganda, of course. The return of Liberalism in the mid-1970s to roll back mere Social Democracy, to impose the undemocratic pan-European project and the repression of the Yellow Vests has emphatically reminded that Western Liberal Democracy is *the party of the bankrupts.*

Must we have a World War III, a 2nd Great Depression and new era of horrific imperialism to remind us of this inevitable conclusion?!

The Yellow Vests are so vital because they refused *to save the party of the bankrupts*, which meant they rendered totally impotent the mystifying absurdities and the obscuration of the class struggle inherent in PFAXIst ideas. Just as one can retort, "the Yellow Vests" to a Western Liberal Democrat who claims the moral high ground over other Socialist Democracy, one can also retort "the Yellow Vests" to Westerners who claim all "populist" movements are far-right xenophobes. These are two major, major achievements.

The Trump movement in the US could never have achieved that: Trump is a completely Fascist leader. He is akin to Adolf Hitler in that Hitler also rejected typical imperialism - his invasions were to gather all the Germanic peoples into one Germanic-only superstate. Hitler famously refused to be bought off by Paris and London with their offers of some of their foreign territories - he wanted to annex only Germanic areas. Trump was the least belligerent American president since World

War II, and his diplomatic overtures to North Korea and Russia (strangled in the cradle by Russiagate, the disproven allegations of Trump's ties to the Kremlin) sent the Western Liberal Democratic elite into an unprecedented fury. Trump generated enormous global popularity mainly due to his rejection of the globalist wing of Western Liberal Democracy and foreign war, but his progressive political bon afides are scant because, again, Fascism is only slightly better than Western Liberal Democracy. The US ultimately has zero interest in political reforms - they are the modern day Whigs in their deluded insistence that they are the world's most truly progressive nation.

The Leave movement in Brexit was a typically British affair in its insularity and it in its latently conservative - and not ardently progressive - motivations. Looking over at a continent in economic and political chaos in 2016, and having a press honest enough to admit the undemocratic basis of the pan-European project (though not being in the euro gave them the most necessary latitude), did indeed produce a progressive and self-preserving result for the UK. It did inspire calls for other nations to leave the EU, which is also progressive. However, simply "-exiting" is not enough: it provides no example for countries not in Europe, for example. This was merely a one-issue movement, after all.

It's vital to recall that "American Fascism" and "English oligarchy" was never discredited as was Fascism on the Continent - they helped win World War II, were never conquered even partially and never openly colluded. Only the intensely racist parts in the US were eventually discredited (thus the end of Jim Crow), as were the intensely autocratic/elitist/pro-monarchy parts of the UK (thus the long, long-delayed acceptance of republicanism within the British Commonwealth, which was established by the London Declaration of 1949, marking the formal beginning of the modern Commonwealth).

But this also means that for decades - quite significantly - there has been no honest discussion about Fascism in these countries. This is evidenced by the fact that, unlike on the Continent, for decades there was no "anti-Fascist" political fight in either Anglophone imperialist nation because they falsely assume that Western Liberal Democracy is inherently anti-Fascist. Indeed, "Fascism" only became a domestic problem in these two countries in 2016! In a world which has become more and more Anglophone and dominated by Anglo culture their 1% neo-aristocratic/bourgeois had never been stopped, until 2016.

However, the world understands politics well enough to understand that both nations are totally incapable of leading a truly progressive and internationalist movement, no matter how much these two nations falsely believe about their own propaganda.

The Yellow Vests, however, were not just a one-issue social movement but a social revolt. The left-wing, transnational basis of this revolt became immediately apparent - they were emulated in some 30 countries. The sale of Yellow Vests had to be banned in Egypt, where the West shamefully helped topple the progressive 2011 Revolution because it progressively demanded a role for Islam in politics.

Had the Yellow Vests not come along who or what would have provided such an easy, accurate retort to the Western Liberal Democratic and PFAXIst claim that all "populist" movements are far-right xenophobes?

The Yellow Vests are primarily an economic movement: taxes, lack of public services, high cost of products of premier necessity - this is the basis of the protest. Contrarily, there is no economic basis of PFAXIsm, thus they are not compatible with the Yellow Vests. PFAXIsm does not care about the incapacity of Western Liberal Democracy to care about the economic concerns of the working poor and middle class.

The political foundation of the Yellow Vests is the anti-democratic autocracy which has been used since 2009. The Yellow Vests do not yet comprehend that Western Liberal Democracy has never cared about the economic and democratic concerns of the working poor and middle class - this book aims to rectify their misperceptions of history.

(For the record: in the quote of Trotsky above I replaced the word "Radical" with "Reformist" because the Radical Party was anti-Socialist, anti-communist and allied with the bourgeois to the hilt. Their name stems from the era when even mere Western Liberal Democracy and republicanism were still considered to be radical. The party was founded in 1901 - it's the oldest active political party in France today, and now on the right-wing - back when when Germanic emperors and kings still ruled autocratically, and thus Liberalist rights for those outside of the aristocratic oligarchy were still "radical". After only a few years, and amid the rise and rise of Socialism, they were quickly replaced further and further on the right of the political spectrum. Their slogan was "Neither reaction nor revolution!" Thus, what could be a better term than mere, inadequate "Reformist"?)

What is the political choice for Yellow Vests and their supporters in a PFAXIst society?

Because of the dominance of PFAXIsm, which attempts to hide how Western Liberal Democracy has subsumed much of Fascism, Trotsky's concern in 1936 that the French would be pushed *"into the embrace of fascism as its sole saviour"* is no longer applicable. Western Liberal Democracy has joined with Fascism - from ex-Nazis in Western German to neo-Nazis in Ukraine - and this is something which would have been difficult for Trotsky to accurately predict. It would have been difficult in large part because he conflated "Bonapartism" with "Liberalism", even though the two are different, the former having genuine grassroots, and thus democratic, support and the latter never really having it.

No politician in France is offering even the semi-Socialist analysis offered by Fascism anymore: Marine Le Pen's genuine National Socialism in 2017 was replaced in the 2022 election campaign with a reversion to "neoliberalism", acceptance of high finance and dead-end reformism for the pan-European project.

PFAXIsm thus can reign forever: Citizens can forever tune in to find scapegoating (in France - of Muslims) or they can find a scapegoating of the scapegoaters, but they will never find what the Yellow Vests are talking about: redistribution of economic and political power, which would be the only way to end the inequalities the scapegoaters of scapegoaters claim to care about. There is no way out if one foolishly accepts the greatly similar tenets of PFAXIsm, Fascism or Western Liberal Democracy.

All experiences of popular fronts - an electoral alliance with elements of the ruling class - have ended in shameful defeat, and 2022 was no different in France. Following the presidential election, the *Nouvelle Union populaire écologique et sociale* (NUPES - the New People's Ecologic and Social Union) gathered together the Communists, Socialists, Greens, Melenchon's leftist *France Insoumise* and the smaller leftist parties (but not some Trotskyists). The goal was to win absolute control over Parliament and to deny the far-right a greater share. The latter was immediately, and foolishly, deemed the more important goal: on the night of his presidential first-round loss Melenchon roared "*not one vote*" for Le Pen in the second round, because he's ultimately a Liberalism-loving PFAXIst. He also began a preposterous and certain-to-fail campaign to force Macron to appoint him as prime minister, which he asserted would happen if NUPES won a parliamentary majority. The NUPES popular front overpromised and then under-delivered, per usual, winning just 25% of seats in the National Assembly, at the very bottom of polling expectations. Contrarily, the far-right National Rally nearly tripled it's best ever score with 15%, which was also a tripling of poll predictions. Macron's coalition actually lost its absolute majority, but because of the far-right. However, such a claim is rendered moot because Macron's coalition will continue to unite with the mainstream conservative party (*Les Républicains*) and they combine for a 53% absolute majority. Thus all issues involving the 3rd Liberalist restoration, the pan-European project and austerity will proceed as they have since 2009. Let's not forget that Macron will also find members of the fake-leftist Socialist and Green parties who have long-been in in favor of such right-wing policies - NUPES is just an electoral alliance, after all, and is widely expected to quickly fracture under the weight of its contradictions and differences. However, these legislative issues are rendered entirely moot because of the certain use of the 49-3 executive decree for centrepiece issues, and also the certainty of Brussels striking down or bypassing legislation they don't want - this also helps explain why not voting was actually the biggest winner of the 2022 legislative elections, with 54%.

NUPES ended in failure, disappointment and discredit, as popular fronts always do. Chapter 7 was published 2 months before the final round legislative vote, and this chapter was published the week before the first round legislative vote, so both proved to be both a prescient prediction of the formation of NUPES and then also an explanation of its certain failure. (Of course, the final vote scores were added here later.) NUPES failure was similar to the "Blue Wave" of United States Democrats in 2020, which also fell far short of its promises - both are fake-leftist, PFAXIst movements which the working poor and working classes, correctly, have no faith in and thus don't bother to vote. As Trotsky wrote: *"a classic definition of the People's Front: A safety valve for the mass movement."*

But it is undoubtedly due to the discrediting example of the Yellow Vests that France's left was forced to do something different. NUPES was the first leftist coalition since the Socialist Party-dominated "Plural Left", which won control over Parliament in 1997. However, all the "*party of the bankrupts*" could offer and achieve was a bankrupt strategy and bankrupt results, again. The upcoming chapter on the unions will point out how the discrediting example of the Yellow Vests forced the unions to actually do something - launch a general strike - but with a similarly wilfully bankrupt strategy and results.

Trotsky promoted something different than the Popular Front: the united front, which is mobilisation of the working class independent of the ruling class and its political parties. This is essentially what the Yellow Vests are, obviously. Indeed, it's so telling that today's Trotskyists are so lost and discredited that they cannot or will not ally with the Yellow Vests?

Trotsky speculated what a good united front would actually aim to do:

> *"The united front does not renounce parliamentary struggle but it utilises parliament above all to unmask is impotence, and to explain to the people that the present government has an extra-parliamentary base, and that it can be overthrown only by a powerful mass movement."*

Only a Yellow Vest party would actually do this in French parliament, not any of the NUPES alliance. The entire history of Western Liberal Democracy is to hide or paper over its oligarchy, which is to say that very "*extra-parliamentary base*" which undemocratically controls policy.

The failure of France's "leftist" Popular Front in the late 1930s proved that Western Liberal Democracy would never cooperate with any kind of leftism, even fake-leftism. Thus, Fascism came to power because the average European realised that Western Liberal Democracy is autocratic, plutocratic and a perpetual dead end.

And yet 2027 cannot be a repeat of 1940 even if Marine Le Pen wins, as expected, because her "Fascism" is not actually Fascism. Human history is not uselessly cyclical but linear: as much as PFAXIsm wants to insist otherwise, post-2016 "Fascism" is not the same as 1930s Fascism.

> Trotsky wrote of France: *"The policy of coalition with the bourgeoisie must be paid for by the proletariat with years of new torments and sacrifices, if not by decades of fascist terror."*

What Trotsky could not have foreseen is the crucial reality I keep stressing: Western Liberal Democracy has subsumed Fascism, thus decades of Fascist terror by France and the West has been the global reality long after the 1930s.

"*On the other hand, if we continue to mark time, the pre-revolutionary situation will inevitably be changed into one of counterrevolution, and will bring on the victory of fascism,* " wrote Trotsky, correctly. Almost a century later the analysis must incorporate the political changes since then: if the French merely tread water from the Yellow Vests' creation of a pre-revolutionary situation (which then became revolutionary with the 2019-20 general strike) then fascism will continue its long victory streak in the West.

In between the first and second rounds of the 2017 election I promoted Macron as the worse choice between him and Le Pen. I was proven totally right that Macron was not some friend of anti-racism/pro-Muslim movements, and that his economic project would gut every Frenchman regardless of color or religion. I was also proven totally right that Macron was as authoritarian as a Fascist - simply look at the Yellow Vests, the normalisation of the state of emergency and his autocratic governing methods.

In between the first and second rounds of the 2022 election I also promoted a vote of Le Pen over Macron. Once again it was the only progressive gain which could have been made: Giving Le Pen power would have shown that Western Liberal Democracy is elitist, Fascist and awful. Donald Trump discredited the US system domestically in a supremely effective way. By re-electing Macron France has merely postponed its similarly honest examination of what their system really is: both Fascist and PFAXIst.

<—>

15

Yellow Vest victory: The death of Western parliamentary democracy as the most progressive government

The fight against autocracy and monarchy - the dominant theme of progressive politics in human history - has always begun with the fight for a parliament: the creation of a group representing some interest beyond the royal executive decree, and with the power to affect the lawmaking process and general governance.

People often do not realise what a historically recent concept this is in human society - the primacy of the people and not just a person.

Perhaps the biggest change for the average Frenchman in the changeover from Charles X of the Bourbons to Louis-Philippe of the House of Orleans in 1830 is that the latter accepted to be the king "of the French" instead of the king "of France". This brand change did nothing on a practical level but it reflected the legacy initiated in 1789: the people's newfound sense that only they bestow legitimacy, instead of a claimed divine theocratic right. Louis-Philippe would be the last unelected royal in France, but it took World War I to wipe away arrogant, unelected royalty in most of Europe (12 monarchs still reign in Europe, which has about 45 nations). Thus the change from millennia of a falsely divine monarchy is a very historically recent one, and much of this book aims to remind that the cultural traits of autocracy - for those who cannot divine it in the governance style of Emmanuel Macron - is pernicious and pervasive today, still.

If, as the last chapter proved, Western voters are herded - or brow-beaten - into supporting parties which falsely claim to be progressive but are merely PFAXIst (Popular Fronts Against Xenophobia but for Imperialism) then is Western parliamentarianism a total sham?

The problem is not in the idea of a parliament of course - which would be to say of representative democracy - but the parliamentarianism habitually produced by Western Liberal Democracy, where power is not based on reflecting the popular will but where power comes from an extra-parliamentary base controlled by an elite. English-style parliamentarianism - French revolutionaries realised in 1789 - does not prioritise representativeness but mere governability of the masses on behalf of an oligarchy which has been only extended only a bit further than the royal family.

The refusal of this "extra-parliamentary base" to care for the needs and will of the working-poor was immediately obvious in 1848, 1871, 1936, 1983 and in the results produced by the culmination of this 3rd imposition of Liberalism - the undemocratic installation of the pan-European project. European Parliament is the only directly elected institution of the European Union.

Marx pegged the perennial problem of of Western Liberal Democratic parliamentarianism at its very start:

> *"In the domain of general bourgeois interests the National Assembly proved itself so barren that, for instance, the discussion over the Paris-Avignon railroad, opened in the winter of 1850, was not yet ripe for a vote on December 2, 1851. Wherever it did not oppress or was reactionary the bourgeoisie was smitten with incurable barrenness."*

Being oppressive and reactionary is a well-known criticism to all, but just as vital is Western parliamentary democracy's "*incurable barrenness*". This is a synonym for more common contemporary terms: "dysfunctional", "paralysis", "ungovernable", "unworkable", "not agreement-capable", etc. These are different ways to stress that Western Liberal Democracy *does not actually want broad economic growth which extends to the working-poor and working classes*: that would empower the average person, and thus encourage them to demand more political and economic power from the ruling post-absolute monarchy oligarchies. Western parliaments are designed to fail the average person on purpose.

As we will see in the next chapter: the best way to make sure a general strike fails is to make sure people don't have any savings to strike with. The same concept applies in non-general strike eras: the Western Liberal Democratic oligarchy wants dependence on bosses and creditors, not empowered and free workers and citizens. Thus wherever Western Liberal parliaments do not oppress or are reactionary its incurable barrenness is rendered obvious by the spectacular and broad creative successes of socialist-inspired nations like China; a century ago the shaming example was the USSR.

Countries victimised by imperialism know that Western Liberal Democracy only overcomes barrenness for projects which are of indispensable economic need to the oligarchy - railroads and highways to move natural resources to ports, military technology, the creation of lavish neighbourhoods in city centres for Western expatriates to enjoy, etc. Barrenness is strictly enforced regarding projects which would lead to the empowerment of the average citizen - well-funded schools, job training, equal pay for women, a dependable social safety net for times of difficulty, etc. and etc.

Indeed, how much of Western culture's existentialism is a result of this certainty of political "*barrenness*"; this ineffectiveness; this apathy which leads to a dull acceptance of the status quo of a society which promises only an endless and rigged competition governed by cruel elites?

The Age of Austerity - which is to say the initial neo-imperial rule of the neoliberal empire that is the EU - is reminding White Europe how they have ruled Brown people for centuries: with disregard for everyone but the 1%.

The Yellow Vests' misplaced hope that RICs can overcome oligarchical parliamentarianism

Overcoming this "*incurable barrenness*", which enforces perpetual difficulty for the working poor class, is the implicit goal encapsulated by the most popular demand of the Yellow Vests which would change France's political structure: a demand for *RICs* (Citizens' Initiated Referendums). Many have even told me they will not stop marching until this is approved. *RICs* are the primary Yellow Vest solution to the failed representativeness inherent in Western Liberal Democracy, but it's already been proven to be a failed solution.

The ability of citizens to initiate referendums is not a revolutionary concept - Switzerland has had it for over 160 years. In their over 160 referendums about 55% have been approved by voters, but most of the time the watered-down government counter-proposal was accepted and not the original initiative idea. It's a mistake that so many Yellow Vests are so invested in this very minor political advance. Emmanuel Macron and French elite are dead-set against even this modest change which has been employed for generations right next door in perhaps the dullest of nations, which reflects how greedily they want to retain their autocratic and nearly-royalist power.

> *Yellow Vest: "There are not enough young people who are joining the Yellow Vests, that is true. I am trying to persuade my friends and*

classmates to join more often, because we must have a convergence of the struggles of both the Yellow Vests and the youth of France."

What is more important is what this demand for *RICs* actually expresses: It is presented as a solution for more representative government in Western Liberal Democracy, and at granting regular citizen involvement in Liberalism's policy-making process. In reality, I believe many Yellow Vests have entirely given up on parliamentarianism in favor of direct rule by the citizen. It's a laudable idea, and maybe one day human society will be so efficient and technologically spectacular that all citizens can take the necessary time to take an effective part in daily governance, but simply cross the border - Switzerland is no egalitarian paradise, and is routinely ranked as the most expensive country to live in in the world. RICs are not a panacea for Western Liberal Democracy's oligarchic and fundamentally anti-democratic structures.

The Yellow Vests' key demand of referendums reflects the fact that since the Lisbon Treaty in 2009 there is now only one route of exchange between lawgivers and citizens in France - the vote. As the writing on the back of one Yellow Vest's vest put it, a bit vulgarly: *"Making love once every 5 years is not a love life - voting once every 5 years is not a political life."* It should be remembered that this is not only a reference to the executive branch vote, but the vote for the legislature as well.

For decades France was exceptional in the West for having the route of exchange of public protests. However, beginning with Nicolas Sarkozy's hiking of the retirement age in 2010 French protests have been almost always fully ignored. The Yellow Vests incarnate the vital insistence that public protests must be a part of the political process, and they have bravely paid a heavy personal price for the benefit of the average Frenchman.

Since the installation of the Lisbon Treaty French protests have been unable to do wrest concessions from their national politicians, who are beholden to Brussels and the rules of the pan-European project. However, Macron went even further in autocratically limiting the circle of influence in policymaking by totally and publicly dismissing any role for any intermediaries - unions, NGOs, grassroots groups, etc. Even the Pope could not have wrested a bit of charity from Macron - religion, infamously, can play zero part in modern French political discourse - thus French policymaking is mostly an affair between a trinity of God, Brussels and Macron.

In Western Liberal Democracy the primacy of parliament is always implied as the heart of their governmental project, as opposed to, say, Islam, the Communist Party, the tribe, etc. However, it's instructive to be reminded how little French parliament has changed from when Edmund Burke examined its very first rolls in 1790:

"Judge, Sir, my surprise when I found that a very great proportion of the assembly (a majority, I believe, of the members who attended) was composed of practitioners in the law." From its very inception, in something that should be obvious to all, Western Liberal Democracy means rule by provincial lawyers. The insult there is not "provincial", but "lawyers".

> *"Who could conceive that men who are habitually meddling, daring, subtle, active, of litigious dispositions and unquiet minds would easily fall back into their old condition of obscure contention and laborious, low, unprofitable chicane*(ry). *Who could doubt but that, at any expense to the state, of which they understood nothing, they must pursue their private interests, which they understand but too well. ... To the faculty of law was joined a pretty considerable proportion of the faculty of medicine. ... Then came the dealers in stocks and funds, who must be eager, at any expense, to change their ideal paper wealth for the more solid substance of land. ... To observing men it must have appeared from the beginning that the majority of the Third Estate, in conjunction with such a depiction from the clergy as I have described* (from earlier: *"mere country curates... habitually guided in their petty village concerns"), whilst*

> *it paused the destruction of the nobility, would inevitably become subservient to the worst designs of individuals in that class."*

Who would disagree with Burke's low estimation of Liberalist parliamentarians: *"men formed to be instruments, not controls"*? Whose "*instruments*" are such legislators? Burke gives the answer: the worst individuals of the de-titled royal class, or - to put it in today's terms - the 1%. In 2017 fewer than 2 percent of legislators in the National Assembly came from the working class. Contrarily, a common Western Liberal Democratic criticism of the parliaments of Cuba, Iran, China, etc., is that there are too many people who are "unqualified". They are accused of this because they lack university degrees, whereas in socialist-inspired democracy morality, devotion to the people and grassroots esteem are seen as good qualifications for public office.

> *Yellow Vest: "Macron simply must not have a legislative majority again. The last five years were such a catastrophe. I hope the French people join us in the streets again because the prices of products even which are totally produced in France have risen shamefully high."*

The incurably barren future of Western Liberal Democratic parliaments was accurately summed up by Burke: *"If possible, the next Assembly must be worse than the present."*

While only today's reactionaries accept Burke's elitist views without skepticism they are useful - we must scroll through Western Liberal Democratic history to remind ourselves that their parliaments have been discredited in every generation.

It's worthwhile to note Marx's assessment of Western Liberal Democracy as practiced in the United States - we see how the complaints about Congress have been monotonously similar for two centuries:

> *"Nowhere do 'politicians' form a more separate, powerful section of the nation than in North America. There, each of the two great parties which alternately succeed each other in power is itself in turn controlled by people who make a business of politics, who speculate on seats in the legislative assemblies of the Union as well as of the separate states, or who make a living by carrying on agitation for their party and on its victory are rewarded with positions."*

The 1852 popular vote in France which sanctioned Louis-Napoleon Bonaparte's self-coup against French parliament was that generation's similar condemnation of English-style oligarchic parliamentarianism. To remind of what Marx wrote in his writings on the Paris Commune:

> *"The* (2nd) empire (of Louis-Napoleon Bonaparte), *with the coup d'état for its birth certificate, universal suffrage for its sanction, and the sword for its sceptre, professed to rest upon the peasantry, the large mass of producers not directly involved in the struggle of capital and labor.* ***It professed to save the working class by breaking down parliamentarianism, and, with it, the undisguised subserviency of government to the propertied classes.*** *It professed to save the propertied classes by upholding their economic supremacy over the working class; and, finally, it professed to unite all classes by reviving for all the chimera of national glory."* (emphasis mine)

Louis-Napoleon Bonaparte was a Bonapartist and not a Socialist Democrat, but he would not have won the biggest popular election in history until that point by professing to save the French sharecropper and small farmer *by defending* a widely-detested, oligarchical parliament full of open royalists. These royalists and elitists colluded with Germanic autocrats to topple Louis-Napoleon Bonaparte in 1871 but ultimately failed to restore an unelected, feudal monarch in France.

However, across the 21st century is the accusation that the West has become a "neo-feudal" society precisely because the ideology of France's first parliamentarians has still not been checked by a victory of Socialist Democracy.

In 1934 Trotsky showed that Western Liberal Democracy still had achieved no record of producing a parliament which puts the needs of the average person first, and not those of the elite: *"On the parliamentary road the socialist proletariat has nowhere and never conquered power nor ever, as yet, even drawn close to it."* As soon as they drew close a Popular Front sprouted to hand power right back to the reactionary bourgeois bloc. We can obviously add 1983, 2012 and the Yellow Vests to this list of Liberalist parliamentary failure in France to remind the problem is not feudalism, but Liberalism.

Whereas elections are now just once every five years, in Western Liberal Democracy with American characteristics elections are perpetual. This has turned politics into something like a competition between two sports teams, and the emphasis on winning votes has totally gutted American politics of any moral substance. Of course taking both the ideology and the morality out of politics renders the average person totally unconnected from the political process.

> As Trotsky wrote: *"As if the fate of the people depended upon a lesser or greater number of municipalities of the 'left' in 1935, and not on the moral, social and political position of millions of workers and peasants during the next period!"*

Starting in 2018 the Yellow Vests had essentially the exact same condemnations as Burke, Marx and Trotsky, even if their primary target was Macron and not parliament. However, to believe that Macron was the main problem with the French executive branch is as misguided as the belief that *RICs* will solve the failures of the French legislative branch.

The autocracy of Macron hid the oligarchy of Parliament

All of France saw in 2017 that the victory of both Macron and of his new parliamentary party was undoubtedly centred around a rejection of the mainstream duopoly, but Macron was legally justified to falsely claim that he held a broad mandate of the people. Macron, in policies and personality, was only elected by a "bourgeois bloc" of around 25%, but nothing could compel Macron to not govern autocratically.

Macron knew this, and did not care. He refused to be hindered by a legislature he dominated and ignored exactly like the kings who followed Napoleon Bonaparte. Macron routinely bypassed a parliament *in which his party held an absolute majority* via using the 49-3 executive decree, simply in order to avoid the bad publicity certain to be created via public debates of far-right economic policies. This is something which should be grasped for how shockingly autocratic it truly was - it is routinely ignored by the Mainstream Media.

There is a second path at influencing the executive in Western Liberal Democracy - intermediaries - but Liberalist lawmakers only listen to paid lobbyists, in a case of obviously undemocratic corruption. Macron has infamously stated that he does not like intermediaries, but what is Parliament but the most powerful intermediary possible between the head civil servant and the citizens/workers? Of course Macron doesn't like any intermediaries - they seek to leaven his autocratic decision-making, and it's shocking he is allowed to persist with such a public admission.

Thus, many Yellow Vests mistakenly believed that France's problem was centred in Macron and not in its Western Liberal Democratic structures. This engendered a widespread desire to speak to Macron in person, which was even caricatured in France's first big-budget movie about the Yellow Vests, *La Fracture*. In the bourgeois artist protagonist's final climax of semi-enlightenment she bestows upon the Yellow Vest character a drawing of him crawling up the sewers to Elysee Palace to finally be able to talk with Macron, which the Yellow Vest character had insisted was the solution which would result in policymaking that favoured the lower classes. When all the checks and balances of Western Liberal Democracy are tested it's clear - autocracy by the 1% is what is preserved, and the average person should just head to the sewers for understanding.

The key is to realise that autocracy did not begin with Macron: An oft-cited concern in France since 2017 is that the 5th Republic (founded 1958) gives the French chief executive power which is unrivalled among his Western peers.

> Edwy Plenel wrote of the Yellow Vest movement: *"It's true motor is a demand for social and political equality where, for the first time, the institutional question of French presidentialism, the power of one to to confiscate the will of all, is swept by a popular anger."*

Critically, Macron comes after Francois Hollande's repeated and flagrant use of the 49-3 executive decree, and both reveal that Western Liberal Democracy with French characteristics no longer puts parliament at the centre of their governance. This evolution would be in line with Western Liberal Democracy's trend towards greater and greater adoption of fascist tactics, and it would also be in line with the historical base of Liberalism: the pro-autocracy view of elitist oligarchs.

> *Yellow Vest: "No I'm not giving up, no. I've not been doing this for 3.5 years just so I can stop tomorrow, no way. Either we win or I die, and these guys will carry on. People should never stop, they should keep going, because that's what the governments - all governments are hoping - that people just give up and let them do their thing."*

Open defiance of the claim of the centrality of parliamentary life in Western democracy makes France today more like the Bonapartism of Louis-Napoleon (rule via the people's mandate but on behalf of the bankers, bourgeois and pro-royalists) and not the more leftist Bonapartism of Napoleon (rule via the people's mandate and on behalf of the moderate wing of the people's revolution).

But this suddenly recognition of an overly-powerful executive branch merely served as a safety valve to obscure the problems inherent and routine in Western Liberal Democracy itself: It's not really presidential power which the repression of the Yellow Vests covered in disgrace, but parliamentary and judiciary power as well.

A necessary and simple question which Western Liberal Democracy wishes to avoid is: Why did the Yellow Vest protests *go on for so very long*? From November 2018 until June 2019 every Saturday represented a disaster of democracy, after all.

After creating an empowered parliament, Western Liberal Democracy's main political advance was to wrest the judiciary from the nobility, and to give it a supposed independence in order to defend the new rights of Liberalism. The failure of the judicial branch to stop the repression of the Yellow Vests could take up an entire chapter in this book, but it takes only one paragraph to recognise the depth of the importance of its obvious refusal to do so:

The protests were not resolved because they were essentially protests against Western Liberal Democracy itself, and thus all branches of government were united against the movement as long as the movement insisted on moving. The executive branch refused to end the crisis if that meant changing its policy-making style away from autocracy; the legislative branch could not or would not intervene - the infamous "anti-Yellow Vest law" showed whose side they were on; the laughable claims of Western Liberal Democracy to have a totally depoliticised (and thus "independent") judicial branch revealed the truth of its obvious bias against the majority's conception of justice and certainly against extending the basic rights of Liberalism to the average citizen. Because the Yellow Vests could not be denounced as "Socialists!" - it's no longer a criminal offence in France - it became so vital to falsely portray the Yellow Vests as hooligans (*casseurs*), i.e. criminals and not political protesters. This absolved the judicial branch, especially.

However, if Western Liberal Democracy is committed to supporting the advantages of and run by ex-nobles and the rich, can we be surprised that any reduction of their rights or powers is considered a crime against the entire nation?

Ultimately, we have a case where the executive, legislative and judicial branches are in total collusion - against permitting the most basic rights of Liberalism. To paraphrase Marx as cited earlier: even the rights of Liberalism are denounced as "Socialism!"

With the legislative, executive and judicial branches thus closed off to democratic input, many concerned French citizens they had only one resort - a direct appeal to the top cop. So we see why the Yellow Vests focused so much on Macron even though the primacy in non-autocratic politics theoretically lays with the legislative branch.

However, presidential power in contemporary France - in the context of a supranational government centred in Brussels - is actually now more comparable to a mere provincial governor. The obfuscation of the actual power in France - the EU and the Eurogroup - has created this confusion among the Yellow Vests and most of the rest of the world.

Stalin was both exasperated and accurate when he famously said, *"Social Democracy and fascism are not opposite - they are twins."* The accurate statement in a post-Lisbon Treaty Europe is that Western Liberal Democracy and fascism are not opposite - they are twins.

Western Liberal Democracy as a false 'Third Way' between autocracy and socialism

Ultimately, the failure lies in the fact that Western Liberal Democracy simply is not a democracy, in the sense that neither majority rule nor the supreme rule of the people is ever achieved, but only consistent Liberalist rights for a minority - namely, a rich oligarchy.

What the Yellow Vests prove is the fallacy of Western Liberal Democracy's implicit claim of being a "Third Way" - first between Socialism and autocracy, and now between Socialism and Fascism. The fallacy was to believe that Western Liberal Democracy is not autocratic in nature, and the repression of the Yellow Vests reminds us of this.

What the Yellow Vests - who are not (yet) revolutionaries for Socialist Democracy - actually greatly resemble in Western Liberal Democracy is a third-party.

A two-party duopoly is inevitably formally created in Western Liberal Democracy. When a new, grassroots, powerful third party actually sprouts one of the duopoly usually absorbs and adulterates them. However, the French political establishment was unable to resolve the embarrassing, long-running Yellow Vest debacle precisely because the only changes allowed in Western Liberal Democracy are those approved by the bourgeois bloc, which the Yellow Vests oppose.

Western Liberal Democracy has always been essentially a mono-party system - dedicated to upholding the elite - and thus it greatly resembles both autocratic oligarchy and modern fascism. There is no "third way" - the choice is either autocracy (rule by one person and his coterie) or Socialism (rule by all). The undemocratic monopoly of power by any small group - oligarchy - has the same practical effect on the 99% as autocracy.

The entire point of Liberalism in 1789 was to finally constrain the executive, and mainly via a parliament that was supposed to reflect and enact the will of the majority.

However, the Macron era confirms the Liberalist trend since 9/11 in the US and since 2009 in Europe of undeniable and seemingly irrevocable executive branch power grabs which neuter the ability of the legislative branch to play a role in policymaking - it's a major return to the monarchical autocracy of 1788.

Parliamentary democracy is certainly a positive progression in political history, but not in the 18th century, elitist conception of parliamentarianism in Western Liberal Democracy.

<—>

16

Yellow Vest Victory: The end of unions as Western leftism's hereditary kings

The 51-day general strike of 2019-20 - the longest labor movement in French history - was the best of times and the worst of times, to use a Dickensian reference regarding progressive France.

It was admirable that train workers thought they alone should or could bear the weight of stopping Emmanuel Macron's self-professed neoliberal *Revolution* - it was pathetic that a general strike didn't appear until December 5, 2019, or 383 days after the Yellow Vests had first revealed the obviously revolutionary sentiment across France.

The vast support for the general strike proves that the situation in France was indeed in a revolutionary situation, as the history of the working class movement proves that a general strike, "*...is the incontestable expression of the revolutionary character of the situation,*" wrote Trotsky. A general strike - but launched far, far earlier - could have incontestably altered French politics.

So why on earth did unions wait so long? The French had been clamouring for a general strike for many years during the Age of Austerity.

During the 2016 Labor Code protests I was talking with the head of the CGT, France's second-largest union and the historic flag-bearer of French unionism. Its solidly-moustachioed president is Philippe Martinez, who is invariably described as a "firebrand" in the mainstream media. I asked him why aren't union leaders calling for a general strike, given the 4,000 arrests, constant police brutality, widespread rejection of the so-called "reforms", etc. He said to me: "Hey, I don't have a button marked 'General Strike' which I can just push!" It was an amusing and perhaps a fair response in 2016, but once the Yellow Vests began marching nationwide with unprecedented popular support it was clear the will among union leadership was simply not there.

I recall interviewing Christiane Lambert of the FNSEA Farmers Union in October 2019. Surely a farmers' union would back the Yellow Vests, no? Not at all. Not wanting to see the unions paint themselves in a bad light, and not wanting to perpetuate the impression that the unions see the Yellow Vests as nothing but *casseurs*/hooligans, I gave her many, many chances to defend the Yellow Vests - she simply never would.

> *"At the beginning of the Yellow Vest movement there were many farmers and rural citizens protesting for the same reasons: the problems of rural citizens being forgotten, poverty, purchasing power,"* said Lambert. *"Given the violence and the evolution of the Yellow Vests it shows that our union was correct to not join forces with them."*

It's a staggering quote from a farmers union leader, one who is surely not reflecting the political wishes of her average member. Of course her richer members - the wealthier farmers - are likely to look down on the rural working poor as much as any city industrialist looks down on the urban poor. Nor was Lambert even accurate: the evolution of the Yellow Vests has been towards greater leftism, civic-mindedness and even more violence against them and not from them.

Union leadership has simply not allowed joining with or has refused to join with the Yellow Vests.

One will respond that the Yellow Vests have prohibited that, but unions exhibit precisely the same failure as the Mainstream Media or political parties: A refusal to actually show up at demonstrations with the banners of reconciliation and the manners of humility for past mistakes. Anyway, unions could have easily avoided the Yellow Vests by simply marching any day of the week except Saturday, of course!

One would assume that unions would have seized the moment and joined in the national protest fervour, but one would be sadly mistaken: March 19, 2019, was the first day of nationwide union strikes - no action until after 18 consecutive Saturdays of nationwide Yellow Vest demonstrations. The strike day was a mere one-off.

Much like France's Trotskyist parties, France's unions cannot even get along with each other: from 2010 to 2018 France's nine major unions did not march together once.

From 2010 until 2019 I covered countless union demonstrations which were staffed with brave, selfless members - they were always at the front lines, and the tough guys whom the French rely on. But one should be clear why Yellow Vests view this essentially nostalgic elevation of unions as anti-revolutionary: The unions also eventually signed off on every major austerity measure, they supported the repression of the Yellow Vests by doing nothing about it and their general strike would be a total failure.

There cannot be any changes in the balance of socio-political power if it's not clear from whom power must be reduced - the failure of the general strike only underscored that.

The general strike of 2019-20: France's longest labor movement ever, but were they trying to lose?

The last general strike, in 1995, was also against pension reform but Macron's version was far more radical.

It was to be a world's first: a universal, "one size fits all" pension system. It was based on a nebulous points system, something which Macron had spent two years shrouding in mystery - for millennia monarchs never felt the need to divulge their plans with the plebes, as well. Also included was a back-door raising of the retirement age to 64.

From the beginning the "universal" plan made sure key groups weren't affected - the military, police, riot police, air traffic control and truckers - so "universal" was always a falsehood.

Unlike in 2010 Brussels wasn't being openly scapegoated for the rollback, but in one of his rare comments during the general strike Macron admitted he was "*advancing our European agenda*". The primary reason given for the pension is that the system was just too darn "complicated" - too "complicated" for whom, it was never explained. It's a nonsensical complaint, because people labor in drastically different conditions and thus require a range of retirement needs - no nation has a universal pension system for this simple reason.

The unions claimed the general strike was Macron's "Thatcher" or "Reagan" moment, and they were right: those Anglophone leaders never faced anything remotely close to the intensity and ideology of the Yellow Vests, so the Yellow Vests obviously belong in a totally different category. Compared to their weekly - and still ongoing - rebellion the union's general strike was just going through the motions. The slogan of the general strike was, "A few weeks of chaos or years of misery" - hardly an inspirational rallying cry.

> *Yellow Vest: "The Yellow Vests have been protesting for a year, so we clearly lit the fuse of this social movement. People are now aware*

that our system is attacking the average person without pity. We aren't on strike only because of the pension, but because of all the right-wing reforms over the past decade."

However, it claimed to be a "general strike" even though only rail-workers were striking the entire time, and even though it was aimed at stopping just one policy: the unions totally ignored the varied and widespread demands prevalent in French society, and expressed via the Yellow Vest's list of 43 demands presented to the government a year earlier.

The strike began on December 5, 2019, and was preceded by enormous repression at the Yellow Vest marches marking their one year anniversary. Polls gave strikers a 70% approval rating, about as high as the Yellow Vests - another example of contemporary France being divided into the bourgeois bloc versus everyone else.

The primary obstacle (other than Liberalism, of course) was resignation to the strike's certain failure, due to the rules of aristocratic and oligarchic Western Liberal Democracy: every Frenchman knew that Macron had absolute control over Parliament, and therefore there was nothing they could really do but hope that he might listen. Furthermore, many workers had already had their pockets emptied by austerity - there's nothing more effective to gutting a strike than keeping workers so poor that they have no savings to strike with.

Thus many Frenchmen could only strike on the days of national protest. The working poor have bills to pay, but they would still respond to calls for solidarity. Incredibly, the unions called only seven days of national protest in over seven weeks of general strike - a major mistake.

Yellow Vest: "There must be a convergence of the different social struggles because of this terrible retirement reform. Yellow Vests are the best catalyst to bring these groups together, and to show our government how determined and angry we are."

Perhaps the biggest catastrophe was fumbling away the news of December 16: Jean-Paul Delevoye, the architect of the pension reform, admitted to receiving huge salaries from private groups after taking public office. French media detailed more than a dozen conflicts of interest between these jobs and his public post, and Delavoye was also accused of lying about the assets of himself and his wife. He resigned to try and save his pension plan, but his pension ideas were obviously now totally tainted and suspect. Yet despite this corruption-induced gift the unions did not immediately apply major pressure and demand the total withdrawal of the pension plan. If they were actually trying to win, this is what they would have obviously done.

The scandal merely forced the government to actually begin talking about the strike - until then Macron and his government spokesperson had essentially refused to discuss the strike in public - and to finally accept meeting with the unions. Such is the autocracy of 21st century Liberalism.

After three days of no progress, on December 20 the government announced no further negotiations were possible until January 7. The unions complacently followed and went on vacation too. The general strike should continue, however. For nearly three weeks there was no movement at all except for the self-sacrificing strikers - it must have been quite aggravating for the strikers. The public transport shutdown made urban areas ghost towns during the holidays. Equally dark was the Anglophone media blackout on France's turmoil, even as it had become the longest labor movement in French history.

The government wasn't just on holiday for three weeks, of course - behind the scenes they were using the same old tactic seen throughout the Age of Austerity: divide the unions in order to conquer them all.

Before the new year the airline pilots union became the first to call off their strike after getting a sweetheart deal for their members.

When the holidays ended the government finally revealed - via press leaks and not during negotiations - some of the finer points of their "points system". Some information had to finally come out - the bill was due to be formally presented to the cabinet on January 24.

Thus after over one month of a general strike France finally learned what the general strike was actually all about! The autocratic silence and secrecy is astounding in its obvious violation of democratic transparency, cooperation and good faith. Union negotiators correctly complained that they had been wasting everyone's time by discussing incorrect facts about the reform! What we have here is not just autocracy but disinformation being used as a normal tool in Western Liberal Democracy.

The disinformation tactic did not stop but continued: as the general strike neared six weeks the government claimed to accept a key compromise - a withdrawal of a two-year hike to the retirement age... but then they said it would only be a temporary postponement. They didn't even clarify when the postponement would start or end. It was clearly a stalling tactic.

The nation's largest union by number of members and always the closest to the right-wing - the CFDT - continued their backing of Macron by immediately embracing the vague postponement, but other unions finally recognised the government's refusal to negotiate in good faith. It had taken them six weeks to reach this point, and they finally scrambled into action: hospital workers called an unprecedented strike and there were calls for three strike days in one week.

But it was too little, too late: on January 20 a key transport union dropped out and rail service returned to near-normal levels. On January 23 in Paris marchers carried torches in a funeral procession for the general strike, and on January 24 unions futilely called a last day of nationwide protest just as the bill was presented to cabinet.

It was over. Another union-led failure in the Age of Austerity.

Yellow Vest: "Every Saturday for 14 months we Yellow Vests have been saying that our unions are part of a deeply corrupt French system which we denounce. Our system lacks democracy and input from public citizens, and our incapable, corrupt unions have been no help to the average person."

Polls gave the biggest unions a disapproval rating of 60%, close to the 70% disapproval for Macron, the prime minister and the mainstream political parties.

Some of the biggest mistakes have already been mentioned, but the biggest is that unions never made the general strike truly "general" - only rail workers went on strike every day. It was the same tactic used in 1995, but they had no laptops or remote work back then. Thus, the general strike failed in a general strike's primary objective: to have a major economic impact on stockholders and the wealthy. The strike only shaved 0.1% off the quarter's economic growth, the same amount as the Yellow Vests, who had infinitely fewer economic levers to pull than unions.

Yellow Vest: "The people did not want the unions to retire from the field of battle. The unions should follow the people, but unions think they are the leaders. Compare the unions with the Yellow Vests - we have won many more concessions and we have been protesting for much longer, even though we face much more oppression."

Months of negotiations were needed in Parliament before the plan would be official, but the pension plan was actually ultimately called off - the coronavirus shut down normal government operations. The coronavirus also postponed Macron's other major reform for his first term - to the unemployment system. Macron has promised to implement his pension deforms immediately in his second term.

The general strike had the trajectory of every labor action during the Age of Austerity in France: Hopes start off high, but then the government buys off one or two key unions with targeted concessions. Those unions rationalise: "We've satisfied our members, as is our duty," and they pull out. Thus, the strikes are now less impactful on the pockets of the 1%, and the 1% becomes more emboldened. Those still striking feel betrayed and see a lack of genuine solidarity, and the strike soon collapses because too many people go back to work to earn money to pay their bills. It's all as easy as pie for the ruling 1% and their politicians, whereas all an increasingly-poor average worker can say each year is: "This time it will be different!" Only the Yellow Vests broke this self-defeating cycle, and they truly did wrest far more concessions than the unions did with the general strike.

Therefore, the three main results of the 2019-20 general strike were that: 1) The Yellow Vests forced France's unions to finally pull out their biggest weapon. 2) The failure to employ that weapon properly smashed another Western fake-leftist totem - that unions are the incarnation of progressive political leftism for at least a generation. 3) Unions failed to properly employ their biggest weapon because they have clearly accepted Liberalism, like the nation's fake-leftist political parties, and are ideologically barren of actual leftism.

This total tarnishing of the image of unions is a key reason behind the rise of the Yellow Vests: their clarity that unions in Western Liberal Democracy do not produce significant changes for society as a whole, only for their own dues-paying members, and thus the French were mistaken to have given unions such clout. Other than the Yellow Vests this key concept is only truly grasped in French politics by some Trotskyists.

All of this explains why Socialist-inspired countries like Iran, Cuba and China ban independent trade unions – for them *the state is the union.* "Independent" trade unions is a legacy of feudalism, not a legacy of Socialism; it is to prioritise competition rather than unity; it is a way for the 1% to easily divide and conquer. The reality is that union leaders always only ever saw the Yellow Vests as competitors for their ever-diminishing slice of the pie - the civic-minded and egalitarian Yellow Vests are above such grasping selfishness.

But the existence of the general strike proves that France's situation was definitely revolutionary, thanks to the Yellow Vests - too bad the unions did their best to stamp out the nation's revolutionary flame.

The Yellow Vests provided the final blow to trade union credibility, not the first

> *"In the old colonising countries, England and France, the labor bureaucracy, directly interested in colonial superprofits, is more powerful and conservative than anywhere else in the world, and the revolutionary masses find it very difficult there to raise their heads,"* wrote Trotsky.

Western imperialism, Western fake-leftism, and Western union failure - how could we have ever expected them to be separate?

However, French union workers are certainly not part of the exploitative rentier class, as Macron falsely campaigned on in 2017, and the Yellow Vests certainly have no direct share in French superprofits.

What's also certain is that French unions have played a key role in sabotaging France's attempts at political progress towards Socialist Democracy for decades - this phenomenon didn't start by their being 383 days behind the Yellow Vests.

> *Yellow Vest: "The average union worker supports the Yellow Vests,*

but not the union leaders, who have repeatedly betrayed us. The unions must finally end their selfishness, because everyone is against this government."

As World War II ended French unions have an ignominious history of failed economic protests, which have distinctly evolved from the early 20th century, Latin Europe-led era of syndicalism (unionism which can have a revolutionary or - more often, now - a reformist bent, where workers gather under the largest, industrial-sized umbrella possible) to a return of the self-interested craft (trade) unionism with its roots in the feudal era.

The post-World War II French trend of a return to craft unionism amid the decreased combativeness and relevance of syndicalism is obvious to all observers: The small businessmen of Poujade in the 1950s (many incorrectly initially called the Yellow Vests "Poujadists"), the artisans led by Gerard Nicoud in the 1970s, the truck driver gas protests in the 1990s following an increase in the price of oil, the public transport-dominated strikes against pension rollbacks in 1995 and 2019-20 - the common theme is that they were limited to one trade and/or one issue.

The broad success of 1968's success came in spite of - not because of - French syndicalist unions. Twenty percent of the population (10 million people) went on strike, but the biggest unions hadn't even called for strikes - the general strike only materialised after grassroots efforts. Philosopher Jacques Derrida even spoke of an "anti-union euphoria". The union-negotiated Grenelle Agreements were famously rejected by workers, which were considered a betrayal of the movement and another self-interested, narrow-minded grab by union leadership.

Syndicalism is a Socialist democracy-inspired theory, but even the left wing of its spectrum contains hugely divisive individualist flaws which will soon be discussed. Dividing unions by craft is the diametric opposite of successful Socialist-inspired countries, where there is one overarching union that is part of the government and not independent from it: in order to permanently reflect the Marxist-inspired totality of the class struggle; to reflect the insertion of the labouring class directly in the structure of the government; to reflect the victory of the working class over the managerial and ownership classes; to decrease societal divisions in the face of bourgeois bloc attacks both domestic and international. How can Socialism not have a vital criticism to make of the two types of unionism promoted and tolerated in Liberalism?

The fundamental difference between unionism in democracies inspired by Socialist Democracy and unionism in Western Liberal Democracy is that in the latter "independence" is considered paramount, despite its inherent tendency towards divisiveness in the face of a united bourgeois bloc. This individualism is rampant in Western society, and ultimately makes it easy for their unions to be divided and conquered. In practice, and as the 2019-20 protest reminds, such divisions mean that non-unionised workers, the retirees, students and lumpenproletariat lowest class are totally forgotten by the higher-skilled trades - except when they call for days of national protest in support of their concerns, but certainly during the decisive negotiations with the government.

> *Yellow Vest: "It's the unions who will be joining the Yellow Vests, because we have not been fighting just for one small group of workers but for the entire country - the pensioners, the unemployed, the handicapped, the students and everyone else. But we all want the same thing: to change not only this government, but also our capitalist system, which does not care for human beings."*

Thus the primary self-conception of Western unionism is the arrogant smugness - both in the quality of his or her work and in the quality of his or her political intelligence - of the self-proclaimed elite craftsman. Indeed, at union demonstrations their members often parade around with the flinty, unfriendly, blinkered combativeness of the very last knights of a forgotten and chivalrous order - contrarily, anyone who appears sympathetic will be warmly welcomed at a Yellow Vest demonstration, especially if wearing a reflective yellow vest. The difference in reception says a great deal, I think, because it can make the difference between someone sourly joining a march one time or becoming a regular part of a sociopolitical movement.

As the 20th century progressed craft unionism was pushed more and more to the forefront by the 1%, while syndicalism - which is rather at ideological, if not open, war with Liberalism and capitalism - was suppressed, but it also withered away due to its own ineffectiveness and mistakes.

It withered in relevance due to their right-wing reformists, naturally, but also because of their left-wing's insistence that the immediate goal of syndicalism should be to transfer all the means of production to the workers themselves. This differentiates reformist syndicalism from anarcho-syndicalism, and no discussion of French leftist history would be complete without an analysis of it.

Anarcho-syndicalism is a combination of anarchism - a rejection of the state - and unionism. It puts absolute primacy on the role of the labor movement and the organised worker, and it looks with permanent skepticism at any civil servant - it combines unionism with anti-statism. It also elevates anarchism's individualistic right of self-determination over anything else. Anarcho-syndicalism's (and libertarian socialism's) biggest mistake is in exaggerating fears of a powerful state in order to wilfully divide themselves and to divide society, rendering both only more easily conquered by the bourgeois bloc.

The ideology is rooted in the ideas of French thinker Pierre-Joseph Proudhon, often called the founder of anarchism, and his influence in the history of French and Latin European leftism is profound. French unionism broadly is not anarcho-syndicalist but we cannot discount the influence of anarchism's skepticism towards hierarchy and bureaucracy as it inundates French leftist culture. Doing so would lead us to misunderstanding French unions, French leftism and also even the Yellow Vests. It would be like ignoring the similarly individualist libertarian thought should we examine American conservatism.

Western anarcho-syndicalism's most famous proponent is Noam Chomsky, who became the world's most quoted living individual by providing a vital Marxist-inspired critique of 20th century Western foreign policy while simultaneously rejecting any actual Socialist-inspired state for daring to be a state. His rise and practical political powerlessness both contrasts and parallels with the decline and practical political powerlessness of anarcho-syndicalism in the 20th century. For Anglophone cultures where unionism has been especially retarded and doesn't play a major social role, such as in the United States, the anarcho-syndicalist ideology finds parallels with the "libertarian socialism" of Murray Bookchin.

Trotsky called anarcho-syndicalism "*the worst of all dictatorships*" because it dangerously and uselessly rallies together workers who combine to refuse to a positive role for governments; its individualistic demands are an inherent rejection of communal unity; it isolates workers from the other sectors of society.

Spain should have been included by Trotsky along with England and France as having unions who are interested in colonial superprofits. Unsurprisingly, Spain is the home of the Confederación Nacional del Trabajo, which France's anarcho-syndicalist CNT is an offshoot of. As someone who has covered countless pro-Palestinian demonstrations in France I can report that you would never see a CGT flag there - and they are considered to be a left-wing union - but you might see the black and red CNT flag. There is also the occasional CNT flag at the Yellow Vests - again, the only union occasionally represented (but I should note that I am based in Paris). France's CNT played a leading role in the social conflicts of the early decades of the 20th century, but it has been reduced to these interesting historical footnotes.

The point here is to show that anarcho-syndicalism contains - like French unionism in general - both good and bad points, and also that some of these virtues and flaws are obviously contained within the Yellow Vest movement itself. These flaws are anarchism's extremism skepticism towards all hierarchy, bureaucracy, a role for the state and self-elevation. However, I believe that the Yellow Vests' primary trait is civic-mindedness, and thus it will eventually overcome this anarchist emphasis on individual empowerment over communal empowerment. I also believe that the Yellow Vests are not going to be just another French clique which insists on its own isolated superiority, but that it is constantly making enduring ties with other social movements, groups and citizens both every Saturday and on-line.

Western anarcho-syndicalism may have been considered revolutionary in the 1910s but it cannot be disassociated from over a century of practical failures.

More broadly, French unionism has obviously embraced Liberalism, just as French leftist politicians embraced Liberalism starting in the 1980s. In another failure of mere Social Democracy in Europe, across the continent unions are allowed to set the level of pay and benefits, which is then to be followed by the non-unionised. This idea that unions should lead the way - with no strings attached for the non-unionised or non-workers - has taken even firmer roots in Germanic countries. The reformism of Social Democracy always amounts to a continuation of the ancient right-wing mantra of "trickle down economics". However, this entire structure has broken due to the incredible greed of the "neoliberal" era, who replaced the more cautious Liberalists during the short era of Social Democracy (1945-75).

The internet has replaced the factory/union hall as the center of leftist politics

Our new historical reality is that social media has supplanted the factory and the union hall as the place to discuss and learn about the historic struggle for solidarity.

France's Yellow Vests perceived all this - that unions and existing political parties are self-interested, out of touch and refuse to lead the progressive way forward - and thus they turned instead to the new factories of discussion: roundabouts and Facebook, which are obviously astonishingly successful new ways of organising, discussing, learning, disseminating effective slogans and ideas, and acting in a common defense.

To paraphrase and add to the observation of Benjamin Bayart, a French militant for internet neutrality and liberty: the printing press permitted the people to read, the phonograph and radio wave permitted people to hear and the internet has permitted people to write. What they are often writing are their political opinions, and thus they are reporting on the perpetual failures and lies of Liberalism. Social media is aggregating these reports, and then also bringing these people together in real life. As Liberalist ideology has captured unions, political parties and the mainstream media, social media has become the most socialistic (and thus democratic) space available to the working-poor and working classes. These are staggeringly democratic changes in human history, and the methods of the Yellow Vests serve as a source of major political innovation for the entire globe.

The West's elite - so isolated and out of touch with the realities produced by first monarchy and then Liberalism - initially expected that social media would only be used to confirm Liberalism, and thus they initially promoted it widely. Their disenchantment with it has been spectacularly swift, and it dates from when the first (but endemic) capitalist bust period arrived in this new digital era. A Metternichian clampdown campaign began in the West in 2016 to ensure that "neo-liberal" ideas and candidates could not be effectively opposed.

The West's future is more clampdowns on social media's anti-Liberalists, and yet it won't be enough. The only ideology which communities agree world-wide that should be censored is far-right thought, and this is why in Socialist-inspired countries censorship of far-right thought is accepted as a necessary good. Censorship of left-wing ideas, however, will never be fully acceptable anywhere, due its obvious aim of benevolence and goodwill to society as opposed to right-wing's elevation of elitism.

The problem is not necessarily that France's unions have led strikes which included pensioners, students, the unemployed, migrants, small businessmen, workers - in short, a totally heterogenous movement - it's that they are correctly perceived as having used these for the gain of only their own members, whereas their propaganda says that they are concerned with the good of the community and country.

The Yellow Vests fully reject - almost a century later - the long-running class-collaborationist model which France initiated in 1934 by calling for a Popular Front. Unions cannot be viewed as saviours, or even as effective leftists. They need to be looked at with the same skepticism which national political parties in Parliament must be looked at: Unionisation as a means of obtaining individual improvements in wages, conditions, safety, etc., ok - but union leaders as political leaders of the working, lower and middle classes? That would lead to the total victory of right-wing Liberalism, as the 2019-20 general strike reminded.

The Yellow Vests said no to union leadership, and that certainly contributed to their ability to produce a political "euphoria" for many months. This decision was not out of mere anarchism - it is because the Yellow Vests refuse to work within the confines of Western Liberal Democracy.

<—>

17

Yellow Vest Victory: Proving that Western Liberal Democracy is the same old autocracy

If we say that the Yellow Vests are not socialist revolutionaries even latently, then what are they protesting about?

To put it the most simply: they are protesting the end of European Social Democracy, with the limited protections it provided.

The Yellow Vests intuited that the pan-European project has ended the era of European Social Democracy (1945-75) and replaced it with elite-driven, free market, winner-take-all Liberalism.

Seeing that their list of 43 demands doesn't include the word "Europe" once, however, the Yellow Vests don't really grasp that the European Union represents the organisational assassin of European Social Democracy. The European Union and Eurozone's response to the Great Recession made it entirely clear: these are institutions which are perfectly hostile to Social Democracy's minor redistributions and protections which fundamentally embolden the average worker and citizen.

Social Democracy was not born after World War II, just as "neo-liberalism" was first on display back in 1871, with what was imposed after the destruction of the Paris Commune. Marx chronicled the birth of European Social Democracy, in 1848, when the Mountain Party (which initially claimed the mantle of neo-Jacobinism) sided with the small-traders in the June Days massacre instead of with the urban proletariat and rural peasantry, as the Jacobins had done in 1789. They went from supporting Socialist Democracy to calling themselves Democratic Socialists (*Démocrate-socialistes*) and this - and not the downward slope from Napoleon Bonaparte to Louis-Napoleon Bonaparte - should be considered the truest essence of Marx's famous line of history repeating itself as farce.

> *"The revolutionary point was thereby broken off from the social demands of the proletariat and a* (social) *democrat turn given to them...."*

That was the birth of Social Democracy: an ideology where the *social* demands of the recently-feudal masses (decent pay, health care, education, pensions, etc.) get only partially addressed while the *political* demands of an aristocracy opposing an absolute monarch (free speech, property rights, trial by jury, etc.) are fully met. Liberalism has always sought to limit progressive changes to the *political* question of how to move on from feudalism, and to stop progressive changes to the *social* question of how to move on from feudalism. The reformist ideology of Social Democracy has operated within Western Liberal Democracy for nearly 175 years and only partially prevailed for 30 of them.

The sooner the Yellow Vests realise that Social Democracy will never be a harmonious solution to the elitism dominant in Liberalism, the better, as Marx did:

> *"The peculiar character of Social Democracy is epitomised in the fact that democratic-republican institutions are demanded as the means, not to remove the two extremes - capital and wage-slavery*

> *- but in order to weaken the antagonism and transform them into a harmonious whole."*

Putting capital primarily in the hands of the recently-feudal masses so they can provide the broad economic stability and success which would end wage- and debt-slavery has never been a goal of Social Democracy, from the Mountain Party to Leon Blum to Francois Mitterrand to Francois Hollande to the "Democratic Socialists of America" led by Bernie Sanders in the 21st century United States.

> *Yellow Vest: "We are not beggars! What is 100 euros only given one time? State taxes compose 60% of the price of gasoline, so calling it 100 euros is totally false - the people truly only receive 40 euros. This is election nonsense, but Macron won't win votes with these crumbs."*

Marx continued in his examination of France and gave us the key to the capitalist culture of both Liberal and Social Democracies: *"This substance is the transformation of society along* (Social) *democratic lines, but a transformation within the boundaries of the small-trader's class."* One extraneous sentence later: *"It believes rather that the special conditions for its own emancipation are the general conditions under which alone modern society can be saved and the class struggle be avoided."*

Trotsky and the Yellow Vests saw that, due to the rise of financial capitalism, a leftist alliance must include the small businessman, but they reject the goal of Social Democracy to elevate their virtues and needs over those of the average worker and citizen.

Thus even when Social Democracy prevails in Liberalist capitalist cultures the virtues of the usually bourgeois-aspiring, individualistic, managerial small-trader class become the highest virtues to be promoted. Everyone must be a self-interested, competitive entrepreneur who aspires to be a boss and a "job creator". This veneration of the small trader is the most obvious in American culture, and it is American culture which has been imposed on France via the pan-European project: at the alleged "end of history", with the fall of the USSR, the United States shepherded the pan-European project, which is rightly said to be even more Liberalist (i.e. Bankocratic) than anything which could be created in the United States.

What we see in the modern era, and as this book proves, is that Liberalism, Social Democracy and Fascism have all joined together and "become bourgeois". This amalgam of 18th century Liberalism, 19th century Social Democracy and 20th century fascism is ultimately not different from the aristocracy of the 17th century and earlier, which which ruled the 99% in an entirely autocratic manner. The extremely modest expansion of wealth and political power from a blood/marriage line to a line of the super-wealthy 1% still results in the exclusion of the recently-feudal masses from policy making, and this is what the Yellow Vests emphatically reminded. Their primary demand was not Socialist revolution but merely to get more public opinion into public policymaking.

The bourgeois bloc continually dangles Social Democracy as a reformist possibility, and thus they secure the loyalty of both the big and the small bosses and owners. However, when the moment of implementation comes, amid the next guaranteed bust in Liberalist capitalism, the response is the anti-Socialist virulence of Liberalism via the ruthless elite domination of a Fascism which has made peace with big capital.

> *Yellow Vest: "Macron's repeatedly evaded the main problems. His solutions are not concrete, and it is certain that in a few months we will just be in the same situation. This is why we will keep protesting, for certain."*

Baudelaire wrote, "The most beautiful trick of the devil is to persuade you that he does not exist," and this is what modern Western Liberal Democracy has done with the elitism, arrogance and autocracy which is the basis of absolute monarchy. Macron's "Jupiterian" remove has pulled the sheet off of Western Liberal Democracy, again, and reminded that the idea of an autocratic ruler remains the preference of a Western elite which has always been totally opposed to Socialist-inspired measures.

The republican lie of Liberalism

When Western leaders communicate among themselves and with their foreign counterparts they use the language of Liberalism; when they implement policy they use the ruthlessness of Fascism; but when they communicate with the masses they know that republican language is paramount.

This is especially true in France and the United States, where royalism has been fully discredited from holding public power. Thus, there is a constant emphasis by contemporary French leaders and their mainstream media on maintaining "republican" values.

However, the republicanism of both is an antiquated one as it is based on Liberal and not Socialist Democracy. A perfect example of the inadequacy of their elite-led republicanism is found in the Orwellian name of the group which wages the actual physical repression of the Yellow Vests: the detested CRS riot police (Compagnies *républicaines* de sécurité – *Republican* Security Companies.) A woman wearing a full-body bathing suit - a "*burkini*" (combination of "burqa" and "bikini") is breathlessly presented as a bigger threat to French republicanism than the repression of the Yellow Vests. Most obviously, there is the mainstream conservative party's name change shepherded by Nicolas Sarkozy in 2015 - from *L'Union pour un mouvement populaire (UMP)* to *les Républicains*: the party had so many corruption scandals that a rebranding was deemed unavoidable.

Such is the false republicanism in Liberal Democracies.

The lip service towards republicanism allows the perpetuation of the outdated notion in France that the world still views them as the brightest beacon of progressive politics. They are different than almost all of Northern Europe, where royals still - bewilderingly - remain on thrones which hide mountains of the public's rightful riches and influence. Indeed, an Iranian can find in France a refuge from the common Western toleration and whitewashing of monarchism.

The elite in the United States uses "freedom", while monarchies like the UK use "human rights" in the same way - to insist that freedom and human rights for their modern aristocracies still represents the pinnacle of progressivism.

The legacy of 1789 exists in France today only in this constant demand to uphold "republicanism", even if it is not at all the spirit of 1789 and only mouths its forms. The Yellow Vest repression will remind all of history that the freedoms offered by the republicanism of Western Liberal Democracy with French characteristics are a fantasy - there is only the autocracy of the bourgeois bloc.

France's 21st century belief that "the republic" must jingoistically unite the French is ultimately a means used to falsely claim the legacy of 1789 while also ensuring that talk for progressive politics ends with this very initial answer to the "political question", and with no answer to the "social question", as well.

This also explains why there is so much forced discussion in France about what a huge threat Islam poses to this immoral republicanism: Islam correctly insists on God and morality being the highest allegiance, and certainly not laws forced through by a Fascist-allying, imperialist bourgeois bloc.

Nothing is more Liberalist than the European Union, and thus the 'Social Fascist' repression of anti-austerity movements and the Yellow Vests

We have already linked the European Union with the birth of neo-liberalism and neo-imperialism, we have established how Fascism was subsumed and its tactics adopted, and we have shown how the goal of the third restoration of Western Liberalism is to roll back the modest gains of Social Democracy.

All that's needed is to show how Western Liberal Democracy wields the power of the state as autocratically as royal families and their coteries used to - for this we simply have to look to the Yellow Vests.

Western Liberal Democracy and pre-1789 autocracy - there is no real difference.

Whether the form is a parliamentary republic based on Liberalism, or an executive-led republic based on Liberalism, or a constitutional monarchy based on Liberalism - the autocracy has been the same. Only the truly elite have the money to buy Liberalist rights and influence in public policy.

> *Yellow Vest: "As usual, no prison for the rich - everything goes fine for them, always. They never know hunger or poverty, but put everything on the average person's back. Benalla should have been treated like anyone else - justice should be equal for everyone."*

Just as the trends of 250 years of Iranian or Chinese history can be summarised so too can the trend of the past 250 years of French and Western history, and this book has aimed to do that. Above all the trend of moving away from an autocratic monarch and towards an empowered people's republic is discerned. The problem has been Western Liberal Democracy's conception of a republic: what they have always had is an oligarchic republic, inspired by the English, which aims for perpetual repression of the recently-feudal (to Asian conceptions of time!) Western masses.

The early years of all revolutionary republics are always fraught with missteps and mistakes, but made with the sincere goal of broad societal progress. In 1789 the move away from absolute monarchy was met with great difficulty and international opposition. In 1848 the move away from a limited monarchy was met with great difficulty, also caused by great inexperience. In 1871 the move towards a social republic was met with great difficulty and international opposition, also caused by great inexperience. But inexperience is not the primary difficulty of the people today - they know how to rule, but they still face great international opposition. As Marx wrote:

> *"The cry of 'social republic' with which the February Revolution* (of 1848) *was ushered in by the Paris proletariat, did but express a vague aspiration after a republic that was not only to supersede the monarchical form of class rule but class rule itself. The Commune* (i.e. the first appearance of Socialist Democracy) *was the positive form of that republic."*

However, the social republic was annihilated by neoliberalism and would not appear until 1917 in the eastern frontier of Europe - Russia.

The Yellow Vests reminded those in the 21st century who believe that the "end of history" had occurred in 1991 that the people's desires for a social republic are no longer vague. However the Yellow Vests have had the misfortune of living in the world's only region - the West - where socialist-inspired revolutionary cultures have never won implantation.

To their great credit, the Yellow Vests created a revolutionary condition for all of France. When it was thwarted by Liberal Democratic politicians, media and unions the Yellow Vests continued to march to keep promoting what may truly turn into a revolutionary culture at the next major uprising over Liberalism's endemic failures. The Yellow Vests have created a vast and reliable network - there's no doubt they will spring into action at the next opportunity.

The next political progression for the Yellow Vests is the realisation that the pan-European project only dangled the illusion of mere Social Democracy, but that its "neoliberal" basis is actually Fascist and autocratic to its very core.

The analysis of that splendidly successful revolutionary Bolshevik, Trotsky, must be remembered today if the Yellow Vests are to break with the perpetual illusion of mere Social Democracy:

> *"The program of the Communist International has the following to say on this subject: '**Side by side** with the Social Democracy, which assists the bourgeoisie to stifle the proletariat and to lull its vigilance, Fascism appears.' The Communist International failed to understand that it is not the mission of Fascism to function **side by side** with the Social Democracy, but to destroy all the existing workers' organizations, including the reformist. The task of Fascism, in the words of the program, is to 'annihilate the **Communist** strata of the proletariat, and their leading cadres.' Fascism, then, does not at all threaten the Social Democracy and the reformist trade unions; on the contrary, the Social Democracy itself plays a "Fascist" role to an ever increasing degree. Fascism achieves nothing more than the consummation of the labours of reformism, by functioning '**side by side** with the Social Democracy'."* (Emphasis his)

The Communist Bolsheviks rejected mere Social Democracy and instead used Socialist Democracy as their guiding structure ideology, as do Socialist-inspired countries today, who then adapt its primary economic and political imperatives to local cultures and mores. They saw that Social Democracy and Fascism work together to destroy not just Socialist Democracy-inspired groups, unions, parties, countries, etc, but also groups, unions, parties and countries which attempt Social Democratic reforms of Liberalism. As time goes on the Yellow Vests will realise, thanks to their own repression, that Liberal Democracy and Social Democracy offer them no solution except the destruction of the Yellow Vests.

One sentence later - in which Trotsky expressed his usual disapproval with the Moscow-based Comintern - Trotsky continued:

> *"We have here before us all the basic elements of the theory of* ***social fascism****. The leaders of the Communist International failed to understand that capitalism in decay is no longer able to come to terms with the most moderate and most servile Social Democracy, either as a party in power, or as a party in opposition. It is the mission of Fascism to take its place not 'side by side with the Social Democracy', but on its bones. Precisely from this there flows the possibility, the need and the urgency for the united front."*
> (Emphasis his)

(Recall that a united front (joining together in society's leftist struggles), is not the same as a popular front (an electoral alliance).)

Call it what you want: Social Fascism, Liberalism, autocracy, Fascism, constitutional monarchy, rule by the 1% - it is all the same oligarchic autocracy for the recently-feudal masses. I call it Western Liberal Democracy to properly place it in a geographic and historical context.

As soon as the Yellow Vests stop trying to win back the Social Democratic measures which Nicolas Sarkozy, Francois Hollande and Macron rolled back, the sooner they will realise that Socialist-inspired countries have shown a better way, method and goal. Without a major reformulation of the pan-European project - which seems impossible to get off the ground in a Liberalist-dominated media - the pan-European project's initial lure of even greater Social Democratic gains should be seen only as a chimera.

The Yellow Vests know enough to reject existing establishment institutions, as well as pathetic PFAXIst (Popular Fronts Against Xenophobia but for Imperialism) electoral strategies - they must realise the monarchist-elitist-reformist-fascist alliance which is Western Liberal Democracy must be rejected in favor of Socialist Democracy.

That, of course, will lead to even more repression.

But their bravery will earn them more and more comrades; their correctness will only increase as the repression accumulates; the guaranteed cycles of failure in capitalism and the clockwork greed of high finance all make the move away from autocratic Liberalism certain.

The combination of royalism, Liberalism and Fascism is doomed, but people must be liberated from the long-outdated and pernicious influence of Liberalism before the next political advancement can take place. Thus the Yellow Vests, and thus this book, which is another humble tally of Liberalism's failures.

> *Yellow Vest: "The people I speak with express absolutely no desire to stop the movement and remain very positive. The Yellow Vests are, above all, the French people, and the French people recognize this and this is why the movement will have a second wind."*

So admirably, The Yellow Vests have cleared the path for France: the despairing working poor, middle and lower classes have a fighting force which can never, ever be called Fascistic. France is back to being the West's leaders of progressive politics.

Marx's most important passage on France - guiding France from 1789 to 2022 and beyond

Here we have the most important passage in Marx's writings on France - from his writings on the Paris Commune - because it historically summarises a century of turbulent political and socio-economic changes and pinpoints the establishment of modern Western Liberal Democracy.

The passage covers the vital and obscured history of France for a century after 1789. The short parentheticals are mine and designed to add clarity to Marx's meaning:

"If the parliamentary republic, as M. Theirs said, 'divided them least' (the different factions of the French ruling class in 1850), *it opened an abyss between that class and the whole body of society outside their spare ranks. The restraints by which their own divisions had under former regimes still checked the state power were removed by their union; and in view of the threatening upheaval of the proletariat they now used that state power mercilessly and ostentatiously as the national* (and imperialist) *war engine of capital against labor.*

In their uninterrupted crusade against the producing masses they were, however, bound not only to invest the executive with continually increased powers of repression, but at the same time divest their own parliamentary stronghold - the National Assembly - one by one, of all its own means of defence against the Executive. The Executive, in the person of (President) *Louis*(-Napoleon) *Bonaparte, turned them out. The national offspring of the 'Party of Order'* (the dominant political party of the 2nd) *Republic was the Second Empire* (of Emperor Louis-Napoleon Bonaparte).

The (Second) *empire, with the coup d'etat for its birth certificate, universal suffrage for its salvation and the sword for its sceptre, professed to rest upon the peasantry - the large mass of producers not directly involved in the struggle of capital and labor. It professed to save the working class by breaking down parliamentarianism and, with it, the undisguised subserviency of government to the propertied classes. It professed to save the propertied classes by upholding their economic supremacy over the working class; and, finally, it professed to unite all classes by reviving for all the chimera of national glory.*

In reality it was the only form of government possible, at a time when the bourgeoisie had already lost, and the working class had not yet acquired, the faculty of ruling the nation. (As they would acquire, starting with the Paris Commune and then later the USSR, China, Iran, etc.) *It* (the 2nd French Empire) *was acclaimed throughout the world as the saviour of society. Under its sway bourgeois society, freed from political cares, attained a development unexpected even by itself. Its industry and commerce expanded to colossal dimensions; financial swindling celebrated cosmopolitan orgies* (Marx uses this last word literally, per scandals of the time)*; the misery of the masses was set off by a shameless display of gorgeous, meretricious and debased luxury. The state power, apparently soaring high above society, was at the same time itself the very scandal of that society and the very hotbed of all its corruptions. Its own rottenness, and the rottenness of the society it had saved* (i.e. the bourgeois elite of the 2nd Republic), *were laid bare by the bayonet of Prussia, herself eagerly bent upon transferring the supreme seat of that regime from Paris to Berlin."*

The globalist descendants of the victors of 1871 would eventually comprise on Brussels instead of Berlin. Belgium - the country fabricated so that France and Germany would have a place to fight their wars, it is often joked - became *"the seat of that regime"*.

> *Yellow Vest: "We are not proud, at least not yet, because we have many more victories to accomplish. We insist on having referendums initiated by citizens, in order to democratically give a voice to all of France and to the Yellow Vests. We will keep marching to ensure that our common future is serene and peaceful."*

If we make only minor substitutions in Marx's passage to include contemporary developments, does this not make an up-to-date history of France and Europe covering over two centuries?

"If the **pan-European project** *"divided them least"* (the different factions of **national** ruling **classes in Europe**) least, it opened an abyss between that class and the whole body of society outside their spare ranks. The restraints by which their own divisions had under former regimes still checked the state power were removed by their union; and in view of the threatening upheaval of the **Yellow Vests** they now used that state power mercilessly and ostentatiously as the **inter**national war engine of capital against labor.

In their uninterrupted crusade against the producing masses they (the pan-European project) were, however, bound not only to invest the **national** executive **branches** with continually increased powers of repression, but at the same time divest their own **national** parliamentary **branches**, one by one, of all its own means of defence against the Executive. The Executive, in the person of **a modern** Louis Bonaparte (**or something new and revolutionary, perhaps similar to the Supreme Leader branch of government in Iran**), **could not be allowed to have** turned them - **Brussels** - out. The national offspring of the **pan-European project** was the **neoliberal** Empire **of the European Union.**

The empire, with the **fall of the USSR** for its birth certificate, **denying the national referendums which rejected the European Union and which were based on** universal suffrage for its salvation and the sword for its sceptre, professed to rest upon the **neo-**peasantry - the large mass of producers not directly involved in the struggle of capital and labor **and who desired to avoid more intra-European wars, free movement around Europe and the strengthening of a Social Democratic safety net**. It also professed to save the working class by breaking down **national** parliamentarianism and, with it, the undisguised subserviency of government to the propertied classes. It professed to save the propertied classes by upholding their economic supremacy over the working class; and, finally, it professed to unite all classes by reviving for all the chimera of **supra**national glory **via colluding with the United States to enforce Liberalist values worldwide**.

In reality it was the only form of government possible, at a time when the bourgeoisie had **fully** acquired the faculty of ruling the nation, **something they had no experience with in 1848.** It (**the pan-European project**) was acclaimed throughout the **West** as the saviour of **European** society. Under its sway bourgeois society, freed from political cares, **such as the profit drags and democratic nuisances created by the era of Social Democracy,** attained a development unexpected even by itself. Its industry and commerce expanded to colossal dimensions; financial swindling celebrated cosmopolitan orgies; the misery of the masses was set off by a shameless display of gorgeous, meretricious and debased luxury. The state power, apparently soaring high above society, was at the same time itself the very scandal of that society and the very hotbed of all its corruptions. Its own rottenness, and the rottenness of the society it had saved - **the royals threatened by 1789, the bourgeois threatened by 1848, the colluding Social Democrats threatened by 1917 and the Fascists threatened by 1945** - were laid bare by the bayonet of **the Yellow Vests,** herself eagerly bent upon transferring the supreme **national** seat of that regime from **Brussels back to Paris**."

France is not Cuba, Iran, China or even Southern Lebanon - it will likely take a civil war for the Yellow Vests to ever use bayonets to finally win political and economic redistribution. However, the Yellow Vests emphatically prove the willingness of Western Liberal Democracy to use violence just as brutally as the autocracies of 1788.

The Yellow Vests also remind that Western Liberal Democracy does not even allow the rights which Liberalism claims to protect - how long can that persist in a country which regularly demands the right to publicly exercise such rights, and whose pens have been freed by the digital era?

If the French elite is not going to permit even the basic rights of Liberalism, then France needs a defensive force which can protect the Liberalist rights of protesters. That is the subject of the next chapter.

<—>

18

What the Yellow Vests can be: A group which can protect Liberalism's rights, at least

"All the chorus of calumny, which the Party of Order never fail, in their orgies of blood, to raise against their victims, only proves that the bourgeois of our days considers himself the legitimate successor to the baron of old, who thought every weapon in his own hand fair against the plebeian, while in the hands of the plebeian a weapon of any kind constituted in itself a crime."

— Marx 1852

The West loves to say is how they are for "law and order" - but what would you choose when you realise that, in truth, the two are actually separable?

It was undoubtedly clear to anyone who actually attended Yellow Vest demonstrations that France's police were incapable of protecting both order and law. Order was preserved - the 5th Republic did not fall - but obviously at the expense of the law, which states that the

French have Liberalist rights such as the freedom of protest, assembly, speech, etc.

The difference between myself and many others is that I found the guaranteed Saturday repression of the Yellow Vests a sufficient crisis to invoke changes of a civil wartime nature which would protect the people and law - others did not, seeing only a sufficient crisis to invoke changes of a wartime nature which would protect property and order. Socialist Democracy privileges the people (equality) and law (rights), whereas Western Liberal Democracy privileges property (inequality) and order (power).

As the right to *social* equality was forcibly abandoned in the 19th century, the rights to *political* equality were the only gains left in France of the French Revolution. Of course, these political rights were never actually allowed in much of Western Liberal Democratic history - they certainly were not considered to be universally enjoyable, especially by women, until the arrival of the era of Social Democracy (1945-75). The repression of the Yellow Vests show how that era has ended.

Given this reality, it's as if 1789 didn't even happen and royalty still rules supreme.

The repression of the Yellow Vests has smashed the appearance of stability, respectability and moral-political superiority which the West claimed they had following the collapse of the Soviet Union. It's an appearance which was routed in 1852, and demolished by the traitorous collusion of the French elite in 1871, the horrors of industrial imperialism, two World Wars and the Great Depression, history reminds.

If even rich people can march with the Yellow Vests and get beaten by police and prosecuted by the judicial system, then the class analysis has lost much of its economic component. What we are then left in the use of class analysis is the political component: only those who support the political agenda of the bourgeois bloc, and are also rich, are granted rights in the 21st century West.

Either those of us not with the bourgeois bloc do not have the right to have political rights, or we do have the right to have political rights and thus the right to defend them.

To put it differently: either the people have rights which are subject to the arbitrary whims of a shah or a "liberal strongman" like Emmanuel Macron, or they have lawful rights which the forces of order themselves must be made to respect - this cannot be disputed.

Yet making such a claim eventually provokes the same old "*chorus of calumny*" even in the 21st century. Marx wrote the above regarding the first Western Liberal Democratic Party in France, the conservative Party of Order. In 175 years Western Liberal Democracy has clearly not evolved away from an oligarchy which jealously guards for their own elite class the political gains of 1789's Liberalism.

What the Yellow Vests remind is that it's still a revolutionary choice in a Western Liberal Democracy to choose "law" instead of "order". They also remind that not only do Liberalist nations not enjoy the social rights of Socialist-inspired nations, but they still do not even have the enjoyment of the political rights of Liberalism. This book has reminded that these rights have been hard won, only recently partially installed, even less recently been actually made universal and only just last Saturday were overturned at roundabouts and demonstrations across France.

> *Yellow Vest: "All of the police violence has made many people afraid to demonstrate. However, they are just as unhappy with the government's choices. We must remember that we protested during winter, which is never done in France, and then all through a very rainy and cold spring. The important point is that there are tens of thousands people protesting despite all these obstacles."*

To many Westerners, with their conception of time perhaps being more recent than that of an Asian or African, these Liberalist rights may seem old; to many Westerners the idea that counter-revolutionaries still act to undermine those rights may also seem to stem from a bygone Cold War mentality; to many Westerners the idea that monarchy still plays a pernicious, un-excised role in Western political cultures seems antiquated as well. This book seeks to give the West a new view of themselves, and from the new perch which is provided by the installation of the pan-European project and subsequent Yellow Vest repression.

What the Yellow Vests have demonstrated, above all, is the long-standing fact of Western imperialism. In neo-imperialism Western people have the rights of what used to be associated with those of a colonised subject - the Yellow Vests should mark the end of the Western individual's sense of exceptionalism. The Yellow Vests show the average Westerner that they are down here with the rest of the world - it's another victory of French egalitarianism, and of the Socialist concept of the class struggle.

What the Yellow Vests should have evolved into - could have evolved into, may still evolve to - is a true protesters' militia which would have safeguarded the right to peaceful protest from both the police and the police-infiltrated black-clad groups, both of whom prevented the exercise of the French people's bourgeois era rights.

The renunciation of militias in the West & the acceptance of fake-leftist militias like Antifa and Black Bloc

The idea of the need for militias empowered to use self-defence was not always so shocking to Western ears.

The very first decree of the Paris Commune of 1871 was to enrol all citizens capable of bearing arms into the National Guard, which replaced the army and police and put power in the hands of the citizens. Marx knew the immediate importance of such an act: "... *the disarming of the workers was the first commandment for the bourgeois at the helm of the state."*

Of course, there is no doubt for what aim that commandment was made: French backers of property and order colluded with the Germans who had just defeated them in the Franco-Prussian War, lay siege to their own capital for over four months, and massacred 30,000 Parisians rather than giving up their monopoly of armed force.

It is not shocking to many non-Western ears, especially in the region currently most set-upon by imperialism - the Muslim world. There are many militias in the region, but almost no Western discernment as to which militia is progressive and has grassroots legitimacy, and which are propped up by foreign dollars and reactionary ideas. The Basij and Al Qaeda are alleged to be the same - reactionary and illegitimate - in shameful propaganda.

Of course Iran has a protesters' militia - it is the Basij. I detailed it throughly in my book, *Socialism's Ignored Success: Iranian Islamic Socialism*, and I drew the innumerable structural and bureaucratic similarities it has with China's protesters' militia, the Chinese Communist Party. Additionally, the China's People Liberation Army is hell-bent against depoliticisation and both allow their republic to average 500 protests a day without police wrecking them, as in France. Cuba has such incredible unity - the protests against the socialist government are so tiny, and the protests in favor of the socialist government so enormous and joyous, as I have reported upon - I'm not sure they even need a protesters' militia at this point, but of course they have the Committees for the Defense of the Revolution (*Comités de Defensa de la Revolución*).

France remains an incredible exception when it comes to protest and violence. It is the rare Western country where police are permitted to use rubber bullets, and with devastating results for scores of French men and women. Violence at protests is presumed, incorrectly, to be totally unavoidable. It's a presumption whose false legitimacy relies on blaming French revolutionary history, but the reality is that protests only grew more and more violent since 2009 because they did not result in any concessions from a disempowered French president in the new pan-European project. For example, the widespread use of preventative arrests was unknown in 1968, but it was also first legalised under Nicolas Sarkozy.

Right now the Yellow Vests are not revolutionary because they do not demand an overturning of property relations, but also because they do not demand the right to armed self-defence. The arming of protesters is verboten in France, and proof that the Yellow Vests accepted this is why Saturday after Saturday they simply took the punishment. The West is unique in that their people have, since the 1960s, totally relinquished to the government the right to self-defence and have been totally swayed by the nonsensical notion that only non-violent protests have political and legitimacy. With the exception of ending their Apartheids, their protests have failed to defend mere Social Democracy much less finally win Socialist Democracy.

"These accusations (that there should be no workers' militia) *reduced themselves, in the final analysis, to the profound that thought that if the oppressed do not balk, the oppressors will not be obliged to beat them. This is the philosophy of Tolstoy and Gandhi but never that of Marx and Lenin,"* wrote Trotsky. Tolstoy, the artist who works in an imaginary and in ivory tower abstract, and Gandhi, the patron saint of the post-colonial status quo and the hardened social caste - they typify the political inspiration of the average Westerner, today. They have these false notions precisely because of anti-Socialist repression, which implies an equal repression of knowledge surrounding the crimes, failures and true aims of Western Liberal Democracy.

And yet a protesters' militia does actually exist in France: Black Bloc and Antifa. The only problem is that both of them exude hate and contempt of the protesters. They are, in turn, hated by the average protester, who does not feel any kinship with them or that their ideals are similar. As someone who has attended many hundreds of protests since 2009 as a journalist I have seen so much questionable behavior from these two groups that I am certain, as many French activists are, that these two unaccountable groups are infiltrated by French police. I say this because I have witnessed many instances of members of these groups committing so many unexpected, ill-timed and unappreciated acts which protesters all knew was only going to discredit them and their cause. Even if that presumption is not true, Black Bloc and Antifa are the opposite of what I am talking about, which is a self-defense militia - those two groups are purely offensive in their tactics and goals; they are playing a game with the cops, not trying to win the support of the marchers/protesters one by one.

I recall Yellow Vests pleading with me at the tear gas-filled Arc de Triomphe roundabout multiple times: "Why aren't the police doing anything to stop Black Bloc?!" Answer: because Black Bloc and Antifa helps police to destroy protests - the don't work to help protests succeed.

Black Bloc and Antifa are thus a safety valve which benefits the government, which is obviously why they are tolerated and not smashed as dangerous and almost universally-despised organisations. As Yellow Vest organisers told me: social media such as Facebook now routes searches for Yellow Vests to these extreme organisations, with the obvious goal of discrediting the Yellow Vests by association.

These two groups are so rejected by French protesters that they are not even worth discussing, except to point out their incapability, their rejection and the ease with which such groups can be infiltrated by reactionary state agents.

Any Yellow Vest protesters' militia would be as sincerely concerned with stopping the shenanigans of Black Bloc and Antifa as they would those of the CRS riot police.

Yellow Vest: "In recent years it has become clear that our police are very violent, and that they murder, hurt and mutilate, yet in the end they are never held accountable."

As time goes on, and as France realises they have been cowed into staying at home and have relinquished their right to protest, then the idea that the Yellow Vests should become the clearly-marked guardians of the rights to assembly and speech will become more acceptable. The idea that the police will be transformed somehow into an organ of the oppressed is without example in history, and it is notable that despite the regular violence for six months the French political establishment never made any efforts to transform their police in a less brutal and lawbreaking manner. Significantly, and as previously discussed, they gave the police even more power and punished police for not being brutal enough.

How many Yellow Vests must die before France comes to its own defense against the bourgeois bloc?

The Yellow Vests undoubtedly created a revolutionary situation, but to call for an armed uprising here would be a failure: even the Yellow Vests would not join, I predict.

Unlike Muslim countries victimised in such a deadly way by Western neo-imperialism, Westerners do not yet see their condition as neo-imperial subjects as being dire enough so as to warrant taking up arms. The fact that the Yellow Vests did not even mention the word "Europe" in their list of 43 demands shows how little understanding there is that the current version of the pan-European project is obviously neo-imperial.

Should the French state ever open fire on the Yellow Vests - then the equation would change.

So far, the 12 deaths at the Yellow Vest demonstrations have been mostly inadvertent - traffic accidents and heart attacks. The killing of 80-year-old Algerian woman Zineb Redouane, hit at her fourth-floor window by what certainly seems to be an intentional tear gas canister fired during a Yellow Vest demonstration, is not viewed the same in France as firing en masse on Yellow Vests.

As the spokesperson of a police union told me during an interview: cops will only stand down if tens of millions of people take to the streets. Only the murder of Yellow Vests could generate that, and then the acceptance that Western Liberal Democracy is obviously a failure. The second *Je suis Charlie* march provoked 4 million to protest.

This exact scenario may actually happen. The Yellow Vests have already been such heroic and wiling martyrs, and the French police such cowardly and reactionary employers of brutality - why should we assume these two trends will discontinue, rather than continuing to a very logical and quite likely conclusion upon the next certain crisis in Liberalist capitalism?

Should this happen the Yellow Vest network will immediately spring to action. France is a nation with plenty of guns (globally they are 26th in gun ownership, with 20 firearms per 100 civilians) and the Yellow Vests are a self-trusting network full of ever-more politically advanced people who are committed to a progressive, not reactionary, France.

The Yellow Vest experience shows that, apparently, only massacres will cause the average Frenchman to realise that they are not even allowed to defend themselves while exercising the Liberalist rights which they are told they enjoy, falsely. Opening fire on the Yellow Vests is the one mistake the bourgeois bloc forces must not make - if they do, then certainly Macron will be forced to resign in order to save Western Liberal Democracy in France, at the very least.

"If one allows for a moment that the army equipped to its teeth will under all conditions be found on the side of big capital, then one must

renounce not only the workers' militia but socialism in general. Then capitalism is eternal," wrote Trotsky (emphasis his), and we can substitute "Western Liberal Democracy" for "capitalism" and "police" for "army" to reflect modern French conditions.

France is like most countries: they naively believe in the benevolence of the national army, even though France's army is not grassroots and defensive but imperialist and offensive. Nor did the army step in to protect the Yellow Vests' - they accepted Macron's order to be deployed against the Yellow Vests.

Many may not realise it, but France is truly at an impasse - what happens in social conflagration produced by the next inevitable bust in Liberalist capitalism?

What is a 'protesters' militia' to protect Liberalist rights?

> *"**The workers' militia** - not by its armaments but by its class consciousness and heroism - **will be the vanguard of the revolution.**"* (emphasis his)

Trotsky isn't describing the Yellow Vests, but the Yellow Vests obviously fit the bill in every way.

The Yellow Vests merit being the political vanguard in French society. The absolute hallmarks of the Yellow Vests is civic consciousness, class consciousness and heroism. Thus they deserve a role in French society, and if the French care at all about their fate in the pan-European project popular acclaim should push them into a vanguard role at protests.

The Yellow Vests desire, I believe, to become an entirely new French institution. They are not sufficiently willing to enter politics - in the

2022 legislative elections they could not even cobble together a "Yellow Vest list" of candidates, though there were individual Yellow Vests who ran for national office - but they are ready to become a fixture of French political culture. The protest is their home, at least for now, and they are undoubtedly needed there.

It would be totally autocratic to presume that public demonstrations are not an indispensable component of modern political life. They are absolutely necessary for any democracy and any society, as they alert both the government and the people to serious problems, and simply must be preserved at all costs. Socialist-inspired democracies such as China and Iran are full of protests for this reason.

A militia is an army made up of regular citizens called to respond during an emergency. What's needed is for the French people to realise that the pan-European project's repression of their Liberalist rights does indeed constitute an emergency.

Barring a massacre of Yellow Vests the French will not easily turn to armed revolution - the average Frenchman is now a neo-imperial subject, but they are still in a much better economic position than most neo-imperial subjects; the propaganda of imperialism falsely tells the French that a revolution would overturn 1789 instead of adding to its achievements. A "protesters' militia" is something which I feel would appeal to the French, and which could lead to the progressive political changes they are obviously clamouring for.

What the Yellow Vests should do is to recreate the National Guard, the group which decided the fate of revolutionary movements until its disastrously wilful disarmament in 1848 and then its disbandment during the 2nd Empire. By drawing on their French Revolutionary heritage the appeal among Frenchmen would be widened. In 2016, France actually reestablished the National Guard - however, it is composed of reservist military forces, serves as the fifth branch of the armed forces, was done as an Islamophobic response to terrorist attacks and is completely shorn of its revolutionary legacy.

What a "National Guard Protesters' Militia" means in 21st century France is that it would be charged with defending Liberalist rights, such as the freedom of assembly, speech and protest - these rights are also a part of Socialist Democracy. They can be a force of conscience and self-defence which presides over protests and debate in order to permit the French to voice their concerns in peace, to raise their political consciousness and to develop French solutions to French problems. Not only would they be present at protests, but they could provide security at nightly protests such as Nuit Debout in 2016. They could even permit the creation of a permanent encampment - a "French Tahrir Square", as was tried at the Eiffel Tower on March 8, 2019, but which was forbidden by police.

To be brief about what a people's militia looks like: it would have to put a citizen's group on the level of the government's armed forces. The Yellow Vests would provide security along with the police. It is not necessary that the protesters' militia would be armed but that the government's armed forces would have to be disarmed. The police would retain their legal rights afforded to them (observation, questioning, detention), but the presence of the Yellow Vests would ensure that riot police, Antifa and Black Bloc cannot cause a degeneration to violence. What are the Yellow Vests if not the watchmen and watchwomen of French democracy?

This is a practical solution, considered within a French culture which is clearly opposed to armed demonstrations, in order to protect the rights of the average Frenchman from further erosion. The solution is not for the Yellow Vests to be run roughshod over again and again and again and again and again.

There's no need to quote the countless heroes of socialist democracy who know that the peoples' best interests are preserved in a peaceful revolution. The proposition of the Yellow Vests as a defensive protester's militia is an opportunity for the peaceful development of progressive politics, and it should be seized upon. If the supporters of the bourgeois bloc refuse it - it is they who are advocating and perpetuating violence, and they should learn from the history of modern revolutionary nations that violent revolutions only occurred as a result of the repeated denial of long-accepted democratic rights. Perhaps above all else the Yellow Vests represent the blatant, repeated denial of accepted democratic rights, and this cannot continue.

This proposition is a peaceful reform of a protest space which the Yellow Vests have proven to be in desperate need of reform - the political *raison d'être* of reformists and Social Democrats is that they insist peaceful reform actually is possible in Western Liberal Democracy, so how can they not champion this?

Quite simply: France either has the Yellow Vests to create a people's militia or they have nobody qualified at all. If they have nobody qualified, then continued repression of French protesters is certain and proves that Western Liberal Democracy will never give even the mere rights of Liberalism to the average French person.

The French government refuses to produce qualified people - French law enforcement has already been totally discredited - and must therefore allow a new institution that will preserve the human and democratic rights of protesting citizens.

If such a group is not created then a massacre of the Yellow Vests will occur - it is the logical endpoint of the combination of a self-sacrificing group and social conditions which have only and will only worsen under this version of a pan-European project.

Calling for the Yellow Vests to be given the right to police demonstrations and to have the right to defend the law is not something which creates more violence - it would prevent it. If the bourgeois bloc feels that even such discussions threaten their dominance and are unacceptable, then they shouldn't look to the Yellow Vests for what the future may hold but to their neo-colonies.

The only area of France which has recently understood the need for citizens to sometimes protect the right of citizens was in French

Guiana, where in 2017 the "500 Brothers against Delinquency" put on masks and did exactly this in order to bring order to France's most violent *département*. Failure to protect the Yellow Vests may led to yet another example of a now-established rule in France: political movements and innovations often begin first in France's overseas territories and then spread to the mainland.

In the 2022 presidential election the majority of France's overseas neo-colonies voted for Marine Le Pen. Which will come over to the continent first: a president from the National Front, the masked 500 Brothers Against Delinquency, the massacre of Yellow Vest protesters or a Yellow Vest protesters' militia to reduce the violence at French protests? Perhaps eventually all four but certainly not none.

What is not also certain to not happen is the promised prosperity and stability of the pan-European project, nor the beginning of a capitalist era without devastating bust periods, nor the complete renunciation by the French of political protests.

France is truly at an impasse: the coronavirus lockdowns have finally faded and the situation has only worsened since January 2020, after the failed general strike. Perhaps the revolutionary situation has passed but it is certain to return - the Yellow Vests have remained a constant.

France must either take steps to reduce its astounding amount of political violence, or else more violence can be the only result.

<—>

19

Postscript: Looking back and looking forward with the Yellow Vests

Western culture has been so prevalent for two centuries that I think much of the world assumes that they already intimately know a major European country like France. Many outside of the West may be saying, "We know the West, but the West doesn't know us!"

It's just not that simple.

A contemporary progressive demand correctly says that local histories must be prioritised and no longer imposed from the outside - stereotypes must be broken. The end of feudalism finally allowed the average person to say the truth in public - there is a class struggle - and using this most high-powered lens we realise: the people of France deserve this right as much as any other people because the history of their working poor masses, too, has been repressed, ignored and slandered.

That didn't all start with the Yellow Vests.

Yellow Vest: "It's not only in Paris, or in France - discontent is international. The poor, the young, the old - so many sectors of society are doing poorly because of a lack of humanity in our social and economic policies. The beauty of the Yellow Vests is that we gather together every weekend to communicate with each other - otherwise, people are just home alone with their misery."

By far the best part of this book, in my opinion, is their words. I hope you have been as delighted as I have been to read their analyses right alongside the deeds of Napoleon, the revolutionaries of 1848, *Communards*, true Trotskyists, etc. Not only do their words tie this humble book together, but they tie together over 200 years of French history. France has this tremendously exciting history of political resistance, but it gets buried, distorted and untaught by the Liberalist elite - the Yellow Vests exhumed it and brought it back to living reality.

After more than a dozen years living in France I must admit that I, too, didn't know France and Europe anywhere as well as I assumed I did before I moved here. What an enormous mistake I made - assuming that I "knew" France even though I knew hardly any French people!

One doesn't have to be on the world's bottom socioeconomic rung to have their culture and history falsely portrayed - every nation without a Socialist-inspired revolution to protect them has their own bottom rung which is silenced, crippled, massacred, etc. This book has been an effort to view modern French history from their ground up and not in the Liberalist fashion - their top down.

Yellow Vest: "Macron has ended so much social assistance to poor people. He tells lies about the poor, and also about his own policies. We are sick of his policies! We must finish the Macron era! We demand more aid for poor people, such as myself!"

Ah, still more progressive Yellow Vest thoughts! Yes, more, because this book is not my book but theirs. This book is not an attempt to give my version of French history, but the version from the average French person.

The average French person has much to learn from this book, I humbly insist, because the history of their working-poor has been so suppressed domestically, and also because the truth of the new pan-European project has been so suppressed.

Admit the truth: the euro has totally failed in its promise to bring about prosperity and economic security. The European Union has totally failed to act in a democratic manner. The pan-European project has not waged bilateral war (perhaps "yet") but it has waged social war on its own citizens across the continent. Many permanently disfigured Yellow Vests would say I am even being too lenient here.

> *Yellow Vest: "By denying that there was any police brutality the government legitimised it. How we can have confidence in a government which cripples its own citizens, or in institutions which do not intervene to stop that? It is truly barbaric violence, which mutilated people because they believe in a better future."*

The immediate, perpetual and ongoing failure of Liberalism; the notion that Western political culture has actually been excised of the influence of immoral, arrogant and unjust monarchism - a misconception which rather turns Iranians apoplectic; the clear goal of modern politics to move from absolutism towards citizen involvement and empowerment; the obvious historical trajectory of Western political structures from absolute monarchy, to aristocratic oligarchy, to a bankocracy which inflicts neo-imperialism on anyone it can reach - I hope this book has clarified these realities. Admit the truth.

I am convinced that what Europeans definitely agree on is that they all want an end to the wars which have gutted their lower classes for so long, to easily move around within Europe and the basic advances of mere Social Democracy. The working classes want peace, ease of movement and a decent social safety net. The pan-European project has manipulated these desires - the 1% has teased with the carrot but just given the stick. The only real success of the pan-European project has been the flexibility of the EU passport - Europeans are quite relieved to be able to move around the continent without the previous hassles.

Europeans, in my experience and according to polls, mostly want a united Europe - it's unfortunate that they are misled into believing that there is no alternative to this thus-far woefully unsuccessful version of it.

Yellow Vest: "I can't tell people how to vote, but I certainly advise them to not vote for Macron. He hasn't done anything for the French people, but has instead worked for the rich bankers, corporations and Brussels."

Even though his autocratic repression of the Yellow Vests should have disqualified him from ever holding public office again, Emmanuel Macron was re-elected, incredibly. The false branding of the Yellow Vests as mere "hooligans" has largely stuck in France, stunningly. There is a dysfunction, a Marxist "*barrenness*", an autocratic schizophrenia which Western Liberal Democracy is forcing the average Frenchman to endure - this book shows how long this sickness has been imposed on the French poor, working poor and working classes.

Without the courage to call things by their rightful names - Western Liberal Democracy means failure for the 99%; Socialist Democracy justly puts the 99% at the forefront of government policy - France as a whole will never heal. How very few political analysts say this!

This postscript was finished the day after France's 2nd-round legislative elections. Macron has not been handed another absolute majority by a slim margin - it's another Yellow Vest victory, but not one which was resounding enough. It's certain that Macron was never a "centrist" but a mainstream conservative, merely with a new logo and of his younger generation. Thus, his coalition will continue to unite with the mainstream conservative *les Républicains* party (and also many fake-leftist Socialists and Greens) for an absolute majority on all issues involving far-right economics, the re-imposition of Liberalism and the pan-European project. French parliament will now be less stable and more combative, but in appearances only - in reality French parliament remains only for appearances on the major questions of economic and political power distribution. It's certain that the reason an absolute democratic majority of France (54%) didn't even bother to vote is because they implicitly know that modern autocracy - rule by the 49-3 executive decree and the overruling of national sovereignty by Brussels - rules, thus rendering Europe's national parliaments a waste of time, their breath and our attention. I would conclude that Liberalism in France is on the verge of becoming so preposterously dysfunctional that it's surely about to be consigned to the dustbin of history but, alas, I recall that Marx and Trotsky wrote the same thing.

It's certain that these analyses will not be popular among my journalist colleagues.

What is so unfortunate is that as early as the summer of 2019 people kept asking me: "You're going to report on a Yellow Vest demonstration? But I thought they had stopped marching?" The media blackout on the group extends beyond the common excuse of the corporate domination of Western media: it doesn't explain the refusal of France's state-owned media to cover the group. French taxpayers deserve better. Capitalism is an issue, but the larger issue is obviously political and cultural - it's elite-driven Liberalism.

Yellow Vest: "We marched as Yellow Vests for two years, and we are still Yellow Vests today, but we all saw that nothing changed! The cost of living is too expensive - we can't pay our bills at the end of the month! We don't want this government - and their violence - any more."

The fact that the Yellow Vests have marched every Saturday for over three and half years (not including the coronavirus pause) is actually more important than how they have been wilfully ignored:

As the West comes out of the coronavirus era, during which they actually employed some Social Democratic-inspired economic measures, they are immediately reverting to extremist Liberalist economic solutions: forced recession, in order to perpetuate the elite's dominance over the working poor. The first half of 2022 was supposed to be a time when France's elections were going to garner great interest, at least in France, but the vote was overshadowed everywhere by total economic disaster - much of it self-inflicted in the West. Betting on a period of economic disaster - always a constant in Liberalist capitalism - seems like a gamble that will pay off quite big, and quite soon, in the world's weakest and least-sovereign macroeconomic bloc.

Yellow Vest: "Things really could explode because prices keep going up but wages do not. If Emmanuel Macron somehow wins re-election then social unrest will go sky-high. The Yellow Vests will really take to the streets then, and it will be much worse than in 2019."

For those who marvel at the insight of these Yellow Vest quotations - they truly are just that politically intelligent and aware! Give them all the credit. The idea that they are just rioting berserkers is… well, this book has already disproven that completely.

The perspective of the daily hard-news reporter is, I think, a unique and useful one. There is an urgency to this particular area of journalism caused by the reality that (after starting from the ideal of objectivity) serious conclusions must be drawn immediately and presented - they cannot be drawn-out, postponed, frittered away by mealy-mouthed relativism. Additionally, I interview and learn the opinion on the day's most vital events from everyone, from hedge fund mangers to think-tank analysts to pensioners to protesters to Yellow Vests and to - most often - the everyday Frenchman and Frenchwoman on the street.

That's not something which can be easily replicated. Personally, my favorite chapters may be Chapters 9 through 11 - covering 2009-2022 - which condensed over 1,500 2-3 minute television hard news reports for PressTV (which equates to more than 3,000 soundbites from French people) and hundreds of columns. That can't be easily replicated, either, nor can my honest claim to have reported on more Yellow Vest demonstrations than any other journalist in any language.

At the next Liberalist-provoked disaster the Yellow Vests will be there - they have never left. That should give France great hope. This book has aimed to share their fundamental message of hope and civic-mindedness.

Yellow Vest: "What voters should do is to not be scared, and to rejoin the Yellow Vests. We have lost our purchasing power, our social services, our individual freedoms - stop crying about these two candidates from behind your television or computer and come join us!"

The ideas of the Yellow Vests are not new - this book examined many different modern French eras to show precisely that. There is obviously a human unity across spaces, and there is also a political unity across time. The interspersed quotes of the Yellow Vests should have given you the clear understanding of: it's been the same political and economic struggle for the past 233 years. It's not complicated: just examine how and why they repressed the Yellow Vests so brutally, and why that failed to stop them.

Yellow Vest: "The government doesn't know what to do because they see that the movement continues despite so much repression. We will not stop until we get the right to citizen-initiated referendums, the end to corporate tax evasion and a rule of social justice so that people can live decently."

That's perhaps the most simple encapsulation of the primary demands of the Yellow Vests. Mine might be a bit different, but I was honoured to be alongside the Yellow Vests to insist on our right to live decently.

The West's best values are not imperialism, elitist Liberalism, oligarchical parliamentarianism, free market chaos, suppressive austerity and a rat race to "become bourgeois". Look at the Yellow Vests for the West's true virtues, and then join them wherever you can.

Ramin Mazaheri
Paris
June 20, 2022

About the Author

Ramin Mazaheri is the chief correspondent in Paris for Iran's 24-hour English-language PressTV, and has lived in France since 2009. He was educated at the University of Missouri-Columbia and holds degrees in journalism and history. He has been a daily newspaper reporter in the United States, and has reported from Iran, Cuba, Egypt, Tunisia, South Korea, Switzerland and elsewhere. He is the author of *Socialism's Ignored Success: Iranian Islamic Socialism* and *I'll Ruin Everything You Are: Ending Western Propaganda on Red China,* which is also available in simplified and traditional Chinese.

Lightning Source UK Ltd.
Milton Keynes UK
UKHW020625281222
414453UK00011B/2115